# MODERN MANAGEMENT IN HOTEL AND CATERING INDUSTRY

# MODERN MANAGEMENT IN HOTEL AND CATERING INDUSTRY

**K.S. Gusain**

**CYBER TECH PUBLICATIONS**
4264/3, Ansari Road, Daryaganj, New Delhi-110002 (India)
Ph.: 011-23244078, 011-43559448 Fax: 011-23280028
E-Mail: cyberpublicationsdelhi@yahoo.com
Website: www.cybertechpublications.com

**MODERN MANAGEMENT IN HOTEL AND CATERING INDUSTRY**

**K.S. Gusain**



First Edition 2010



*Published by :* Asian Offset Printers

**G.S. Rawat** for **Cyber Tech Publications**
4264/3, Ansari Road, Daryaganj, New Delhi-110002 (India)
Ph.: 011-23244078, 011-43559448 Fax: 011-23280028
E-Mail: cyberpublicationsdelhi@yahoo.com
Website: www.cybertechpublications.com

# Preface

Beginning with an introduction to the travel and tourism industry, the book goes on to discuss various types of tourism, tourism infrastructure, telecommunications, tourist transport, and Indian and international tourism organizations. The book explains how to set up travel agencies and tour operations and their role in the tourism industry. Key topics, such as tourism product, tourism marketing, customer service skills, economic, environmental, sociocultural, and political impacts of tourism, and planning, managing, and developing a tourist attraction are discussed at length. The emerging trends in tourism, such as GDS, e-ticketing, and web marketing are also explored.

Catering is the business of providing food (and often, service) for events. According to the National Restaurant Associations 2000 Restaurant Industry Forecast, social caterers are one of the fastest-growing segments of the restaurant industry, with sales expected to reach $3.6 billion in 2000 - a 5.7 percent increase over its 1999 level. There are an estimated 80,000 caterers in N. America. The updated, comprehensive guide to successful catering business management. In addition to creating and executing a great menu, successful catering also takes know-how for marketing your business, keeping costs in line, and ensuring the entire operation runs smoothly. Hotel catering industry--such as small business management and running your own catering industry. It presents fresh information on menu design and pricing, complete with illustrative menu examples and tips for using software tools to create enticing menus.

— *Author*

# CONTENTS

# 1

# Introduction

The travel and tourism industry is by its very nature global in scope. By the beginning of the twenty-first century, however, travel destinations and vacation activities were changing. Perhaps the hottest trend in travel is the rise of "ecotourism." According to the Quebec Declaration on Ecotourism, ecotourism "includes local and indigenous communities in its planning, interprets the natural and cultural heritage of the destination to the visitor, and lends itself better to independent travellers."

Not so long ago many of the now-popular ecotourism destinations were either unknown to the outside world or fairly inaccessible. For most people places such as the Amazon rain forest, Africa's savannas, and the Himalaya and Andes mountains were simply out of reach. But many countries are now promoting their remote environmental treasures to travellers looking for something out of the ordinary. Tour operators are developing special packages for the environmentally minded traveler, and local groups are organizing tourism associations that attract tourists to out-of-the-way places.

Archaeological tourism is another growing trend. Ancient sites in destinations such as Egypt, Israel, and various other places in the Middle East are attracting visitors who only a short time ago had little knowledge of that region of the world. In 2005 Archaeological Tours in New York City offered packages that allowed travellers to explore the ancient Silk Road of China, the Byzantine monuments in southern Italy, and the legendary statues of Easter Island. Most of the tours were led by archeologists or university professors.

The development of ecotourism and archaeological tourism has coincided with an increase in travel to the United States by foreign tourists. Along with a global economy has come a growing middle class in Asia and Latin America. Latin America's outbound travel market has grown almost 33 percent since the mid-1990s, according to a 2004 on-line article by the Travel Industry Association of America. A good number of these newly prosperous travellers will eventually make their way to the United States.

Another travel trend has its roots in America's history as a country of immigrants. In recent years many Americans have begun searching for relatives or ancestors both at home and abroad. As distant parts of the world grow closer together, travellers are finding more opportunities for what has come to be called "heritage travel" to Europe, Asia, Africa, and Central and South America.

No innovation has affected the hotel industry more than the automobile. With the invention of the automobile, locations throughout the country became far more accessible to travellers. Motels, or "motor hotels," were built to accommodate drivers as they explored America. Early motels were usually small, family-owned businesses with a few roadside cabins. Air travel has further expanded the possible locations to which people can travel. Moreover, the Internet has had a profound impact on tourism. Potential travellers can explore vacation packages and make reservations online. According to a 2005 article published in Revenue, travel researcher PhoCusWright noted that half of flight and hotel reservations were made online by the end of 2005.

**Trends in the Hotel Industry**

In the first five years of the twentieth century hotel chains dominated the industry. In 2000 chains controlled nearly 70 percent of the hotel market share in the United States while less than 40 percent of all hotels were independently owned and operated. Just ten years earlier in 1990 nearly 55 percent of all hotels were independent. Hotel chains have flourished because they offer consumers a reliable and predictable visit. Each hotel in a chain offers similar facilities and services. Many are adding services from nationally known franchises such as pizzerias or Starbucks coffee shops. This similarity makes them popular because travellers going to an unfamiliar city know what to expect if they have stayed in another hotel or motel in the same chain. The hotel industry faces fierce competition due to an oversupply of hotel rooms. A construction boom in the 1980s was followed by a decline in the number of travellers during the early 1990s. Hotel occupancy fell from a high of 72 percent in 1979 to just 59.2 percent in 2003, leaving more than one-third of all hotel rooms empty on any given night. The result of this oversupply has been increased market segmentation. Rather than running huge, five-hundred-room hotels to fit the needs of every traveler, many hotels today target one market segment such as business or budget travellers.

Some innovative hotel designs have also captured markets successfully. One popular trend has been the all-suite hotel. Each unit in an all-suite hotel provides a living area and a separate bedroom. Some also offer a cooking area. Another development is the environmentally conscious "ecohotel," which highlights features such as low-flush toilets, refillable containers for toiletries, and recycled stationery. One of the most popular promotions in resort locations is the all-inclusive package, which offers travellers not only lodging but all meals, drinks, and entertainment for one price.

The growth of the global economy has also affected the hotel industry. Many hotel chains based in the United States have expanded overseas. At home the hotel industry made a slow recovery from 9/11 but was still coping with the effects of the recession through the first decade of the new century. According to a March 2005 report in the Fairfield County Business Journal, the typical U.S. hotel achieved an estimated 13.3 percent increase in yearly profits in 2004. Moreover, an increased confidence in airport security, a decreased fear of a terrorist attack, and a weak U.S. dollar has led to an increase in foreign travel to the United States. During the first half of

2004 international spending in America rose for the first time since 9/11.

In 2004 the U.S. Commerce Department estimated that foreign tourism accounted for over $71 billion in economic activity in the United States-a figure larger than the profits from U.S. automobile, engine, and parts exports. With that much at stake, it is little surprise that President George W. Bush approved a $50 million ad campaign aimed at tourists in England, Japan, Germany, Canada, and Mexico.

Hotels make foreign travellers feel welcome by serving international cuisine in their restaurants and by providing room directories and menus printed in several languages. Some hotels now employ multilingual concierges to help guests with making reservations, arranging tours, and answering questions about the region. This trend increases the demand for workers who speak several languages and who have experience with different cultures. In April 2005 Wyndham Hotels announced it would implement an English language education program for its Spanish-speaking employees.

## BUSINESS TRAVELLERS

One major market segment for the hotel industry is business travel. Hotels in all price ranges compete to attract these guests and keep them as clients. Employees who have sales and marketing experience can help a hotel compete successfully.

Hotels seek business travellers by providing special features or services designed to make it easier to work away from home. During the 1980s many hotels built business centers that included computers and copiers. Portable technology has lessened the popularity of these centers, and now many business travellers prefer to work in their rooms using their own notebook computers. By the early 2000s popular hotel amenities included free newspapers, a complimentary breakfast, a large work desk, high-speed or WiFi Internet access, and exercise facilities. Efficiency is a primary concern for all business travellers whose tight schedules require quick service. Many hotels provide computerized services for speedy check-in and check-out.

Employees are trained to help visits run smoothly and to handle problems swiftly. As in any service industry, pleasing the customer is of foremost importance.

Some business-oriented hotels offer facilities for companies to conduct extended staff meetings. It is also common for businesses to schedule "retreats" where employees stay at the same hotel and discuss business strategies in designated meeting rooms, then spend time together participating in leisure activities such as golf, tennis, or swimming. Many hotels are designed to cater to these meetings, especially those at popular resort destinations.

Earning customer loyalty is a key feature of serving business travellers. If a hotel satisfies a business client, the long-term return can be great. One way that hotels promote customer loyalty is through frequent-guest programs. Travellers earn points for every dollar they spend at the hotel. When they have accumulated enough points, they can redeem them for gifts such as free lodging or a vacation at an exotic resort.

Like all aspects of the hospitality industry, business and convention travel was hit hard by 9/11 and the sagging economy. From 1998 to 2003, business and convention travel experienced a 14 percent drop-off; however, business travel grew more than 4 percent in 2004 and should experience even more growth in the next few years, according to the Travel Industry Association of America.

## CONVENTIONS

Guest rooms are only one source of revenue for many hotels. They can make large profits by renting meeting rooms and exhibition space and by hosting banquets and receptions. Trade shows and conventions draw hundreds of customers at a time to a hotel.

Many different industries and business organizations hold trade shows and conventions each year. Political, civic, religious, and social organizations also have annual meetings. Hotels hire convention planners to attract conventions, to help businesses plan events, and to negotiate prices. During a convention service managers supervise every stage of the event. Because a hotel's reputation for efficiency and good service is often the key to its success in attracting conventions, the work of the convention staff is critical.

## HOTEL WORKER TEAMS

The workers in a large hotel generally are organized into teams according to the department in which they work. There are currently more than 170 different careers in the hospitality industry. Common departments include sales, food and beverage, housekeeping, and accounting. Each department is run by a manager, who usually reports to a general manager in charge of the hotel. Hotel workers are traditionally described as "front-of-the-house" or "back-of-the-house" employees, depending on whether they have direct contact with the guests. Front-of-the-house workers include bellhops, desk clerks, and concierges. Back-of-the-house workers are the behind-the-scenes employees who keep the hotel running smoothly. They include kitchen workers, housekeepers, and accountants.

## FOOD SERVICE INDUSTRY

Any business that prepares and serves meals, snacks, or beverages is part of the food service industry. The largest segment of the industry includes restaurants serving full menus and offering table service. The second-largest segment is limited-menu, or fast food, outlets. Although large fast food chains are a familiar sight all across the United States, more than seven out of ten eating and drinking places are single-unit, independent operations. Other segments of the food service industry include school and employee cafeterias, catering businesses, hotel restaurants, and vendors at sporting events and concerts.

The food service industry in the United States is booming and appears to be immune from the weak economy of the twenty-first century's first decade. Sales have increased from about $43 billion in 1970 to $426 billion in 2003. The National Restaurant Association estimates that more than 54 billion meals were eaten in restaurants and school and work cafeterias in 2002. Social scientists suggest that the boom is the result of people's busy schedules. They also point out that dual-income families have limited time for cooking. Although the rapid food service boom of the 1970s and 1980s may be slowing, the employment outlook is still very good. In 2002 the food service industry employed about 11.7 million workers, making it the largest U.S. employer besides the government. Food and beverage service employment is expected to reach 13.3 million by 2012.

## Trends in Food Service

The growth of the take-out food market is a major trend in the food service industry. This market segment is called the "off-premises sector" because food is eaten away from the restaurant where it is cooked. It includes take-out, delivery, and drive-through restaurants. Many traditional restaurants that offer table service attempt to cash in on this expanding market by offering delivery service. Take-out and delivery accounted for 51 percent of total restaurant business in 2002. The Internet has also had a profound influence on the food service market; many workers now order their lunches online. After rapid expansion in the 1980s the number of fast food restaurants remained stable through the 1990s. New restaurants are likely to be full-service restaurants, which cater more successfully to America's older population. In fact, the full-service sector is expected to be the fastest-growing sector in the industry. The number of Americans between the ages of fifteen and thirty-four-the age group that generally thrives on fast food-is decreasing, whereas the food service industry includes any business that prepares and serves meals, snacks, or beverages. Many older diners have more time for a leisurely meal and do not seek out fast food.

Like any other business, fast food restaurants must adapt to changing times. Many fast-food chains are offering a wider range of choices and emphasizing low-fat items such as salads and grilled foods to appeal to health-conscious Americans. Another significant trend is the growth of the ethnic food sector. Whereas many Americans once limited their exploration of ethnic foods to Italian or Chinese cuisine, today they seek out traditional foods of Latin America, India, Africa, the Caribbean, and other cultures.

### Food Service Workers

The people who work in the food service industry include food and beverage managers, restaurant managers, bartenders, chefs and cooks, bakers, dining room and cafeteria attendants, hostesses and hosts, waiters and waitresses, fast food franchise workers, caterers, stewards, dishwashers, and other kitchen workers.

The food service industry employs large numbers of relatively unskilled workers. Restaurants traditionally have depended on young people to fill these positions; however, low birthrates in the 1970s and 1980s limited the number of youths looking for employment in the 1990s. The food service industry was forced to attract workers from other age groups. It became common for food service businesses to offer more full-time employment, higher wages and bonuses, and more training for career advancement than before. The industry also began recruiting more women and minorities, as well as nontraditional workers such as seniors and mentally and physically challenged individuals.

## RECREATION INDUSTRY

From aerobics and hiking to rock climbing and parachuting, the recreation industry helps millions of Americans enjoy their leisure time. Workers in this industry organize and lead activities, provide instruction and equipment, and maintain facilities.

## SUMMER JOBS IN HOSPITALITY AND RECREATION FOOD SERVICE

Summer jobs are available for kitchen and dining room workers, particularly servers, dishwashers, kitchen helpers, cooking staff, cashiers, and hosts and hostesses. Contact:

- hotels
- restaurants

- caterers
- amusement parks
- employment agencies

## HOTELS

Summer positions in hotels include housekeepers, bellhops, porters, desk clerks, and doorkeepers. Hotels with other amenities such as room service, tourist information desks, and social programs need additional staff. Contact:

- hotels
- motels
- summer resorts
- cruise operators
- employment agencies

## RECREATION

Summer jobs in this area include camp counsellors, lifeguards, and recreation workers. Some parks and museums offer summer internships. Guides are needed for parks, historic sites, and public monuments. Contact:

- local parks and recreation departments
- historic sites
- camps
- tourism offices
- museums
- community centers

### Trends in Recreation

In the 1990s sociologists identified a trend called "cocooning." If this trend continues more and more Americans will stay at home for relaxation and recreation. Climbing sales of home gym equipment and rentals of DVDs suggest that cocooning will continue for at least the first decade of the twenty-first century. However, some U.S. consumers still seek out a diverse range of activities offered by the recreation industry. Because many Americans have a limited amount of leisure time, they are very selective about how they spend it.

Instead of participating in several leisure activities, many people prefer to focus on just one. More and more people are choosing to take shorter vacations as well; for example, weekend and getaway trips are becoming more popular than traditional two-week vacations.

### Physical Fitness Programs and Participatory Sports

The physical fitness movement of the 1980s was led by baby boomers-people born from 1946 to 1964. As members of this generation have reached middle age and become more interested in maintaining their physical fitness, they have devoted more time to working out in gyms, health clubs, and community centers.

The interest in physical fitness continues, but the focus has shifted from workouts to wellness.

In addition to building their muscles and toning their bodies, aging baby boomers seek to improve their total mental and emotional well-being. "Total care" health clubs are responding to this trend by offering seminars and counselling in nutrition, stress management, smoking cessation, weight loss, and self-esteem.

Baby boomers seem to have turned to less strenuous sports that can be practiced safely throughout life. Within this age group, "lifetime" sports such as hiking, bicycling, walking, golf, and doubles tennis are increasing in popularity as more strenuous or hazardous sports such as running, jogging, downhill skiing, and singles tennis decline. Sporting goods stores employ instructors to teach customers basic skills and safety precautions pertaining to their sport of choice.

### Movie Theatres

For decades the only place anyone could see a movie was in a theater. By the dawn of the twenty-first century theatres were competing fiercely with cable television and DVD sales and rentals. Movie theatres try to attract audiences by offering amenities such as improved audio and projection systems and concession stands that sell a wide range of food and drinks. Some chains are experimenting with special ultra-large screens that produce a thrilling and vivid viewing experience, and many theatres have added online information, reservation, and prepay ticket sales systems to make ticket purchasing easier. Such improvements are designed to attract an older, more affluent crowd.

Another continuing trend is the multiplex, a theater complex with many screens. Each theater offers In addition to providing traditional exercise facilities, many health clubs offer seminars and classes in nutrition, stress management, and self-esteem.

Multiplexes encourage impulse viewing and increase customer satisfaction. By showing a popular film on more than one screen, multiplexes can increase the size of the audience and avoid the risk of selling out while patrons are still waiting for tickets. Movie theatres provide jobs for managers, projectionists, cashiers, ushers, and concession-stand workers.

**Museums**

The rich cultural history of the United States is reflected in its variety of museums. In addition to museums of art, many American cities support museums devoted to history, science, culture, and children's studies.

According to the 2004 Museum Attendance Report compiled by Morey and Associates, the average total attendance at more than eighty museums in the United States increased 2.6 percent between 2003 and 2004. Most museums are seeking to attract wider, more diverse audiences. One common strategy is to plan exhibits that reflect the ethnic or cultural interests within a community. Some museums are dedicated entirely to particular themes, such as the Charles H. Wright Museum of African American History in Detroit, the Museum of Tolerance in Los Angeles, and the Holocaust Memorial Museum in Washington, D.C.

Many museums now use interactive technology-once limited to children's museums-to increase accessibility and encourage more active, hands-on experiences for visitors. This technology includes displays and kiosks that provide museum maps and helpful information about museum displays.

As Americans' travel habits shift from long family vacations to shorter, more frequent outings, museums need to find new ways to attract visitors. According to a 2002 report by the New England Museum Association, museums that "have diversified their offerings to include changing attractions along with special events and new experiences" have been the most successful.

Museums hire curators to plan and maintain exhibits. In a large museum a curator is usually in charge of one department such as photography or African American art. Updating museums requires the services of professional designers and educational specialists. Museums also hire clerks who sell tickets and work in museum stores, as well as tour guides, guards, maintenance workers, and fund-raising experts.

## Spectator Sports

Millions of fans regularly attend professional and amateur sporting events. Baseball, basketball, ice hockey, and football grew in popularity during the 1980s. Spurred by Americans' interest in professional sports, many leagues have expanded in recent years or plan future expansion.

At the beginning of the twenty-first century women's professional sports were attracting many new fans as well. The Women's National Basketball Association was founded in 1997, the U.S. women's soccer team enjoyed national attention when it won the 1999 Women's World Cup, and women's professional tennis maintained a decades-long period of popularity.

However, men's professional organizations like the National Football League, National Basketball Association, National Hockey League, and Major League Baseball continue to be so popular that they have cultural significance as well as entertainment value.

## Top-Earning Jobs in Hospitality and Recreation

These are some of the high-paying jobs described in this volume. The figures represent typical salaries or earnings for experienced workers.

| | |
|---|---|
| $100,000-$25,000,000 | * Professional Athlete |
| | * Professional Athletic Coach |
| $30,000-$80,000 | * Athletic Trainer |
| | * Caterer |
| | * Corporate Travel Manager |
| | * Lodging Manager |
| | * Meeting and Convention Planner |
| | * Museum Conservator |
| | * Museum Curator |
| | * Property, Real Estate, and Community Association Manager |
| | * Restaurant Manager |

Professional athletes are the highly paid stars of spectator sports, but many other people work in this sector of the recreation industry, including coaches, managers, trainers, ticket sellers, and stadium workers. Sales and marketing personnel create special promotions and events that help get fans into the stands. Even the steroid scandal that rocked American baseball could not drown fan interest: advance ticket sales for the 2005 season were up 6.5 percent from 2004. Sports still has its problematic economic issues, however, as evidenced by the lockout that cancelled the 2004-05 National Hockey League season. The lockout affected many local businesses and left thousands of employees out of work.

## Community Recreation

Community recreation is the most widespread recreation field in the United States. Just about every community and county in the nation has a public recreation center where residents can swim, learn arts and crafts, put on a play, or participate in sports. Many "controlled" communities such as retirement centers also employ recreation staffs. Jobs available in community recreation facilities include recreation director, program director, lifeguard, playground supervisor, and recreation aide. Opportunities also exist for people who can teach activities such as dancing, crafts, drama, and sports.

### Zoos

The Bronx Zoo in New York is a prime example of the changing role and function of American zoos. Its official name-the Wildlife Conservation Park-emphasizes its ties to the Wildlife Conservation Society, formerly known as the New York Zoological Society. Stressing their role in the preservation of animals and their ecosystems, modern zoos have replaced the old-fashioned animals-behind-bars environment with wildlife parks where animals roam free in replicas of their natural habitats. The pioneering and best-known of these zoos, the San Diego Zoo, is noted for its breeding programs for endangered animals. Wildlife park directors feel that today's zoos play a vital role in helping to conserve endangered animals, as well as in teaching the public about the importance of conservation efforts throughout the world. Wildlife conservation parks require many skilled workers, including directors, curators, veterinarians, and zoologists. Zoos also hire animal caretakers, guides, maintenance workers, and public relations personnel.

### State and National Parks

The United States has a well-developed system of county, state, and national parks. The National Park Service administers many frequently visited parks throughout the nation, from Gulf Islands National Seashore in Florida to Yosemite National Park in California. Since the 1950s visits to national parks Zoos are increasingly providing habitats for animals have jumped 500 percent. The park system employs thousands of workers to maintain the parks and help visitors enjoy camping, hiking, picnics, historical tours, and nature studies.

## THE SNAPSHOTS

### Hotels

Competition in the hotel industry is intense. Many hotels are targeting their services to particular market segments such as business-people or budget travellers. Expansion of smaller budget hotels is expected through 2014. Other trends include the all-suite hotel and the ecohotel. Increased international tourism makes cultural sensitivity and adaptability especially important in this field.

### Food Services

Busy Americans rely heavily on the restaurant industry to provide satisfying meals. Although the fast food boom has slowed, take-out establishments that offer a wider and healthier selection of foods are still experiencing growth. A rise in the number of parents and children who dine out, combined with a more affluent population of diners age fifty-five and older, are expected to spur growth in restaurants offering traditional table service. Franchise outlets will continue to be a significant part of the industry, but small, independently owned businesses will still hold the largest market segment.

### Recreation

Americans are being more selective when deciding how to spend their limited amounts of leisure time. All forms of recreation-movies, museums, zoos, parks, sporting events, and so on-compete to attract consumers. Recreation that meets the needs of an aging and culturally diverse population will be important in the first two decades of the twenty-first century.

### Travel

An increase in both business and leisure travel is expected to continue, though it may not reach pre-9/11 levels until the end of 2006, according to the Office of Travel and Tourism Industries. Many travellers are opting for shorter but more frequent trips. With the broadening scope of choices and decisions to be made when planning a trip, some travellers will continue to seek out the services of travel industry workers.

The increase in the number of senior citizens-many of whom have the free time and disposable income to devote to travel-will most likely spur the growth of leisure travel designed to appeal to older Americans.

## Technology

Workers throughout the field of hospitality and recreation rely on computers. Museums and zoos feature multimedia exhibits and interactive displays. Travel agents and reservations clerks use computers to determine the availability of flights and accommodations. Restaurants use computers to keep track of inventory and table charges. Hotel managers can use computers for yield management-a process that reveals when to discount rates rather than have empty rooms.

## Training

Many hotel and restaurant managers find that hospitality training is beneficial to their employees and their establishment. Employees who have completed training in the hospitality field are said to feel empowered and more capable of meeting their clients' needs. These programs go beyond teaching specific skills-they cover broad topics such as setting goals, developing communication skills, reducing stress, and building self-confidence. By promoting a good working environment, hospitality training contributes to worker and customer satisfaction. These programs need trainers as well as people to develop computerized training programs and instructional videos.

According to the National Park Service Office of Communications, in 2004 more than 276 million people visited America's national parks. Since then many parks have faced a crippling budget crisis. In an April 17, 2006 article, WashingtonPost.com contributor Matt Stearns reported: "The Bush administration has ordered America's national parks to show that they can function at 80 percent or less of their operating budgets." National park superintendents have to make some hard choices concerning ranger staffs, services, and visitor center hours, according to an article in National Geographic News. Prior to President Bush's budget-cutting announcement, environmentalists and conservationists were urging the government to purchase more land for parks-a proposal that seemed unlikely to gain acceptance in light of the 20 percent cut in park funding set for 2007.

## Camps

Summer camps are changing to adjust to new population and cultural trends. Camps still offer traditional activities such as swimming, boating, and hiking, but many also offer unique learning opportunities. Some camps focus on developing skills in specific areas, including computers, tennis, music, drama, and foreign languages. Others cater to children with special needs such as those with chronic illnesses or disabilities. Modern camps provide job opportunities for instructors and therapists, as well as directors, counsellors, lifeguards, nurses, and cooks.

The characteristics of camp-age children are expected to shift in the twenty-first century, with far more attendees coming from urban areas and different cultural backgrounds. The goal for the future is to find new ways to attract an increasingly diverse range of campers.

## EMPLOYMENT OUTLOOK

The health of the hospitality and recreation industry and the coinciding employment outlook is greatly affected by fluctuations in the U.S. economy. During a recession such as the one that began in 2000, consumers have less income for travel and leisure pursuits and they are usually more cautious about spending money for nonessential items. They also are less likely to contribute money to support historic sites, museums, and zoos.

As less money is spent on hospitality and recreation, fewer workers are hired and the number of available jobs decreases. This scenario characterized the beginning of the twenty-first century. On the other hand, during strong economic times, people have more discretionary income (extra money) and the hospitality and recreation industry generally flourishes. Consequently, the employment outlook for the field becomes favourable.

Changing demographics and lifestyles also have a major impact on employment in hospitality and recreation. As the United States entered the twenty-first century, about 25 percent of the population was over the age of fifty-five. This growing market segment has the money and the time to travel and pursue leisure activities. For this reason many analysts predict strong growth in leisure travel designed to appeal to retirees; this in turn will spur employment growth in the field.

Technology and training will be vital for workers in the hospitality and recreation industry. As in all fields, new technology will help people work more efficiently. Training programs can help workers keep pace with new trends and changing needs.

Despite continued economic problems and the aftereffects of the 9/11 tragedy, employment opportunities in hospitality and recreation still exist. Candidates committed to the principles of customer service-those who display patience, knowledge, enthusiasm, and a willingness to go the extra mile for a client-are in the best position to enter, succeed, and advance in this field.

## GETTING INTO HOSPITALITY AND RECREATION

Good jobs do not magically appear. Anyone who has been in the job market knows that landing the right job takes planning, preparation, perseverance, and patience. This is true whether you are looking for your first job, reentering the job market, trying to get a new job, or planning a mid-career change. This essay is designed to guide you through the process of finding a job, from helping you define your career objectives to suggesting ways to prepare yourself for interviews.

Use the advice and checklists below to help identify the kind of work that fits your personality, skills, and interests. Then learn how to locate job openings that match your criteria. Finally, use these tips to help you create a resume and prepare for the interview that helps you land the job that's right for you.

### Planning your Career

What are your unique skills? What kind of workplace appeals to you? What do you find most rewarding in your daily life? Answering these questions can help you identify a career path that will enrich your life, financially and otherwise. Most people enjoy doing a job well. There is an inner satisfaction that comes from taking on a challenge and accomplishing something worthwhile. Whether you are just starting out in the working world or you are at the midpoint of a career, it is worth taking some time to consider whether or not you are in the right kind of work-or looking for the right kind of job. If you are unhappy or dissatisfied in your daily work and are just trying to do enough to get by, you may not be in the right job or the right field. The following ideas can help you match your skills and interests with the kind of work you will find most rewarding.

## Evaluate Yourself

Before you make any career decisions, think about subjects or topics that interest you and tasks you do well. This can help you pinpoint the kind of work you would be happy doing. One way to go about this is to compile a self-inventory chart. Such a chart will be helpful as you decide which jobs you want to consider. Including details about your work history and educational background will also make the chart useful to you as you compile your resume, write cover letters, complete job application forms, and prepare for job interviews.

Begin your self-inventory chart by listing all the jobs you have ever had, including summer employment, part-time jobs, volunteer work, and any freelance or short-term assignments you have done. Include the dates of employment, the names and addresses of supervisors, and the amount of money you earned. Then compile a similar list of your hobbies and other activities, including any special experiences you have had, such as travel. Next, do the same for your educational history, listing schools attended, major courses of study, grades, special honours or awards, courses you particularly enjoyed, and extracurricular activities.

At this point, you may see a career pattern emerging: perhaps your list is already suggesting a direction for your career search. If the picture still lacks detail or focus, expand your self-inventory chart by compiling a list of standard workplace aptitudes, and rate yourself above average, average, or below average for each one. Some skill categories to include in your list are administrative, analytic, athletic, clerical, language, leadership, managerial, manual, mathematical, mechanical, sales, and verbal abilities. Also rate your willingness to accept responsibility and your ability to get along with people. In combination with your educational background, work history, and list of personal interests, this information should help you understand why some kinds of work appeal to you and others do not.

### Evaluate Workplace Characteristics

Another tool to help you find a rewarding job is the "Work Characteristics Checklist" below. Some of these characteristics will be attractive to you. Some will not. Perhaps you will discover that having a workplace with flexible hours, for example, is more important to you than being able to work outdoors. Or maybe you will find that these are both very significant issues in your quality of life.

This checklist can be useful as a guide as you compile your own list of what is important to you in a job or workplace. Do not expect a job to meet all your requirements, however. Focusing on the job characteristics that are most important to you will help you identify the type of work you would find most rewarding. It will also be helpful when it is time to decide whether or not to apply for jobs you discover during the search process.

### Evaluate Career Options

Now that you've evaluated your personal skills, aptitudes, interests, and experience, and you've identified the kinds of workplace characteristics that are important to you, do you feel confident that you know what kinds of jobs you'd be good at? If not, you may wish to consult an experienced career counsellor or take advantage of online resources that can help you find a good career field match.

Most high schools, vocational schools, and colleges provide vocational testing and career counselling guidance for students and alumni. Some local offices of the state employment services affiliated with the federal employment service offer free counselling. Commercial career centers also offer guidance services. There are many tools available to test your interests and aptitudes for the purpose of career counselling. The personal profile that emerges from a skills inventory can be matched with potential career fields to show you what kinds of jobs might be good matches for your interests. These assessment tools will also show you what kind of training is necessary to qualify for jobs in these career fields. You may find programs like this online that you can try for yourself.

For a more comprehensive approach, you may prefer to look into aptitude tests that are administered and interpreted by a career counselor. Most major cities have professional career consultants and career counselling firms. You should make sure to check their reputations before paying for their services. A list of counselling services in your area is available from the American Counselling Association in Alexandria, Virginia.

You can also search the Internet for many services that career counsellors provide. Some sites have online counsellors who can help you with a variety of tasks, such as obtaining information on jobs, careers, and training. They may be able to provide information on available services, including housing assistance, day care facilities, and transportation. A list of career planning resources, including Web sites, is available at the end of this volume.

## Evaluate Specific Jobs

After you have considered what you do well and what you enjoy doing, and identified some career options that provide a good match with your interests and abilities, you're ready to focus on the specific types of jobs that may be available to you. First, make a note of all the jobs in this volume that interest you. Then examine the education and training required for these jobs. Decide whether you qualify or would be able to gain the qualifications. If possible, talk with people who have the kinds of jobs you are considering. Firsthand information can be invaluable. Also look through the appropriate trade and professional journals listed at the end of this essay and check the section at the end of the volume called "Resources" for books and Web sites that contain more detailed information about the jobs. In addition, counsellors usually are helpful. Once you have found out all you can about a particular type of job, compare the features of the job with your work characteristics checklist. See how many characteristics of the job match your work preferences. By completing these steps for all the jobs that appeal to you, you should be able to come up with a list of jobs that match your interests and abilities.

### Work Characteristics Checklist

Do you want a job in which you can

- work outdoors?
- be physically active?
- work with your hands?
- be challenged mentally?
- work with machines?
- work independently?
- work on a team?
- follow clear instructions?
- earn a lot of money?
- have a chance for rapid advancement?
- have good benefits?
- travel in your work?
- work close to home?
- work regular hours?
- have a flexible schedule?
- have a variety of tasks?
- have supervisory responsibilities?
- express your own ideas?
- be a decision maker?

### Finding Job Opportunities

Once you've decided what kind of job suits you, the next step is to look for available positions. Obviously, the more openings you can find, the better your chance of landing a job. People usually apply for many job openings before they find the right employment match. There are many ways to find out about or apply for job openings. Some of these job-hunting techniques are explained on the pages that follow, along with information about how to follow up on job leads.

### Applying in Person

For some jobs, especially part-time or entry-level jobs, you may be able to find employment by visiting the company or companies for which you would like to work. This works best when a company is expanding or jobs are plentiful for other reasons, or when a "help wanted" sign is posted at the company. Applying in person can sharpen your interviewing techniques and give you a chance to see a variety of workplaces. This direct approach is best for hourly labour or service jobs; when applying for other types of work, it is not the method to use unless you are directed to do so. Applicants for professional or supervisory jobs should always send a letter and resume to the company.

### Phone and Letter Campaigns

To conduct a phone campaign, use the business listings of your telephone directory to build a list of companies for which you might like to work. Call their personnel departments and find out whether they have any openings. This technique is not useful in all situations, and it has its drawbacks: you may not be able to make a strong impression by phone, and you will not have a written record of your contacts. Letter writing campaigns can be very effective if the letters are well thought out and carefully prepared. Your letters should always be typed. Handwritten letters and photocopied letters convey a lack of interest or motivation.

You may be able to compile a good list of company addresses in your field of interest by reading the trade and professional publications listed at the end of this essay. Many of the periodicals publish directories or directory issues. Other sources you can use to compile lists of companies are the trade unions and professional organizations listed at the end of each job profile in this volume. The reference librarian at your local library can also help you find appropriate directories. You can also e-mail letters to human resource departments of many companies. Be sure to follow all the same guidelines as you would for traditional letter correspondence.

### Job Finder's Checklist

The following list of job-hunting tips may seem obvious, but getting all the bits and pieces in order beforehand helps when you're looking for a job.

### Resume

Find out whether you will need a resume. If so, bring your resume up to date or prepare a new one. Assemble a supply of neatly printed copies and have an electronic version ready to e-mail to prospective employers.

### References

Line up your references. Ask permission of the people whose names you would like to use. Write down their addresses, phone numbers, and job titles.

### Contacts

Put the word out to everyone you know that you are looking for a job.

### Job Market

Find out where the jobs are. Make a list of possible employers in your field of interest.

### Research

Do a little homework ahead of time-it can make a big difference in the long run. Find out as much as you can about a job, the field, and the company before you apply. A knowledgeable job applicant makes a good impression.

### Organization

Keep a file on your job-hunting campaign with names and dates of employers contacted, ads answered, results, and follow-up.

### Appearance

Make sure that the clothes you plan to wear to an interview are neat and clean. You may need to dress more formally than you would on the job, particularly if you are visiting a personnel office or meeting with a manager. Keep in mind that people will form an opinion of you based on their first impressions. Whether they are paper or electronic, your letters should be addressed to the personnel or human resources department of the organization. If possible, send the letter to a specific person. If you don't know who the correct person is, try to find the name of the personnel director through the directories in the library. You can also call on the phone and say, "I'm writing to ask about employment at your company. To whom should I address my letter?" If you can't find a name, use a standard salutation. It's a good idea to enclose a resume (described later in this essay) with the letter to give the employer a brief description of your educational and work experience.

Keep a list of all the people you write to, along with the date each letter was mailed, or keep a photocopy of each letter. Then you can follow up by writing a brief note or calling people who do not reply within about three weeks.

### Job Databases Online

The World Wide Web can be an excellent resource for job hunters. The Internet currently has thousands of career-related sites where you can read about job openings or post your resume in a database for a possible match with available jobs. Some sites, such as The Monster Board, help you build a resume and post it online as well as allow you to search through a massive database of help-wanted listings. Others employ a search engine to find jobs that match your background, then post your resume online for employers. The Web site called CareerBuilder uses an interactive personal search program that lets you select job criteria such as location, title, and salary; you are then notified by e-mail when a matching position is posted in the database.

Many companies post job openings in their human resource Web pages. You can usually access these lists by visiting the

Web site of a company and clicking on a link called "jobs," "careers," or "employment opportunities." If you find a job that interests you during your online search, whether it's posted at a company's own Web site or on a general listing of jobs, follow the directions given for applying for the position.

Some online ads will provide the contact information you need to send your resume Many career-related Web sites can be found on the Internet. This hypothetical site allows job-seekers to search for a position by location and by job description (for illustration purposes only) and cover letter directly to the employer, either by e-mail or by traditional mail, but other ads direct job hunters to apply directly through a link at the job description.

Job hunters can often find job listings through the Web sites of the professional associations in their career fields. State government Web sites may also provide links to job listings- or to non-government sites that list available jobs.

**Help-Wanted Ads**

Many people find out about job openings by reading the "help-wanted" sections of newspapers, trade journals, and professional magazines. Employers and employment agencies often, though not always, use these classified ad sections to publicize available jobs.

Classified ads use unique terms to convey basic information. You will find some common abbreviations in the chart in this essay titled "Reading the Classifieds." You can usually decode the abbreviations by using common sense, but if something puzzles you, call the newspaper and ask for a translation. Classified ads usually list the qualifications that are required for a particular job and explain how to contact the employer.

As you find openings that interest you, answer each ad using the method requested. Record the date of your contact, and if you don't hear from the employer within two or three weeks, place another call or send a polite note asking whether the job is still open. Don't forget to include your phone number and address in your initial contact.

Some help-wanted ads are "blind ads." These ads give contact information for replying but provide no name, phone number, or address that would identify the company. Employers and employment agencies may place these ads to avoid having to reply to all of the job applicants or being contacted directly by job-seekers.

## Situation-Wanted Ads

Another way to get the attention of potential employers is with a situation-wanted ad. You can place one of these in the classified section of your local newspaper or of a trade journal in your field of interest. Many personnel offices and employment agencies scan these columns when they're looking for new employees. The situation-wanted ad is usually most effective for people who have advanced education, training, or experience, or who are in fields where their unique skills are in great demand.

A situation-wanted ad should be brief, clear, and to the point. Its main purpose is to interest the employer enough so you are contacted for an interview. It should tell exactly what kind of job you want, why you qualify, and whether you are available for full-time or part-time work. Use the same abbreviations that employers use in classified ads. If you are already employed and do not want it known that you are looking for a new position, you can run a blind ad. A blind ad protects your privacy by listing a box number at the publication to which all replies can be sent. They are then forwarded to you. You do not need to give your name, address, or phone number in the ad.

## Networking

A very important source of information about job openings is networking. This means talking with friends and acquaintances about your area of interest. If any of them have friends or relatives in the field, ask if they would be willing to speak with you. There's nothing wrong with telling anyone who will listen that you are looking for a job-family, friends, counsellors, and former employers. This will multiply your sources of information many times over. You can use the Internet to make contacts, too. You can meet people with similar interests in news groups, which are organized by topic. Then you can correspond individually via e-mail. Many fields have professional organizations that maintain Web sites. These can help you keep current on news affecting your field, including employment opportunities. Sometimes a contact knows about a job vacancy before it is advertised. You may have an advantage, then, when you get in touch with the employer. Don't, however, use the contact's name without permission. Don't assume that a contact will go out on a limb by recommending you, either. Once you have received the inside information, rely on your own ability to get the job.

### Placement Services

Most vocational schools, high schools, and colleges have a placement or career service that maintains a list of job openings and schedules visits from companies. If you are a student or recent graduate, you should check there for job leads. Many employers look first in technical or trade schools and colleges for qualified applicants for certain jobs. Recruiters often visit colleges to look for people to fill technical and scientific positions. These recruiters usually represent large companies. Visit your placement office regularly to check the job listings, and watch for scheduled visits by company recruiters.

### State Employment Services

Another source of information about job openings is the local office of the state employment service. Many employers automatically list job openings at the local office. Whether you're looking for a job in private industry or with the state, these offices, which are affiliated with the federal employment service, are worth visiting, online or in person, if there are offices locally.

State employment service offices are public agencies that do not charge for their services. They can direct you to special programs run by the government in conjunction with private industry. These programs, such as the Work Incentive Program for families on welfare, are designed to meet special needs. Some, but not all, of these offices offer vocational aptitude and interest tests and can refer interested people to vocational training centers. The state employment service can be a valuable first stop in your search for work, especially if there are special circumstances in your background. For example, if you did not finish high school, if you have had any difficulties with the law, or if you are living in a difficult home environment, your state employment service office is equipped to help you.

## PRIVATE EMPLOYMENT AGENCIES

State employment services, though free, are usually very busy. If you are looking for more personal service and want a qualified employment counselor to help you find a job, you might want to approach a private employment agency.

Private employment agencies will help you get a job if they think they can place you. Most of them get paid only if they're successful in finding you a job, so you need to show them that you are a good prospect. These agencies will help you prepare a resume if you need one, and they will contact employers they think might be interested in you.

Private employment agencies are in the business of bringing together people who are looking for jobs and companies that are looking for workers. For some positions, usually mid-and higher-level jobs, the employment agency's fee is paid by the employer. In such cases, the job seeker pays no fee. In other cases, you may be required to pay the fee, which is usually a percentage of your annual salary. Paying a fee can be a worthwhile investment if it leads to a rewarding career.

Some agencies may also ask for a small registration fee whether or not you get a job through them. Some agencies may demand that you pay even if you find one of the jobs they are trying to fill through your other contacts. Be sure to read and understand the fine print of any contract you're expected to sign, and ask for a copy to take home. Since the quality of these agencies varies, check to see if an agency is a certified member of a state or national association.

Some employment agencies, called staffing services, operate in a different way. They are usually paid by employers to screen and refer good candidates for job openings. They earn money when they refer a candidate who is hired by the employer. The employee pays no fee. Staffing firms, however, only spend time on candidates they think they may be able to place. Private employment agencies are usually helping many people at one time. They may not have the time to contact you every time they find a job opening. Therefore, you may need to phone them at reasonable intervals after you have registered.

### Civil Service

In your search for work, don't forget that the civil service-federal, state, and local-may have many jobs in your field. You may contact the state employment office or apply directly to the appropriate state or federal agency. The armed services also train and employ civilians in many fields. Don't neglect these avenues for finding jobs. Civil service positions usually require you to take a civil service examination. Books are available to help you prepare for these exams, and your local civil service office can also provide information.

### Unions

In certain fields, unions can be useful sources of information. If you are a member of a union in your field of interest, you may be able to find out about jobs in the union periodical or through people at the union local. If you do not belong to a union, you may contact a union in the field you are interested in for information about available employment services. You will find addresses for some unions in the job profiles in this book.

### Temporary Employment

A good way to get a feel for the job market-what's available and what certain jobs are like-is to work in a temporary job. There are both private and state agencies that can help place people in short-term jobs. Some jobs are seasonal, and extra workers may be needed in the summer or at another busy time.

Temporary employment can increase your job skills, your knowledge of a particular field, and your chances of hearing of permanent positions. In today's tight labour market, many companies are using the services of temporary workers in increasing numbers. In fact, temporary agencies may sign multimillion-dollar contracts to provide businesses with a range of temporary workers. In some cases, temporary workers are in such demand that they may receive benefits, bonuses, and the same hourly wages as equivalent permanent employees. Some temporary agencies are even joining with companies to create long-term career paths for their temporary workers.

### Marketing Yourself

An employer's first impression of you is likely to be based on the way you present yourself on print. Whether it is in an application form or on a resume, you will want to make a good impression so that employers will be interested in giving you a personal interview. A potential employer is likely to equate a neat, well-written presentation with good work habits, and a sloppy, poorly written one with bad work habits.

### Writing an Effective Resume

When you write to a company to follow up a lead or to ask about job openings, you should send information about yourself. The accepted way of doing this is to send a resume with a cover letter.

2

# Managing the Hotel Organisation

## INTRODUCTION

A hotel is an establishment that provides paid lodging, usually on a short-term basis. Hotels often provide a number of additional guest services such as a restaurant, a swimming pool or childcare. Some hotels have conference services and meeting rooms and encourage groups to hold conventions and meetings at their location. Hotels differ from motels in that most motels have drive-up, exterior entrances to the rooms, while hotels tend to have interior entrances to the rooms, which may increase guests' safety and present a more upmarket image.

In Australia, a hotel may also be an establishment that serves alcoholic drinks, and usually meals in a casual setting but which does not necessarily provide accommodation. This type of establishment would more usually be called a pub or bar in other countries. In general use in Australia the terms "'hotel" and *pub* are usually taken to be synonymous. In India, the word may also refer to a restaurant since the best restaurants were always situated next to a good hctel.

## ORIGINS OF THE TERM

The word *hotel* derives from the French *hotel*, which referred to a French version of a townhouse, not a place offering accommodation (in contemporary usage, *hotel* has the meaning of "hotel", and *hotel particulier* is used for the old meaning).

The French spelling (with the circumflex) was once also used in English, but is now rare. The circumflex replaces the 's' once preceding the 't' in the earlier *hostel* spelling, which over time received a new, but closely related meaning.

## SERVICES AND FACILITIES

Basic accommodation of a room with only a bed, a cupboard, a small table and a washstand has largely been replaced by rooms with en-suite bathrooms and, more commonly in the United States than elsewhere, climate control. Other features found may be a telephone, an alarm clock, a TV, and broadband Internet connectivity. Food and drink may be supplied by a mini-bar (which often includes a small refrigerator) containing snacks and drinks (to be paid for on departure), and tea and coffee making facilities (cups, spoons, an electric kettle and sachets containing instant coffee, tea bags, sugar, and creamer or milk).

In the United Kingdom a hotel is required by law to serve food and drinks to all comers within certain stated hours; to avoid this requirement it is not uncommon to come across "private hotels" which are not subject to this requirement.

However, in Japan the capsule hotel supplies minimal facilities and room space.

## CLASSIFICATION

The cost and quality of hotels are usually indicative of the range and type of services available. Due to the enormous increase in tourism worldwide during the last decades of the 20th century, standards, especially those of smaller establishments, have improved considerably. For the sake of greater comparability, rating systems have been introduced, with the one to five stars classification being most common.

## BOUTIQUE HOTELS

"Boutique Hotel" is a term originating in North America to describe intimate, usually luxurious or quirky hotel environments. Boutique hotels differentiate themselves from larger chain or branded hotels by providing an exceptional and personalized level of accommodation, services and facilities. Boutique hotels are furnished in a themed, stylish and/or aspirational manner. Although usually considerably smaller than a mainstream hotel (ranging from 3 to 100 guest rooms) boutique hotels are generally fitted with telephone and wi-fi Internet connections, honesty bars and often cable/pay TV. Guest services are attended to by 24 hour hotel staff. Many boutique hotels have on site dining facilities, and the majority offer bars and lounges which may also be open to the general public.

Of the total travel market a small percentage are discerning travellers, who place a high importance on privacy, luxury and service delivery. As this market is typically corporate travellers, the market segment is non-seasonal, high-yielding and repeat, and therefore one which boutique hotel operators target as their primary source of income.

**Famous Hotels**

Some hotels have gained their renown through tradition, by hosting significant events or persons, such as Schloss Cecilienhof in Potsdam, Germany, which derives its fame from the so-called Potsdam Conference of the World War II allies Winston Churchill, Harry Truman and Joseph Stalin in 1945. Other establishments have given name to a particular meal or beverage, as is the case with the Waldorf Astoria in New York City, USA, known for its *Waldorf Salad* or the Raffles Hotel in Singapore, where the drink *Singapore Sling* was invented. Another example is the Hotel Sacher in Vienna Austria, home of the *Sachertorte.*

There are also hotels which became much more popular through films like the Grand Hotel Europe in Saint Petersburg, Russia when James Bond stayed there in the Blockbuster, Goldeneye. Cannes hotels such as the Carlton or the Martinez become the center of the world during Cannes Film Festival (France).

A number of hotels have entered the public consciousness through popular culture, such as the Ritz Hotel in London, UK ('Putting on The Ritz') and Hotel Chelsea in New York City, subject of a number of songs and also the scene of the alleged stabbing of Nancy Spungen by her boyfriend Sid Vicious. Hotels that enter folklore like these two are also often frequented by celebrities, as is the case both with the Ritz and the Chelsea. Other famous hotels include the Beverly Hills Hotel, the Hotel Bel-Air and the Chateau Marmont, in California, Watergate complex in Washington DC, the Hotel Astoria in Saint Petersburg, Russia, the Hotel George V and Hotel Ritz in Paris, Palazzo Versace hotel on the Gold Coast, Queensland, Australia, Hotel Hermitage and Hotel de Paris in Monaco (in the French Riviera), Peninsula Hotel in Hong Kong and Hotel Leningradskaya in Moscow.

### Unusual Hotels

Many hotels can be considered destinations in themselves, by dint of unusual features of the lodging and/or its immediate environment:

### Treehouse Hotels

Some hotels, such as the Costa Rica Tree House in the Gandoca-Manzanillo Wildlife Refuge, Costa Rica, or Treetops Hotel in Aberdare National Park, Kenya, are built with living trees as structural elements, making them treehouses. The Ariau Towers near Manaus, Brazil is in the middle of the Amazon, on the Rio Negro. Bill Gates even invested and had a suite built there with satellite internet/phone. Another hotel with treehouse units is Bayram's Tree Houses in Olympos, Turkey.

### Cave Hotels

Desert Cave Hotel in Coober Pedy, South Australia and the Cuevas Pedro Antonio de Alarcon (named after the author) in Guadix, Spain, as well as several hotels in Cappadocia, Turkey, are notable for being built into natural cave formations, some with rooms underground.

### Capsule Hotels

Capsule hotels are a type of economical hotels that are quite common in Japan.

**Ice Hotels**

Ice hotels, such as the Ice Hotel in Jukkasjarvi, Sweden, melt every spring and are rebuilt out of ice and snow each winter.

**Snow Hotels**

The Mammut Snow Hotel in Finland is located within the walls of the Kemi snow castle, which is the biggest in the world. It includes The Mammut Snow Hotel, The Castle Courtyard, The Snow Restaurant and a chapel for weddings, etc. Its furnishings and its decorations, such as sculptures, are made of snow and ice.

There is snow accommodation also in Lainio Snow Hotel in Lapland (near Yllas), Finland.

**Garden Hotels**

Garden hotels, famous for their gardens before they became hotels, includes Gravetye Manor, the home of William Robinson and Cliveden, designed by Charles Barry with a rose garden by Geoffrey Jellicoe.

**Underwater Hotels**

As of 2005, the only hotel with an underwater room that can be reached without Scuba diving is Utter Inn in Lake Malaren, Sweden. It only has one room, however, and Jules' Undersea Lodge in Key Largo, Florida, which requires scuba diving, is not much bigger.

Hydropolis is an ambitious project to build a luxury hotel in Dubai, UAE, with 220 suites, all on the bottom of the Persian Gulf, 20 meters (66 feet) below the surface. Its architecture will feature two domes that break the surface and an underwater train tunnel, all made of transparent materials such as glass and acrylic.

**Other unusual Hotels**

The Library Hotel in New York City is unique in that its ten floors are arranged according to the Dewey Decimal System. The Rogers Centre, formerly SkyDome, in Toronto, Canada is the only stadium to have a hotel connected to it, with 70 rooms overlooking the field.

The Burj al-Arab hotel in Dubai, United Arab Emirates, built on an artificial island, is structured in the shape of a sail of a boat.

The RMS Queen Mary in Long Beach, California is the only 1930s ocean liner still in existence. Its elegant first-class staterooms are now used as a hotel. The Oriental Pearl Tower in Shanghai houses an extremely expensive hotel with only 20 rooms.

## WORLD-RECORD SETTING HOTELS

### Tallest

The tallest hotel in the world is the Burj al-Arab in Dubai, United Arab Emirates, at 321 metres, which however will soon be surpassed by the nearby Rose Rotana Suites at 333 meters (1,091 feet). The Ryugyong Hotel in Pyongyang was intended to reach 330 meters (1,083 feet), but is unlikely to be completed; it has been under construction since 1987 and was abandoned in 1992.

The highest hotel rooms are in the *Grand Hyatt* in the Jin Mao Building in Shanghai, the highest floor being at around 350 m.

### Largest

The largest hotel in the world is the MGM Grand Las Vegas in Las Vegas, Nevada, USA with a total of 6,276 rooms as of December 20, 2006. On December 18, 2006 Guinness World Records listed the First World Hotel in Genting Highlands, Malaysia as the worlds largest hotel. It has a total of 6,118 rooms and is part of the Genting Highlands Resort and Casino.

The First World Plaza which is joined to the two hotel towers boasts 500,000 square feet of indoor theme park, shopping centres, casino gaming areas, and eateries. Previously, Guinness had listed the MGM Grand Las Vegas in Las Vegas, Nevada, USA with 5,005 rooms as the largest hotel in the world.

### Oldest

According to the Guinness Book of World Records, the oldest hotel still in operation is the Hoshi Ryokan, in Awazu, Japan. It opened in 717, and features hot springs.

## HOTEL OCCUPATIONS

The owner, chairman, or CEO of a hotel or hotel group is known as a *hotelier*.

### Living in Hotels

The American billionaire Howard Hughes lived much of his life in hotels. He moved with his entourage from hotel to hotel and from Beverly Hills to Boston before deciding to move to Las Vegas and become a casino baron. Less than a month after his November 27, 1966 arrival, Hughes made a public offer to buy the Desert Inn.

The hotel's 8th floor became the nerve center of his empire and the 9th floor penthouse became Hughes's personal residence. Hughes moved to the Bahamas, Vancouver, London and several other locations — always taking up residence in the top floor penthouse of the hotel. Between 1966 and 1968, he also purchased several other hotel-casinos from the Mafia: Castaways, New Frontier, The Landmark Hotel and Casino, Sands and Silver Slipper.

Coco Chanel made the Hotel Ritz in Paris her home for more than thirty years, until the day of her death, at 87, in a suite now named "Coco Chanel Suite".

King Peter II of Yugoslavia spent much of the Second World War at Claridge's, a hotel in London. His son, Aleksandar Karadordevis, was born in the hotel.

Prince Felix Yusupov lived in the Hotel Vendome in Paris.

Alois Brunner, Austrian Nazi war criminal, is believed to have lived in the Meridian Hotel in Damascus, Syria, under the name Georg Fischer.

Sultan Said Bin Taimur of Muscat lived at Dorchester Hotel in London after he was deposed by Qaboos of Oman in

1970, He died in the hotel in 1972. Eleftherios Venizelos, Greek statesman and diplomat, lived in the Hotel Ritz Paris while he was in exile in France from 1935-1936.

## HOTELS IN FICTION

Hotels have been chosen by authors as settings for crime fiction, farce and mystery works. A hotel is perfect as a mysterious, anonymous setting where various characters may gather. Hotels also feature in films, television series, songs and even theme park rides.

### Taj Hotels

Taj Hotels Resorts and Palaces is the largest Indian luxury hotel chain. A wholly owned subsidiary of the Tata Group, Taj Hotels Resort and Palaces comprises 57 hotels in 39 locations across India with an additional 18 international hotels in the Maldives, Mauritius, Malaysia, Seychelles, United Kingdom, United States of America, Bhutan, Sri Lanka, Africa, the Middle East and Australia.

Their first and most well known property is the Taj Mahal Palace & Tower in Colaba, Mumbai. The Taj Mahal Palace & Tower, Mumbai was opened on December 16, 1903, by the founder of the Tata Group, Jamshetji Nusserwanji Tata. Taj President-a business hotel and Taj Land's End-an ultimate luxury boarding are also located in Mumbai.

It operates TajAir, a luxury private jet operation with state-of-the-art Falcon 2000 aircraft designed by Dassault Aviation, France; and Taj Yachts, two 3-bedroom luxury yachts which can be used by guests in Mumbai and Kochi.

### Falaknuma Palace

Falaknuma Palace is situated on a hill 650 meters in height, in the Old City of Hyderabad, India. It was built by Nawab Vikar-ul-Umra. It was purchased by the then Nizam VI during 1897 for use as a royal guest house. The palace provides a good view of Hyderabad.

The palace is spread out in a scorpion shape with two pincers spread out as wings on the north. The middle part occupies the main building. The Harem quarters and the kitchen stretch towards the south.

The palace was designed by an Italian architect. The palace boasts of lavishly decorated interiors made of the Italian marble, and follows a western architectural style. It took almost nine years to complete. This famous palace houses a large collection of rare treasures, paintings, statues, furniture, manuscripts and books collected by the Nizam. The jade collection displayed here is considered to be unique in the world. Some old models of artillery are also exhibited in the front. The Palace is being converted into a heritage hotel by the Taj Hotels group.

## OPERATIONS OF THE HOTELS

No hotel company operating today can be unaware of the swift pace of global change and its impact on every facet of the hospitality industry. With just five years left in this century, we can expect change to be the only constant. New business practices are evolving virtually as fast as our technologies, while resistance to change has become one of the primary causes of business failure.

The specter of constant change raises fundamental questions as to the creation of shareholder wealth in a capital-constrained, highly competitive environment. How will hotel organizations build shareholder wealth, and what key drivers will result in success? What future products and services will be essential in a technology-driven, global environment marked by rising customer expectations? Moreover, what alternative approaches and skills must organizations develop to ensure market success? The future success of hotel organizations will be driven in large part by the ability to foresee--and capitalize--on change. Beyond this truism, however, there is an urgent need to identify what will be required in the competitive environment of the future with its intense focus on serving customer needs.

The hospitality industry--as is the case with business generally--is subject to deep currents of change set in motion as economic and social systems shaped in the industrial era evolve to a knowledge-based era driven by technology advances.

In this period of global transition, it behooves hotel organizations to examine the key factors that will not only define success, but the ability to survive in coming years. Many of these issues were spotlighted in a global study undertaken by the Economist Intelligence Unit and co-sponsored by Arthur Andersen. The Successful Corporation of the Year 2000 surveyed more than 600 senior executives around the world. Its mission was to identify the characteristics needed to lead successful businesses in the next century. These executives offer a number of compelling messages regarding the key success factors of the future.

Customers will have the strongest influence on the corporation in the year 2000. Indeed, these executives believe that the customer will be "king" in the new century. Exceptional leadership was by far the attribute most frequently cited by CEOs and senior executives; the consensus appears to be that successful companies in the year 2000 will be led by corporate visionaries.

A strategic planning focus is not only essential, but must embody a concept of planning for the future that anticipates change, rather than being based exclusively on historical models. In structuring organizations for the future, companies must build management capabilities to deal with one of the most critical challenges--diversity in the marketplace. Employing information technology to drive business success in this information-driven era is not only the path of least resistance, but vital to virtually every aspect of operations.

The study's top-line results create an excellent backdrop to address key issues confronting the hotel industry, and what factors will lead to membership--rather than rejection--in the elite club of the world's corporate success stories in the year 2000.

## FROM AN ASSET TO CUSTOMER FOCUS

Recognizing that the hotel industry has a somewhat split personality reflecting the inherent conflicts between its real estate and operational aspects, it is important to understand the industry's real estate origins and how they are shaping the challenges ahead. The origins of the industry's real estate persona are embodied in the classic theory of location-"if we build it, they will come." As a result of this "building" complex, the industry has tended to have a real estate and asset orientation, rather than a customer focus. From the hotel company perspective--especially that of the brand-oriented "chain"--the varied interests of a diffused property ownership group can be quite different than the singular interest of the chain that operates and markets the properties.

Even when the ownership of geographically dispersed hotel properties is controlled by a single hotel organization, the financial structuring tends to be property-specific. Corporate financial strategies are frequently subjugated to the needs of the last property deal brought into the company's fold.

Each property in a so-called "chain," is frequently the subject of a unique and distinctive ownership and financial structure. This phenomenon--quite common in the real estate sector, but unusual for business enterprises generally--makes for elusive economies of scale in the structuring and financing of property-driven expansion.

Collectively, these factors have produced low comparative returns in real estate, although criticism leveled at commercial real estate returns is somewhat less germane to the hotel industry, where management and franchise fees can produce high returns for those companies where property ownership is held by third parties. Nevertheless, average returns in the real estate industry in the United States, for example, are just over 10 percent, compared to small company stock returns at almost 20 percent and large company stocks at an average of about 15 percent.

While hotel chains have adopted traditional corporate frameworks, there are a number of predominantly real estate-driven, family-owned businesses in the hotel sector that continue to operate as relatively unstructured organizations. In meeting the future, these businesses will need plans, people and processes in order to establish viable corporate forms that can compete in tomorrow's marketplace and capitalize upon its opportunities.

In today's changed environment, the hotel organization must deal with a number of new realities. Investors in our industry are no longer satisfied with long-term capital appreciation and psychic income that heretofore were often the justification for otherwise seemingly uneconomic investments in hotel property or, indeed, hotel chains.

The first reality is that there is a very specific and identifiable relationship between bottom line performance and value. Improvements in business operations raises values. It is not surprising, therefore, that the new owners attracted to this industry in recent years have new sets of demands. This transformation from an old-guard group of investors and owners to income and return-driven newcomers has meant that the once "quiet enjoyment" of operators in their management of hotels for third parties is being disturbed, interrupted and overturned.

These challenges all take place in an environment where capital has become extremely selective in markets that have little stability. A global shortage of capital will not remain a short-term problem, and future hotel organizations must have a stronger alignment to capital providers--a critical "customer" group. Hotel companies will need to compete by offering better returns and performance than in the past. Hotel chains have found their development timetables quashed in recent years, making it difficult to achieve goals of critical mass often required to improve performance. These factors are driving consolidation in the brand "sweepstakes." Capital markets, therefore, continue to favour well-established companies, a reality that must drive entrepreneurial organizations to meet the future now by planning for an evolving corporate context in which to operate.

## KEY SUCCESS FACTORS

Within this broad context, hotel developers, owners and management companies will all need to develop new strategies, skills and processes that look forward to the competitive demands of the future. These ultimately must address issues related to vision and planning, as well as organizational skill sets and processes to attract and retain customers. To stake a claim in the future, current business practices should be examined in light of what can be expected to be the key success factors in the year 2000.

Embrace a global change orientation. As the information age produces greater worldwide integration of business activities, a global knowledge base will become invaluable. Success in local and regional hotel markets will be shaped decisively by a global business environment that defines capital movement, customer expectations and applications of new technologies.

Focus on the Customer. If the customer is "king" in the 21st century, hotel organizations will be best served by focusing less on their hotel assets as measures of success, and more on their customers.

This involves a fundamental shift in viewing the real estate asset as the wealth creator--to the customer as the key to building shareholder wealth. A customer focus must imbue business decisions at all levels of developing and operating a hotel organization. Pursuing such a course will inevitably impact shareholder wealth. To accomplish this, however, customers need to participate in the product development process.

Fully realizing a customer focus in the industry poses a significant challenge. The hotel industry must confront problems due to conflicts between operational needs and real estate goals. Quite simply, an operator must remain customer-focused, but the short-term strategies to meet these needs may be inconsistent with the long-term objectives of property owners. Balancing those goals will be essential. A customer focus implies a significant shift in what drives hotel development--placing primary emphasis on the customer with the locations to follow. Nevertheless, a hotel organization with its large investment in fixed assets--the real estate--can never be as nimble as a consumer products company in adjusting products and services to match rapid shifts in the marketplace.

The Japanese taught us that the concept of "zero defects" in products and services can yield tremendous benefits. But today an even more rigorous standard dominates--quality that surprises. In practical terms, the hotel industry finds it extremely difficult to meet the standard of zero defects in service. Hotel services are based primarily on people, not computers or other equipment. Quality that surprises takes the concept of zero defects a step further. Yesterday's surprising product or service is today's status quo.

Twenty years ago, a business executive did not expect a consistent and predictable level of service wherever he or she travelled in the world. Today that is a standard--not the exception--as is the expectation for sophisticated technology in hotel rooms to support business needs. With customer discrimination so acute, it is not surprising that brand loyalty is a diminishing "commodity" in the hotel industry.

Find the ingredients for visionary leadership. Today's hotel organizations need to recognize the need for visionary leadership. The ability to forecast the future--to anticipate change rather than react to it--will be one of the single greatest determinants of market dominance in the years ahead. The old "command and control" model of leadership is giving way to a focus on leadership in ideas, information, inspiration, vision and teamwork. Warren Bennis, an authority on leadership in the U.S., puts it this way--"For the most part, failing organizations tend to be over-managed and under-led. The leader sets the tone for the moral character, the vision, the corporate culture and the fiber of the institution."

While visionary leadership is essential, it must be linked to business operations and foster a risk bias, rather than a procedural bias. This will allow the organization to stretch and, in turn, change. And it must be shared by empowered professionals and staff throughout the organization, including those who meet the customer. Overcoming the resistance to change can be a daunting task, particularly in large hotel organizations in which diversions from the status quo may threaten established management lines. It suggests that a culture based on conformance may need to be replaced by an emphasis on flexibility, learning and cooperation. Management competencies will need to be aligned in order to achieve the desired result. For many organizations, this may mean a shift from traditional hierarchies typical of companies in an industrial era to a flatter organization with a more transparent interface between leadership, organizational functions and employees.

Create a defensible position through corporate strategy. For many of the industry's leaders, vision is driven by the strategic planning process, a function which has become critical for success.

Strategic planning, however, has at times been a step-child in the hotel industry, and it is often the first to be cut when organizations are downsized. It is clearly in transition. There also has been a tendency to decentralize and simplify this function--both actions of potential benefit. Strategic planning must be led by the top people in the organization--the CEO and COO. On the other hand, it should be close enough to the customer to ensure that planners can "listen" to and be influenced by customer needs.

**Empower Management**: Beyond the ability to envision the future, core management capabilities will make the difference--they are essential. A clear vision without the management skills to support it cannot be a recipe for success. First and foremost, hotel management must have strategic development skills and the ability to integrate complex factors affecting success. Market volatility has become the norm, in part caused by the rapidly changing tastes of customers. Customers are increasingly approaching the hotel industry with widely different social, economic and political backgrounds, to say nothing of employees. Being able to deal with these diversities in a positive and constructive fashion that capitalizes on the differences, rather than working to find ways to mitigate them, is the clear path for successful management in the future.

The organization will also need to be imbued with a sense of entrepreneurship that reacts proactively to the market's diversity. Traditional organizations that follow well-documented rules must give way to leaders who can balance a sense of discipline with that of flexibility. Talent and resources must be marshalled and leveraged. In an industry with high fixed costs and labour intensity, the concept of leverage in the hotel business is an all-important one. Improving labour productivity through technology must be a goal for today's forward-looking hotel organization.

Management must also be able to narrow the gap between the employer and the employee, forcing a flatter organization in the process. This will put management closer to the customer and speed the two-way communication process up and down the organization.

**Be in the Information Fast Lane**: The traditional role of information technology (IT) as a back office support for accounting and bookkeeping has clearly moved front and center stage.

IT today influences all aspects of business from corporate strategies to organizational structure--and from the very business processes it is designed to support to performance measurement. In a world where the customer is "king," IT must also deliver in two critical areas: sales and marketing and customer service.

Technology was once viewed as a way to reduce costs by replacing people. That attitude has been firmly supplanted by one that seeks IT support for the creative work that all organizations must pursue. IT must allow organizations to react more speedily to market needs and, of course, produce the fulfilment of customer demands both quickly and accurately. To do this IT must operate on a decentralized basis. IT delivers, but it has to be the right information to the right people, and it needs to be done on a timely basis.

## IMPROVING MANAGEMENT (GEF) PROJECT

Improving Management of NGO and Privately Owned Nature Reserves and High Biodiversity Islands in Seychelles Project funded by the Global Environment Facility through the World Bank

The Seychelles is known world wide as a storehouse of rare biodiversity. Historically, most of the islands and ecosystems have been severely impacted by human activities. Nevertheless, a few examples of whole island ecosystems have been protected and restored. These islands are Cousin, Cousine, Aride, Fregate and Aldabra, all managed, surprisingly, by civil society organisations. Nevertheless, there are significant barriers to sustainability of conservation efforts by these organisations.

The focus of the project is two islands, Cousin and Cousine, which are host to numerous rare and endemic species, and immense biodiversity. These include shared resources such as 10 species of breeding seabirds, 5 species of endemic land birds, rare floral species, 8 species of reptiles and hundreds species of invertebrates, the most important population of hawksbill turtles in the Western Indian Ocean and the highest biomass of reef fish in the granitic islands of Seychelles.

The project is to ensure the islands' function as a reserve for the preservation of globally important biodiversity through understanding processes and changes in sites, species and habitats in the islands for better management and decision-making on activities to preserve this globally important biodiversity.

Cousin and Cousine are adjacent to Praslin-the second most populous island of the Seychelles. Cousin was purchased in the 1960's through a world wide appeal at a time when unique biodiversity in Seychelles was in jeopardy. An international NGO held the title to the island because land tenureship was the only method of securing the island for perpetuity and thereby restoring the ecosystems. This NGOs also assisted the previous owners of Cousine in the early years to conserve its biodiversity. This proved to be a very wise move because the islands are remarkable in that unlike other granitic islands of Seychelles, endemic and globally important fauna and flora have been saved.

They have been protected by NGO/private resources and management, and at least for Cousin, through national legislation and policy.

The ownership and management regimes by civil society organisations and the relative remoteness, which are the main reasons why biodiversity has been saved, are now proving to be constraints for not only continuing with established activities but also for initiating new programs; the civil society organisations cannot source adequate resources from the local private sector, governmental or international sources. In addition, anthropogenic impacts and lack of knowledge of ecosystem-level changes, all mean that science and conservation action on each of them cannot move beyond present capacity and limits.

The project assumption is that conservation of island biodiversity can be sustained and at the same time greatly improved through an inter-island integrated and collaborative approach geared to clear management outcomes and also to the development of public education and community buy-in. The project recognises the importance of developing financial sustainability to maintain these conservation programs. The project intends to build long-term capacity for sustainable conservation and use of island biodiversity through program and capacity building, infrastructure acquisition and installation, co-management, and education and advocacy.

The two islands are small, close to each other, and share similar and sensitive ecosystems, associated conservation activities and problems. They are both focused on biodiversity conservation, chiefly concerning globally threatened endemic land birds and internationally important colonies of breeding seabirds. Each island also hosts similar important reptile, botanical and invertebrate species. Both islands have a distinguished conservation history and offer a slightly different model and philosophy for biodiversity conservation. Cousin Island is owned by an international NGO but managed by an independent, locally registered, not-for-profit Association. Cousine Island is owned and managed by a private limited company registered in Seychelles. Management of the islands are supposed to be undertaken with in-country resources.

## PROJECT VISION

The project will remove barriers that currently prevent civil society organisations from augmenting and enhancing their capacity to conserve and restore species, sites and habitats. The project will aims to create partnerships between neighbouring islands which have shared globally important biodiversity and similar environmental issues. This will be done through a substantial number of new and improved linked programs, the creation of a common resource and management center, institutional strengthening and capacity building, and public education and advocacy. The ultimate aim of this model partnership is to catalyze further collaboration and public buy-in, to remove other barriers and to mitigate negative ecosystem changes. The process set in motion by the project will improve the management of high biodiversity islands as well as increase the number of managed conservation sites in Seychelles. This project will thus have global biodiversity benefits, lead to greater sustainability of biodiversity and permit the sharing of these benefits to be directed principally at local levels. The vision mirrors the three principal objectives of the 1992 Convention of Biological Diversity.

## OVERALL GOAL OF THE PROJECT

The Goal of the project is to improve management of biodiversity-rich islands by installing a shared multi-pronged programme framework and infrastructure for enhanced and sustainable conservation, financing and use of biodiversity. The project vision and overall goal will be delivered through two principal components namely Small Island Ecosystem Management, and Public Education and Advocacy.:.

### *Component 1: Small Island Ecosystem Management*

A. Improved management of terrestrial and marine habitats and important species.

B. Establish collaborative management and resource center on Praslin

C. Institutional strengthening

D. Capacity building and training

### *Component 2: Public Education and Advocacy*

A. Develop biodiversity awareness and advocacy programs

B. Establish community outreach, partnerships and stakeholder participation programs

## PROJECT PARTNERS

Nature Seychelles, formerly known as Bird Life Seychelles, is a local not-for-profit association registered in Seychelles. It is currently the largest independent environment organisation in Seychelles. The association is involved in a suite of activities including species and habit conservation, monitoring, research, island restoration, eco-tourism, education and awareness and advocacy. Nature Seychelles manages Cousin Island Special Reserve and has a presence on several other islands. It has a multi-stakeholder and result-oriented approach through its programs such as the Seychelles Magpie-robin Recovery Team (SMART) and the Seychelles Seabird Group (SSG) as well with other organisations such as the Wild Life Clubs of Seychelles, Ministry of Environment and Ministry of Education.

Its donors and partners include the World Bank/GEF and the Royal Society for Protection of Birds. It is a member of the Bird Life International network, WIOMSA, the African Bird Club and IUCN, works in close collaboration with WWF, the Mauritian WildLife Foundation and many others. Cousine Island LTD (Owner and Manger of Cousine Island): is a private limited company registered in the Seychelles. The company has built a very small and ecologically friendly luxury hotel. The island is not legally protected and the owner is not obliged to conserve its biodiversity. The company has voluntarily put in a system for biodiversity conservation using its own resources. It delegates management responsibility for the island to a Conservation Warden.

The Warden works in close collaboration with the hotel manager. The purpose of setting up the small hotel is to bring in sufficient revenues to maintain the conservation and research programs on the island and to maintain it as a high biodiversity area. The company supports other conservation programs in Seychelles, for example the Magpie Robin Recovery Program and the Seychelles Rare Birds Committee.

## LANDMARKS ACHIEVEMENTS

Hotel Association of India, established on 24th October 1996, within a short span of less than a decade of its inception, has successfully provided an integrated hospitality platform produced ground breaking results and recorded several notable 'firsts' for the hospitality industry described in the ensuing pages:

## Export House Status for Tourism and Hospitality Industry

Among the path breaking industry 'first' initiatives of Hotel Association of India is the unique recognition secured for tourism and hospitality sectors in India as 'export industries'. This was an unparelled achievement of the Association which undertook the entire groundwork and created consensus in support of according export status for hospitality industries.

HAI organized series of inter-active meetings with the concerned Ministries of the Government of India, culminating in a high level Conclave presided over by Shri Ramakrishna Hegde, then Hon'ble Minister of Commerce, Government of India, on 16th July 1998 at the Oberoi Hotel, New Delhi which cleared the decks for the action plan blue-printed by HAl receiving the official seal of approval of the Government of India manifested in the a Gazette Notification of November 26th, 1998 declaring Hotels and Tourism Units eligible for the benefits of Service Export House/International Service Export House/International Star Service Export House/International Super Star Service Export House categories on the basis of their quantum of foreign exchange earnings.

This extraordinary recognition placed hotels and tourism units on par with industries engaged in export of products for imports of projects and products against their foreign exchange entitlements and facilitated hotels in acquiring competitive edge vis-a-vis hotels overseas in providing world class facilities.

## Tourism Export Promotion Council

Another notable first for hospitality and tourism industries, synchronizing with the grant of Export House Status, was notched by the Hotel Association of India by formulating the Constitution of the Tourism Export Promotion Council (TEPC) on 20th November 1998. The approval of the Company Law

Board was also secured for the new body under Section 25 of the Companies Act 1956. TEPC represented an unique experiment in bringing together for the first time all constituents of the tourism sector-hotels, travel agents, tour operators, transporters, airlines, tourism finance companies-under a single umbrella on a common platform.

## Establishment of SAARC Hotel Association

HAI reached beyond the national boundaries to provide regional co-operation aiming hotels in South Asia and became the prime mover in the formation of the SAARC Hotel Association.

This was achieved by developing close synergy between the hospitality industry organizations of Bangladesh, Bhutan, India, Maldives, Nepal, Pakistan and Sri Lanka. The SAARC Hotel Association was formally launched at Mumbai on 7th April 1999 with Nepal being assigned the responsibility of hosting the SAARC body for its initial two years and later by rotation by other member countries.

## International Code of Conduct to Govern Relations Between Hoteliers, Travel Agents and Tour Operators

For the first time in the history of travel trade in India on 28.4.2000, HAI successfully evolved consensus among the Travel Agents Association of India (TAAI) and the Indian Association of Tour Operators (IATO) and the Hotel Association of India (HAI) resulting in the signing of the International Code of Practice governing the relations between Hoteliers, Travel Agents and Tour Operators.

The code represents a watershed for the tourism and travel industry in India, as protracted negotiations for adopting a code of practice for over three decades had not yielded any results till HAI took the lead and crafted consensus in favour of adopting the global practice. It's signing by the three national bodies signalled to the international travel fraternity and business travellers that India had opted for internationally approved policies of hotel bookings, cancellations, refunds, claims etc.

## Legal 'First' for Hotel Industry

The Hotel Association of India took the lead in invoking the intervention of the High Court of Delhi in protecting the interests of hospitality industry in India on a matter of vital importance to the hotels as well as to the foreign and domestic tourist staying in hotels. Hotel Association of India filed a writ in the High Court Delhi against an arbitrary and ad hoc administrative directive requiring the hotels in approved categories, classified by the Ministry of Tourism, to follow a Single Tariff system. The directive would have proved detrimental and counter productive to national tourism interests. The industry perspective presented by HAI was accepted by the High Court of Delhi which granted a Stay in favour of hotel industry, signifying an unique legal validation of hospitality industry system of operation across the country.

## Seeking Repeal of Anti-women Legislation

The Punjab Excise Act enacted during the British rule in India in 1914 contains an archaic and anti-women provision prohibiting the employment of women in licenced premises, i.e., bars and restaurants in hotels. The Hotel Association of India challenged the validity of this ancient legislation before the Hon'ble High Court to protect the interest of women. The HAI's Writ against the constitutional validity of the provisions of the Punjab Excise Act, 1914

## Media Centric Initiatives

The large number of foreign correspondents stationed in India, representing powerful and popular foreign publications, newspapers, journals, T. V. Channels, Broadcasters play a major role in making or marring the image of India as a peaceful tourists destination country through their news reports and dispatches. HAI took the lead in organizing the first ever hospitality industry meeting with the foreign correspondent stationed in New Delhi.

The event was organized with the objective to discuss adverse the impact of Travel Advisories issued by foreign Governments on the State of Indian hospitality and tourism industry and correct their perspective to restore consumer confidence in travel, tourism and hospitality sectors adversely affected by global events of preceding years. Because of the unique nature of the special event and its potential for future tourists arrivals in India, the Ministry of Tourism fully associated with HAI.

## Survey on the Impact of Travel Advisories in Hospitality Industry

Foreign Embassies and Missions are often instrumental in advising their respective countries to issue "Travel Advisories" to caution their citizens from undertaking visits to specific countries owing to adverse conditions of safety and security. Travel Advisories against visiting India were issued by several countries following global events like the terrorist attacks on 9/11 in USA and 13/12 in New Delhi, War in Afghanistan and tension on Indo-Pak borders etc. The adverse travel advisories affected tourists arrivals to India over a prolonged period.

The Hotel Association of India stepped in by organizing an innovative Survey among foreign tourists staying in hotels to obtain their reactions to such advisories issued by the foreign governments.

The HAI Survey brought out that a preponderant majority of tourists declared India as a safe and peaceful destination and foreign travellers viewed the travel advisories and warnings as "coloured by political considerations" and based on "inadequate knowledge of ground realities". Some of them opined that they found New Delhi "safer than Manhattan". HAI Survey facilitated the Governments of the respective countries in reviewing and withdrawing the adverse travel advisories and re-assured tourists of their safety and security in India.

## Setting Up of Confederation of Indian Travel and Tourism Industry

Another first initiative mooted by the Association related to the need for creating a Confederation of Indian Travel and Tourism Industry (CITTI) as an umbrella organization to represent all components of the Travel & Travel industry in

India. Unlike other industries, there has never been an umbrella organization in the tourism industry. To fill this gap, HAI proposed the setting up of CITTI which would address the policy issues and concerns of the industry. The Constitution of the proposed new body has been drawn up and made available to all sectoral associations to facilitate its establishment in the future.

## Study of Tariff System in Hotels

The first ever 'While Paper' on Tariff Systems in Hotels in India, produced by a Central Government Autonomous Organisation the National Institute of Public Finance and Policy (NIPFP), was undertaken at the behest of the Hotel Association of India. The NIPFP headed by eminent economists of the standing of Dr. Raja J Chelliah, former Chief Economic Advisor of the Government of India and Dr. C. Rangarajan, former Governor of the Reserve Bank of India, provided the Indian hospitality industry with its most appropriate perspective and authentic study of tariff systems.

## First Afro-Asian Infotech Hotels Expo

HAI-led initiative resulted in Afro-Asian Region's first Conference-cum-Exposition on Information Technology being institutionalized as 'an annual event in New Delhi for countries in the South Asian Region.

The first Conference-cum-Expo organized by HAl on April 10-11, 2000 at the ITC Maurya Sheraton Hotel, New Delhi received support from the United Nations Economic and Social Commission for Asia and the Pacific, and the SAARC Tourism Council. The Ministries of Tourism and Information Technology, Government of India, extended official support to HAl as Co-sponsors of the event.

## Second Afro-Asian Infotech-hotels Expo

The Second Conference-cum-Exposition on Information Technology in Hotels was organized on March 15-16, 2001 at the Taj Palace Hotel, New Delhi. This Afro-Asian conference was supported by United Nation Economic and Social

Commission for Asia and like the front conference the Pacific (UN-ESCAP); Ministry of Tourism, Ministry of Information Technology, Government of India, SAARC Tourism Council and SAARC Hotel Association, Pacific Asia Travel Association (PATA) and International Hotel & Restaurant Association (IH&RA).

### Creating a National Network of HAI Chapters

The Hotel Association of India, established in April 1997, enlisted co-operation on a voluntary basis of professional hoteliers in twenty five State and fifty three cities to monitor hospitality related developments to enable the Association to address the concerns of the hospitality industry at the grass-roots level.

### Going Global with Knowledge Exchange Partners

Knowledge Exchange partnerships were formed with international organization such as the World Travel and Tourism Council (WTTC); the Pacific Asia Travel Association (PATA); World Tourism Organisation (WTO); the International Hotel and Restaurant Association (IH&RA); the United Nation Economic and Social Commission for Asia and the Pacific (UN-ESCAP); the South Asia Association of Regional Countries (SAARC), the World Health Organisation (WHO) and the European Union's South Asia Integrated Tourism Human Resource Development Programme (EU-SAITHRDP).

### Inter-sectoral Linkages With Apex National Fora

At the National level working partnerships were established with apex industry for a like the Federation of Indian Chamber of Commerce and Industry (FICCI); Associated Chamber of Commerce and Industry of India (ASSOCHAM); Confederation of Indian Industry (CII); to provide hospitality industry perspective in the formation of national industrial policies and development.

### Affiliation with World Health Organisation (WHO)

HAI's pioneered the concept of 'Healthy Hotels' in line with WHO's 'Healthy Cities' campaign by initiating programmes for the hospitality industry on 'Hygiene Management in Hotels' at Agra in 1997. The WHO representative in India delivered the keynote address at the First Hygiene Management Seminar.

### Innovative-"India Quiz Contest" at ITB Berlin 2002

A new promotional first was scored by the HAI at ITB Berlin, held from 16th to 20th March 2002. This was the first time 25 leading Indian hotels were brought together by HAI on the industry net to sponsor prizes of FAM Holiday Tours to Travel Trade visitors at the ITB. The India Quiz Contest brochure of HAI provided a high visibility to the Indian hospitality industry products among visitor to the ITB, Berlin. The participating hotels received excellent marketing exposure of their properties in the Quiz brochure. This also offered unique opportunities for prospective agents and operator for the familiarization and experience of the hotels.

### Guidelines for Provision of Disabled Friendly Facilities in Hotels

The Association undertook a pioneering role in formulating a comprehensive set of Guidelines for provision of Disabled Friendly facilities in Hotels, especially in parking and Approach Areas, Lobbies, Public Areas, Lifts, Rooms, Bathrooms and to install special Fire Prevention measures for the disabled.

### Promoting Public-Private Partnership

The Association in a step towards promoting the public-private partnership called upon its members to extend their full corporation to the Archeological Survey of India in the maintenance of the National monuments, which has translated into following public-private sector partnership:-

(i) Illumination of Humayun's Tomb at Delhi by the Oberoi Group of Hotels.

(ii) Development of facilities for visitors at the Agra Fort by the ITC Hotels Ltd.

(iii) Main entrance of the Jantar Mantar observatory at New Delhi by the Apeejay Surrendra Park Hotels Pvt. Ltd.

(iv) Illumination of the Safdarjung Tomb, New Delhi by the Grand Group of

### 62 Special Promotional Packages in Hotels

A major initiative undertaken by HAI galvanized the entire Indian hospitality industry to come together under the Association's banner to offer for the first time in the history of the industry as many as 62 special promotional packages in hotels for marketing averages in association with Air India.

### Memorandum of Undertakings Signed with the Hotel Association of Nepal and the Uganda Investment Authority

The Hotel Association of India signed two Memorandum of Understanding which aimed at fostering and promoting tourism in their respective countries by inter alia agreeing to exchange information in respect to development and trend in the fields of tourism, hospitality and hotel sectors and encourage interaction between their respective hotels and Hospitality Association of India for Tourism Promotion and exploring investment opportunities in these sectors.

### India Quiz Contest Brochure at 51st PATA Annual Conference

Encouraged by the overwhelming response received from the ITB Berlin, HAI launched its exclusive India Quiz Contest at the 51st PATA Annual Conference held in New Delhi from 14.04.2002 to 18.04.2002 offering opportunities of FAM Holiday in 14 leading Hotels.

### Study Project on Management of Cross-cultural Tourists Movements in Hospitality Sector

HAI initiated a study project on Management of cross-cultural tourism movements in hospitality sector to assess and promote awareness among staff in smaller hotel and upgrade their knowledge and skills for handling of foreign tourists.

### Grant of Fiscal Benefits to the Hospitality Industry

For the first time the tourism industry's aspirations elaborated in the Hotel Association of India's various memoranda to the Central Government were translated into "tourism-friendly", measures in the Union Budget of 2003-04.

These measures were aimed at making India more affordable destination, fuelling growth of hospitality infrastructure, facilitating business re-organisation, re-structuring hospitality industry and motivating State Governments to rationalize tourism tax regime. The major incentives extended to hospitality industries included and exemption of Service tax in hotels relating to Conference and Banquet business, which have been excluded from the service tax net.

### Encouraging Investments

Hotel Association of India orchestrated the strategy leading to announcement in the Union Budget 2003 of benefits under Section 10(23) (g) on loans to hotels (3 star and above categories) for increasing the availability of funds for the hotel industry.

This provision has allowed lending institutions to make available funds to hotel projects at reduced rates of interest. The financial institutions will get a tax break on the interest income they earn on loans extended to such borrowers.

Inclusion of finance to the hotel projects of three star category and above for the first time under Section 10 (23)(g) of the Income Tax Act "signals" the positioning of hotels on the threshold of securing full infrastructure status as granted to other industries. HAI is now carrying this agenda forward to securing the wider benefits of infrastructure under Section 84 I/A of Income Tax Act.

### Restructuring Hospitality Business

#### *Amalgamation and Merger*

It is at the behest of HAI that the Finance Ministry constituted a Working group under Chief Commissioner of Income Tax Mumbai which recommended the grant of benefits under Section 72 A of the Income Tax Act (which relates to the set-off of accumulated losses and depreciation on amalgamation), for the hotel industry to help loss-making hotel companies in re-organising their business. The facility of mergers and acquisitions was hitherto available only to industrial undertakings and manufacturing units. With its extension to hotel companies, it has facilitated moves towards consolidation with the hospitality industry and releasing of resources blocked in non-performing assets. This measure has now enabled smaller hotel units to enter into franchisee arrangements with established hotel groups/chains which in turn has led to improvements in occupancy levels and service standards.

### Zero Duty Facility for Imports by Hotels

HAI pursued with the Ministry of Commerce, Government of India for grant of the zero duty import facility to hotels and standalone restaurants. The Industry has now been granted under the "Served from India Scheme", the zero duty facility to all hotels including one star, two star hotels for import of food items and alcoholic beverages sell which would make India an affordable destination.

### HAI Directory of Hotels Going Global

The exclusive HAI Directory of Hotels is an annual publication promoted with a singular aim of fulfilling the promotional need for tourists and visitor coming to India for an authentic compendium of leading Indian hotels recognized by the Ministry of Tourism. For the first time in 2005 the Directory was utilized by the Ministry of Tourism for distribution among foreign travel agents and tour operators in 12 countries through the Government of India's Tourist Offices abroad.

### World Tourism Day Celebration

A new promotional first was scored by HAI for creating awareness about the World Tourism Day on 27th Sept. 2005 amongst not only the member-hotels but also the school children. To encourage and facilitate the member-hotels in celebrating the World Tourism Day on 27th September 2005, HAI outlined a bouquet of activities to be organized by the member-hotels. The member-hotels came forward in large numbers and organized the activities with enthusiasm and excitement. In New Delhi, HAI collaborated with the Sanskriti School to launch a Quiz Contest on Tourism for school children on the World Tourism Day.

**Members Services**

Variety of professional member-services are provided by HAI to its members these include:-

(i) INFORMATION BULLETINS sent out regularly with updates on latest developments concerning hotel industries, policy changes and pronouncements by Ministry of Tourism, Ministry of Finance, Ministry of Commerce, CBEC, CBDT, State Governments and affiliate international organizations such as WTTC, IH&RA, WTO etc.;

(ii) HAI TODAY-the first hospitality industry magazine of its kind in India;

(iii) HAI DIRECTORY OF HOTELS-an exclusive high quality reference manual of recognized hotels in India;

(iv) HAI PRIVILEGE CARDS which are offered to members in the Gold and Silver Categories entitling them to discounts on hotel room tariffs and restaurants outlets in all member hotels on reciprocal basis;

(v) HAI LEGAL SERVICES which enables members to avail benefits of highest calibre legal advice on issues of concern them and interventions on their behalf in courts.

**HAI GREEN WEEKS**

HAI has successfully institutionalized the concept of celebrating annual green weeks in hotels to exhibit its commitment to conservation of environment through use of bio-degradable and environment-friendly products by efficient management of waste generated and by adopting measures for efficient utilization of day light to conserve upon electricity etc. HAI has this year celebrated its ninth annual green week, reaching out to large number of tourists, employees, their families, school children and society with its environment message.

### *Fundamentals of Revenue Management will be Revealed in a Special Report Commissioned by HSMAI Special Interest Group*

MCLEAN, VA The Hospitality Sales & Marketing Association International (HSMAI) Revenue Management Special Interest Group has taken on an ambitious project to produce the first-ever comprehensive "Fundamentals of Revenue Management" special report.

The report will be a practitioner-friendly publication that addresses the fundamentals of revenue management for a broad audience of hospitality professionals. With comprehensive content that is both readable and actionable, it will deliver tools and information for revenue management education, incorporating expert advice from interviews with industry executives and educators, case studies, and practical checklists for implementing successful revenue management strategies at the property level.

"Creating relevance for members and the industry at large through groundbreaking initiatives such as this Revenue Management Special Report is in keeping with HSMAI's mission to be the leading source for sales and marketing information, knowledge and business development for professionals in tourism, travel, and hospitality," states Robert A. Gilbert, CHME, CHA, president and CEO of HSMAI.

"We are very excited about this debut project, and expect it will be a springboard for other initiatives including certification and revenue management research," notes Tim Wiersma, vice president of revenue management for Host Marriott and chair of HSMAI's Revenue Management Tangible Resources Committee.

The publication will be produced in a manner similar to the recent special report produced by HSMAI and TIG Global entitled DeMystifying Distribution, widely praised by the industry for its insight, accuracy and comprehensive coverage of the topic.

The commissioned report, which will be released at the third annual HSMAI Revenue Management Strategy Conference on June 19, 2005 in Minneapolis, will be co-authored by Caryl Helsel and Kathleen Cullen of the Solutionz Group, a business development and strategic consulting group based in Florida. Helsel heads the hospitality practice and previously held executive positions with Kimpton Hotels, Pegasus Solutions and Mandarin Oriental Hotel Group, and is the former president of the Hotel Electronic Distribution Network Association (HEDNA). Cullen is a lead consultant on the hospitality team and is a hospitality revenue management and distribution veteran, holding executive positions with Swissotel and Raffles Hotels, as well as past vice president of HEDNA.

Delving deep into the fundamentals, nuances and specifics of revenue management, the special report will address the following:

- Ideas and initiatives to maximize revenue opportunities, optimize profits by managing revenues and develop an infrastructure (strategies, policies, procedures, reports, etc.) to make informed decisions about accepting or rejecting business.
- An overview of the external market such as segmentation, demand forecasting, revenue strategy, operational forecast, interdepartmental integration, strategic pricing, inventory control strategies and internal performance analysis.
- Tactics including rate-level maintenance, inventory management and rate offer assessment (for group and negotiated rates).
- The optimal environment, characteristics and descriptors.

The Revenue Management Special Interest Group is made up of a group of HSMAI members who advance the revenue management discipline through education, certification, participation, resources and guidance, enabling leaders to optimize revenue and performance within their own organizations.

# 3

# Personnel Management for Hotel Industry

Summer employees hired by local recreation departments or by amusement parks are often high school students or individuals with no education beyond a high school diploma. Specialized training in a particular field, such as athletics, music, or first aid, can be an asset when seeking employment in the recreation industry.

## GETTING THE JOB

High school students interested in careers in amusement and recreation should try to get summer, seasonal, or part-time jobs with local sports centers, amusement and theme parks, recreation centers, or other facilities offering recreation programs. It is best to inquire about positions at recreation departments or amusement parks well before the start of the summer season.

## ADVANCEMENT POSSIBILITIES AND EMPLOYMENT OUTLOOK

Employment in this industry is expected to grow faster than average for all occupations through 2014, although competition for full-time positions will be strong. Overall, about 30 percent of amusement and recreation positions are part time, and many jobs are seasonal.

Amusement and recreation attendants wishing to make a lifelong career in the industry should study the field at the college level. Specialized training, combined with experience in seasonal or part-time jobs, will improve a candidate's chances for landing a full-time position. Advancement opportunities within the field of amusement and recreation vary according to the needs of the population being served. Expect job growth within athletic clubs, camps, sports clinics, and commercial recreation enterprises.

### WORKING CONDITIONS

Amusement and recreation attendants typically spend most or all of their time outdoors in all sorts of weather. Most recreation attendants put in a forty-hour workweek, although many jobs do not feature typical 9-to-5 schedules. The work can be physically challenging, and park attendants are at risk for injury. Being responsible for the safety and well-being of participants can also place emotional stress on amusement and recreation attendants.

### EARNINGS AND BENEFITS

Recreation attendants earn less on average than attendants in other fields. According to the U.S. Bureau of Labour Statistics, the average wage for amusement and recreation attendants is $7.69 per hour. Self-employed attendants in the amusement and recreation industry are rare.

## BARTENDER

### Definition and Nature of the Work

Bartenders prepare alcoholic drinks for patrons of restaurants, bars, cocktail lounges, and other places where drinks are served. Alcoholic drinks are made up of many combinations of ingredients, and each drink may be made in several ways. The bartender's main job is to know the standard drink recipes and be able to mix them quickly and accurately. Occasionally, customers have their own preferences or recipes for a bartender to follow. Bartenders also check the identification of customers seated at bars to ensure that they meet the minimum drinking age. Most bartenders take drink orders, serve drinks, and collect money for drinks. In restaurants bartenders fill drink orders placed by the diners, but the drinks are usually served by waiters. Bartenders may have additional duties. Sometimes they arrange bottles and barware, wash glasses, and clean the bar. Bartenders also remove empty bottles and trash and replace empty beer kegs. In large bars and restaurants they may be assisted by a bartender helper.

Bartenders stock the bar by bringing liquor bottles, mixed drink ingredients, and other bar supplies from the storeroom to the bar. They keep track of wines, beers, liquors, and other supplies. Some bartenders do the actual ordering of bar supplies. Others report what is needed to the owner or to a purchasing agent. In very large restaurants and bars the ordering of supplies is done by a wine steward or a beverage manager.

In addition to bars and cocktail lounges, bartenders work in hotels, in private clubs, aboard ships, and on trains. Many bartenders work in restaurants that have a liquor license. About one-fifth of all bartenders own their own bars.

### Education and Training Requirements

Most bartenders learn their trade on the job. Some vocational schools offer courses in bartending. Working as a waiter is good experience for someone who wishes to become a bartender. Waiters can learn how to tend bar by watching the bartender work.

Bartenders must be aware of state and local laws concerning the sale of alcoholic drinks. In some states bartenders must have a bartender's license or a state health certificate. Bartenders usually must be at least twenty-one years old, but many bars prefer to hire individuals who are twenty-five or older. Bartenders must have a neat and clean appearance and a pleasant, agreeable manner. They often interact socially with the patrons, which works to their advantage as far as tipping is concerned.

### Getting the Job

Many bars will train prospective bartenders who do not have bartending skills. Interested individuals can apply directly to bars in which they would like to work. Newspaper want ads often carry advertisements Bartenders work in a variety of locations where alcoholic drinks are served for bartending jobs. Many bartenders belong to labour unions. A union's local office can help candidates find out about jobs in the bartending field.

### Advancement Possibilities and Employment Outlook

Many bartenders gain experience by working in small restaurants or bars.

Then they look for jobs in large luxury hotels, restaurants, or cocktail lounges that offer higher wages. In hotels large enough to have many bartenders, one may advance to the position of head bartender. Skilled bartenders who have a knowledge of accounting can become wine stewards or beverage managers.

The employment outlook for bartenders is expected to grow as fast as the average through the year 2014. The overall number of bartenders is large and the turnover rate is high. There is always strong competition for positions in expensive restaurants where potential tip earnings are greatest. It is important to note that the consumption of alcoholic beverages outside of the home has been declining in the United States-a trend that is certain to affect employment. Opportunities will be best for bartenders with the most training and experience.

### Working Conditions

Working conditions vary widely. Bars in luxury hotels, restaurants, and resorts offer more plush surroundings than do neighbourhood bars. Bartenders must be able to get along well with the public. They should also have good judgment and be willing to stop service to a customer who has had too much to drink. Bartenders must be prepared to work long hours on their feet and lift heavy cases and beer kegs.

Bartenders may work more than forty hours per week. They often work until very late at night and on weekends and some holidays. Some bartenders work split shifts; that is, they work for a few hours, take a long break, and return to work a few hours later. Part-time positions are often available. Many bartenders belong to labour unions.

### Earnings and Benefits

According to the U.S. Bureau of Labour Statistics, bartenders earn a median salary of $7.42 per hour plus tips. Like waiters, bartenders who work in public bars may receive more than half their earnings as tips. Very popular bartenders, especially those who know their customers well and socialize with them at the bar, can make even more in tips. In some bars and restaurants workers contribute all or a portion of their tips to a tip pool, which is distributed among the staff. The tip pool allows workers who are not usually tipped to share the rewards of good service.

Some bars supply bartenders with jackets or uniforms. Bartenders who work in restaurants are usually given free meals while they work. Many bartenders receive paid holidays and vacations. Bartenders who work in large hotels and restaurants may receive health insurance, sick pay, and retirement benefits.

## CAFETERIA ATTENDANT

### Definition and Nature of the Work

Cafeteria attendants work in schools, colleges, clubs, hospitals, other institutions, and office buildings. Their main job is to serve food at a counter. Depending on the organization of the cafeteria, cafeteria attendants may serve all the items offered or only one or two items, including salads, soups, desserts, vegetables, or main dishes. Some attendants are in charge of beverage machines. Food servers must be careful to serve just the right amount of food to control the amount of waste.

Some cafeteria workers have specific tasks. Dining room attendants put out clean trays and silverware and refill napkin dispensers. After meals they may remove dirty dishes and wipe down tables. Food runners carry food from the kitchen to the serving line. They tell the cooks how many more people to expect.

Some cafeteria attendants are responsible for several tasks in the kitchen. They make coffee and tea, toast bread, cut pies and cakes, slice meat and cheese, or make sandwiches. They often cook foods to order such as eggs, bacon, and grilled cheese sandwiches. In some cafeterias attendants calculate the customer's bill, receive money, and give change; however, most cafeterias have cashiers who handle all of the money transactions.

Between serving hours, cafeteria attendants clean the kitchen, serving and dining areas, tables, and equipment. They may wrap and restock prepackaged items. They refill salt and pepper shakers, sweep, mop, vacuum floors, and get ready for the next meal shift.

### Education and Training Requirements

Cafeteria attendants typically are trained on the job and need no special education; however, most employers prefer applicants who have a high school education. Cafeteria attendants should be patient and cheerful and able to get along well with other workers and the public. They should also have a neat, well-groomed appearance. Many states require a health certificate stating that they have no communicable diseases. Cafeteria attendants who calculate customers' bills and handle money must have good mathematical skills.

### Getting the Job

Interested individuals should apply to the cafeteria in which they would like to work. Office buildings, hospitals, and airports often have large cafeterias, and prospective cafeteria attendants can apply directly to the establishment's manager. Cafeteria jobs are frequently listed in newspaper want ads and at state and private employment agencies.

### Advancement Possibilities and Employment Outlook

Experience in a small cafeteria may lead to a higher-paying job with more responsibility in a large cafeteria. In addition, cafeteria attendants Cafeteria attendants serve food at schools, colleges, clubs, institutions, and office buildings. Although the work can be monotonous, attendants meet and interact with many people each day may become supervisors in charge of training workers. Some attendants become menu planners, cooks, or food and beverage managers. It has become increasingly necessary to take courses in cooking, nutrition, and food services to get these advanced jobs.

The employment outlook for cafeteria attendants is expected to grow as fast as the average through 2014. People who lead busy lives like the speedy and nutritionally balanced meals that cafeterias offer, so the demand for cafeteria attendants is expected to grow. There is a high turnover rate in this field, with many people using it as a short-term source of income.

### Working Conditions

Cafeteria attendants work in clean, well-lighted kitchens and dining rooms. Kitchens usually are warm and noisy. Food servers stand almost the entire day and may often be pressured to work quickly. The work can get monotonous, although attendants are always meeting new people. Cafeteria attendants also have to do a lot of lifting, carrying, and bending. Most kitchens have modern equipment that is simple and convenient to use. It can be a pleasant job for those who like to work around food.

Cafeteria work can be either part time or full time. Some attendants work only during meal hours and go home between meals. Many workers belong to labour unions.

### Earnings and Benefits

According to the U.S. Bureau of Labour Statistics, cafeteria attendants earned an average of $7.10 per hour in 2004. Unionized workers and those with experience earned more. Attendants often receive uniforms. Many workers are provided with health and accident insurance, retirement plans, paid holidays, and free meals while at work.

## DINING ROOM ATTENDANT

### Definition and Nature of the Work

Dining room attendants, formerly called busboys or bussers, work in restaurants, cafeterias, and hotel dining rooms. Attendants clear tables and unload their trays in the kitchen, separating the dishes, silverware, and linen. Then they reset the tables, laying tablecloths, arranging the silverware perfectly, lighting candles if appropriate, and filling flower vases. Dining room attendants may have to arrange tables and chairs to make room for large groups. They are responsible for seeing that the dining room is well stocked with utensils, napkins, glasses, tablecloths, table decorations, and foods such as butter and crackers or bread.

Dining room attendants may also be expected to dust woodwork, wash mirrors, vacuum carpets, clean and wax floors, and help to clean up spills. They are usually assigned to a station, which consists of several tables, but may help other attendants whose stations get very busy.

In addition to these duties, attendants act as assistants to waitresses and waiters. They get high chairs for children, help serve food, carry heavy trays, and fill water glasses. They clear dishes from tables between courses. Dining room attendants also act as messengers between the dining room staff and the kitchen staff. Dining room attendants are usually supervised by other restaurant workers. Sometimes the supervisor is the waiter who works at the station with the dining room attendant. More often the supervisor is the headwaiter who manages the dining room. Sometimes the restaurant host instructs the dining room attendants.

## Education and Training Requirements

Dining room attendants are not required to have a high school diploma. They typically receive on-the-job training, learning all about the operation of the kitchen and dining room. Their positions are considered starting points for other jobs in a restaurant, hotel, or cafeteria business. Some fine hotels offer training programs for all their employees, including dining room attendants, so that their customers receive the very best service. Many chain restaurants send their employees to a short training session. Dining room attendants should have a neat, clean appearance, a pleasant manner, and the ability to follow directions. Many states require a health certificate stating that the attendant has no communicable diseases.

## Getting the Job

Prospective dining room attendants can apply directly to hotels, restaurants, or cafeterias and answer want ads in the newspaper. The opening of new restaurants provides more opportunities for work. Individuals interested in working during the summer months only should apply to resorts well in advance of the tourist season.

## Advancement Possibilities and Employment Outlook

Dining room attendants may be promoted to other positions. They may become waiters or waitresses. If they are interested in preparing food, they may become kitchen helpers. Because of the expansion of the restaurant business, a good worker will have many opportunities for job advancement. Positions for dining room attendants are expected to grow about as fast as the average through 2014. There is one trend to note, however: although the number of restaurants is growing, waiters and waitresses are increasingly assuming the duties of dining room attendants.

## Working Conditions

Dining room attendants work at a fast pace and often under pressure. They have to perform a variety of tasks quickly and efficiently. Their surroundings are usually pleasant, well lighted, clean, and comfortable. However, the area where they unload dirty dishes may be hot and noisy. Dining room attendants should have plenty of energy and strength to lift heavy trays and move furniture. In order not to disturb customers, they must work very quietly. Candidates must be good multi-taskers, meaning they are capable of doing many things at once. They have an opportunity to meet many interesting people, both fellow workers and customers. Full-time attendants may work forty to forty-eight hours per week. Some work on a part-time basis. Many dining room attendants belong to labour unions.

## Earnings and Benefits

According to the U.S. Bureau of Labour Statistics, dining room attendants earned a median hourly wage of $7.17 in 2004.

New dining room attendants often begin at the minimum wage. Those who assist waiters or waitresses usually receive overtime pay. In some restaurants they may also receive a share of the wait staff's tips. Dining room attendants generally receive free meals while they work. Full-time workers may receive paid vacations and holidays, health and accident insurance, and retirement benefits.

## DISHWASHER

### Definition and Nature of the Work

Sparkling glasses and clean silverware make a good impression on restaurant customers. A clean table setting suggests that the restaurant will offer good service and wholesome food. The person responsible for providing clean tableware is the dishwasher. After customers have completed their meal, a dining room attendant takes the dirty dishes to the dishwasher. Dishwashers scrape, sort, and stack the dishes, and then load them into dishwashing machines. Dishwashers fill the machines with soap and turn them on. When the dishes are clean, dishwashers unload them and put them in their proper places so that other kitchen workers and waiters and waitresses can find them.

In very large establishments dishwashers may perform only one or two jobs. For example, one dishwasher may scrape plates, while another dishwasher may be in charge of washing large pots and pans. Dishwashers often are responsible for other cleanup jobs. Sometimes they clean floors, cabinets, sinks, and counter-tops. Occasionally they perform some of the tasks of dining room attendants such as clearing tables and assisting waiters and waitresses.

Dishwashers work in every establishment that serves food, including restaurants, buffets, hotels, coffee shops, hospitals, and schools.

### Education and Training Requirements

Dishwashers learn all their duties on the job. Some states require that dishwashers have a health certificate stating that they are free of communicable diseases.

## Getting the Job

The best way for an interested individual to get a dishwashing job is to apply directly to restaurants or other places where they would like to work. Newspaper want ads often have listings for dishwashers. The state employment office may also list job openings. Dishwashers must be strong enough to lift heavy dishes and pots and pans, and they must have enough stamina to stand or bend for long periods.

## Advancement Possibilities and Employment Outlook

After obtaining some experience, dishwashers may advance to other jobs such as kitchen helper, dining room attendant, cook, or waiter or waitress. Taking courses in cooking and food service is helpful to those who wish to advance to a better job. The employment outlook for dishwashers is expected to be good through the year 2014. The turnover rate for dishwashers is very high because about half of all dishwashers are students who change jobs when they graduate. Prospective dishwashers can almost always find jobs.

## Working Conditions

The dishwashing area in a kitchen is often hot, damp, and noisy. Sometimes the work gets hectic when the restaurant is busy. This job requires lifting heavy baskets of dishes along with heavy pots and pans. In addition to strength, dishwashers need stamina because they stand for long periods during the workday. Restaurants are open for long hours to best serve the public. As a result dishwashers are often required to work evenings, weekends, and holidays. Sometimes they work split shifts, in which they work for a few hours, leave, and return to work a few hours later. Full-time dishwashers work from forty to forty-eight hours per week; however, about half of all dishwashers work part time. The average workweek for dishwashers is less than thirty hours. Many dishwashers belong to labour unions.

## Earnings and Benefits

Dishwashers typically start out earning the minimum wage. They may make more money if they work in a large, upscale restaurant. Dishwashers who belong to labour unions generally earn higher pay. According to the U.S. Bureau of Labour Statistics, dishwashers earned a median hourly wage of $7.35 in 2004.

## DOORKEEPER

### Definition and Nature of the Work

Doorkeepers are stationed at the entrances of most large city hotels, restaurants, and luxury apartment buildings, as well as country resorts. These uniformed greeters create a welcoming atmosphere for guests or tenants arriving at their doors. Doorkeepers must be diplomatic, courteous, and helpful to all guests. Their responsibilities include opening the doors of cars and taxicabs for guests who arrive at their establishment, helping the guests out of cars, shielding them from rain or snow with an umbrella, and opening the door of the building so that the guests can step inside. In exchange for these services, guests frequently tip doorkeepers.

Doorkeepers also hail taxicabs for guests and tenants, carry packages, and watch for unauthorized people who might try to enter the building. They report suspicious people to the building manager or the police. In addition, doorkeepers direct delivery workers to the delivery entrance of the establishment. Those who work in apartment buildings may notify tenants that visitors have arrived by calling the tenants on the telephone.

### Education and Training Requirements

A high school diploma is not necessary for this position, but a good command of the English language is necessary to make the best impression on guests and tenants. Doorkeepers are usually trained on the job by experienced doorkeepers. They can start as bellhops in hotels or as kitchen helpers in restaurants. Doorkeepers must have a neat personal appearance and a pleasant and agreeable manner. They should also be polite, helpful, and responsible.

Doorkeepers assist hotel guests and apartment building residents who are in transit. They hail taxi cabs, carry packages, and open building and taxi cab doors for people.

### Getting the Job

Interested individuals can apply directly to hotels, restaurants, and apartment buildings for a job as a doorkeeper. The want ads in local newspapers are also a good source for job listings. Candidates who are unable to find work as a doorkeeper can apply for a job as a bellhop or a kitchen helper and advance from that position.

### Advancement Possibilities and Employment Outlook

There are very few advancement possibilities for doorkeepers; however, an experienced doorkeeper may be promoted to supervisor of all lobby employees, including bellhops, floor cleaners, and window washers. The employment outlook for doorkeepers is fair. Although openings develop quickly for many hotel and restaurant employees, most hotels and restaurants employ only a few doorkeepers. Turnover is low, so few job openings occur. Additional doorkeeper jobs will likely come from the development of new hotels.

### Working Conditions

Doorkeepers typically work a five-day, forty-hour week. They sometimes work evenings or weekends and often work in shifts so that the door to an establishment is covered at all times. Most doorkeepers wear uniforms. Some doorkeepers are provided with uniforms or a uniform allowance. Others must purchase their own.

Since hotel and restaurant doorkeepers are stationed outside, they must endure all kinds of weather. All doorkeepers stand for long periods, which may be very tiring. In spite of physical discomforts, doorkeepers must remain cheerful and courteous at all times.

### Earnings and Benefits

Doorkeepers generally start at minimum wage. Those who belong to unions may earn higher wages. Experienced doorkeepers earn an average salary of $17,000 to $19,000 or more per year. Doorkeepers in New York City earn much more-according to an April 19, 2006 article in the Christian Science

Monitor, about twice as much as the average. Those who work night shifts generally receive extra pay. In addition, a large portion of doorkeepers' incomes come from tips given by patrons of the hotel, restaurant, or apartment that employs them. Doorkeepers generally receive benefits such as paid vacations, sick leave, health insurance, and retirement plans.

## FAST FOOD FRANCHISE WORKER

### Definition and Nature of the Work

Fast food franchise workers are employed by fast food restaurants throughout the country. The most popular restaurants of this type specialize in hamburgers, fried chicken, fried fish, roast beef sandwiches, and other easily prepared food items. Fast food franchise workers prepare and serve food, keep the restaurant clean, and make sure that the customers are satisfied with their service.

In many fast food restaurants the food is prepared in an assembly-line fashion. Workers in some franchises are trained to do all of the jobs in the restaurant; in others each worker learns a specific task.

In a typical fast food chain, a counter worker takes the orders and gives them to the cook, who prepares the food and places the order on a plate or packages it in a box or paper wrapper. The counter worker then completes the order with beverages and processes payment. Some fast food restaurants have one counter worker who works as the cashier and takes all of the orders and another who fills them. A counter worker may also prepare sundaes and other ice cream dishes, cook french fries, and toast buns.

Dining room attendants are in charge of clearing and wiping the tables, filling the salt and pepper shakers, stocking packets of ketchup, mustard, and other garnishes, and making sure the napkin and straw dispensers are filled. They also sweep and mop the floors. Sometimes counter workers assist the dining room attendants by cleaning kitchen equipment, sweeping, mopping up spills, and carrying out trash. All fast food franchise workers are supervised by a manager or an assistant manager. Sometimes the owner of the franchise acts as the manager. Managers hire Fast food franchise counter workers take customers' orders, receive payment, and make change. They deliver the order to the cooks, who prepare the food in an assembly-line fashion and fire workers as necessary, oversee the running of the franchise, and make sure the customers are satisfied. The majority of fast food franchise workers are students who work part time. Managers must set up schedules that cover all work shifts.

## Education and Training Requirements

There are no formal educational requirements for fast food franchise workers. Most skills are learned on the job. Counter workers, however, should speak proper English and be able to do simple arithmetic. Most counter workers use a cash register or a computerized system for taking orders, totalling the check, and making change. Fast food franchises provide training in the use of these machines. It is helpful but not necessary for cooks to have some cooking experience. Dining room attendants need no special training.

Most fast food franchises have their own training programs in which they teach workers what to say when customers reach the counter and exactly how each food-related task should be done. This is the company's way of making sure that customers get fast, courteous service. In these training programs, cooks gain experience preparing the foods served by the franchise, counter workers practice greeting customers, using the cash register, and making change, and dining room attendants learn how to work efficiently. Training programs may last from two days to two weeks. Counter workers must be able to get along with people and have a pleasant personality and a neat appearance. All positions require good health and physical stamina. State laws often require health certificates stating that workers are free from communicable diseases.

## Getting the Job

Interested individuals should apply directly to fast food franchises in their area. Job listings often appear in newspaper want ads or on the windows or signs of franchises that are hiring. New restaurant openings are another source of job leads. The turnover rate for employees in the fast food business is very high, so potential workers are likely to find job openings.

### Advancement Possibilities and Employment Outlook

Workers who show enough ability and enthusiasm can become assistant managers or managers. Some workers advance by taking other jobs in the food service industry.

Jobs for fast food franchise employees are expected to grow as fast as the average through the year 2014 because the lifestyle of many Americans is increasingly fast paced and because healthier items are being added to the menus of many fast food restaurants.

### Working Conditions

Fast food franchise employees must work quickly and efficiently. They rarely get a chance to rest, and they are always on their feet. The work can be monotonous. Job hazards include falls, cuts, and burns, although injuries are seldom serious. Fast food franchise workers typically have to work their share of weekends, evenings, and holidays. Students must arrange work schedules that allow them to attend classes. Most counter workers and dining room attendants work fewer than thirty hours per week. Cooks may work as many as forty-eight hours per week, although part-time work is available. Workers generally wear uniforms. Most employers provide uniforms or a uniform allowance, but some workers may have to purchase their own uniforms.

### Earnings and Benefits

Earnings vary depending on the location of the franchise and the experience of the worker. According to the 2004 Occupational Employment Statistics survey, fast food franchise workers earn a median salary of $7.06 per hour. A few workers also receive tips. Many receive free meals during work hours. Full-time workers generally receive paid vacation time and other benefits.

## GAMING CAGE WORKER

### Definition and Nature of the Work

Gaming cage workers or cage cashiers count the money at casinos and other gaming establishments. They work in a secure place, known as the cage, which is the central depository for money, gaming chips, and casino paperwork. Cage workers exchange real currency for playing chips used in dice, card, and roulette games. They also buy these tokens back from patrons for cash, verify credit references for patrons who want to open a credit account at the casino, and cash checks.

Because the gaming industry is highly regulated, the cage cashiers must keep precise records. Transactions involving large sums of money must be reported to the Internal Revenue Service for tax purposes. Gaming cage workers use computers to calculate and keep track of all transactions. They must balance their money drawers at the end of each shift.

### Education and Training Requirements

There are no formal educational requirements for the job, although most employers require a high school diploma or the equivalent. Casinos usually provide on-the-job training to acquaint cage workers with the establishment's procedures. They also may offer classroom training in rules and regulations. Employers expect applicants to speak clear and proper English and to have excellent math skills. Some employers administer a math test to job applicants. Experience in handling money or other employment in gaming establishments is helpful in getting a job as a gaming cage worker.

Gaming cage workers must be well organized, detail oriented, discreet, and trustworthy. They often handle confidential material. Good customer service skills are essential.

Gaming cage workers, like all casino employees, must have a license issued by a regulatory agency such as a state gaming control board or commission. To get this license applicants must show photo identification, provide proof of residency in the state in which they plan to work, and pay a fee. The fee may vary by geographical area. Age requirements for the job may vary by state as well. All gaming job applicants should expect a background check.

### Getting the Job

People interested in casino work should contact the personnel offices of casinos directly for information on openings and entry-level requirements. Working part time or as a seasonal employee during major tourist seasons is a good way to move into full-time employment.

### Advancement Possibilities and Employment Outlook

Gaming cage cashiers can advance to supervisory roles by maintaining spotless work records and by demonstrating professionalism and good customer relations skills. Additional education and training may be required for advancement.

The job outlook for gaming cage workers is only moderate through the year 2014, partly because of technology. All gaming establishments are finding ways to reduce the amount of cash handled by employees. Cash-out machines, change machines, and automated teller machines (ATMs) are common. Some slot machines make payouts in tickets instead of coins. The tickets can be read by other slot machines and the amount on the ticket transferred to a new machine. By reducing the amount of cash needed to play, fewer workers are needed in the cage.

Gambling is legal in eleven states and the number of gaming establishments is growing. The largest growth will probably be in Native American-owned casinos and in racetracks that offer casino games. A fair number of openings for gaming cage workers should result from the continuous turnover in this occupation, which is usually due to the high level of scrutiny these employees receive.

### Working Conditions

Most gaming cage cashiers work eight-hour shifts five days per week. Because casinos are typically open twenty-four hours a day, shifts are usually staggered, and cage workers are expected to work some nights, weekends, and holidays. Cage workers are on their feet throughout their shifts but are usually given two short breaks and a mealtime break. They must work quickly and be able to concentrate for long periods in a noisy and hectic environment. Stress is particularly high for gaming cage workers because they are always being observed by supervisory and surveillance personnel. Cage workers must be tactful when dealing with unruly and frustrated patrons. In establishments that are not smoke free, they must also deal with exposure to cigarette, cigar, and pipe smoke. They are sometimes expected to lift and carry heavy bags of money.

### Earnings and Benefits

Wages for gaming cage workers vary according to their level of experience, training, location, and the size of the gaming establishment that employs them. According to the U.S. Bureau of Labour Statistics, the median hourly salary of gaming cage workers was $10.74 in May of 2004.

## GAMING DEALER

### Definition and Nature of the Work

The most high-profile workers in casinos and other gaming establishments are the dealers, or croupiers, who run the games of chance. Dealers explain and enforce the rules and wagering guidelines for games, ask patrons to place their bets, conduct the games, make payoffs to the winners, and collect losing bets. Some games, such as dice, craps, baccarat, and roulette, require more than one dealer to run. Dealers are frequently moved from one gaming table to another during a shift and often switch between two or more games per day.

### Education and Training Requirements

There are no formal education requirements for dealers, although employers do prefer to hire people with high school diplomas or the equivalent. They expect dealers to speak clear and correct English and to have strong mathematical skills. Some employers administer a math test to job applicants.

Gaming dealers are required to have a certificate or appropriate training from a dealer school. Some technical schools offer classes to train workers in specific games and skills. Other schools offer a Professional Casino Croupier certificate to students who have learned to run all of the games. Some colleges offer programs that include formal training for the casino industry. Casinos may provide dealer training, especially for employees who wish to change jobs.

Dealers, like all casino employees, must have a license issued by a regulatory agency such as a state gaming control board or commission. To get this license applicants must show photo identification, provide proof of residency in the state in which they plan to work, and pay a fee. The fee varies by geographical area. Age requirements for the job may vary by state as well. All gaming job applicants should expect a thorough background check.

### Getting the Job

Individuals interested in working as dealers should contact the personnel offices of casinos directly for information on openings and entry-level requirements. Working part time or as a seasonal employee during major tourist seasons is a good way to move into full-time employment.

### Advancement Possibilities and Employment Outlook

Dealers can advance by maintaining clean work records and by demonstrating professionalism and good customer relations skills. Dealers may be promoted to a higher wage table or to a more desirable work shift. With additional education and training, they may become supervisors.

The employment outlook for casino dealers is good, with jobs expected to grow faster than the average through the year 2014. As more states are legalizing casino gambling, more casinos are being planned and built, which will increase the number of dealer jobs. The largest future growth will probably be in Native American-owned casinos and in racinos, which are racetracks that offer some casino games. Part-time and seasonal positions will be most readily available.

Gaming dealers must work quickly and remain alert for long periods of time.

### Working Conditions

Casino dealers usually work eight-hour shifts five days per week. Because most casinos are open twenty-four hours a day, shifts are usually staggered, and dealers are expected to work some nights, weekends, and holidays. Dealers are on their feet throughout their shifts but are usually given two short breaks and a mealtime break.

Casino dealing is a high-pressure job. Dealers must work quickly in a noisy, hectic environment; knowing that they are being observed by supervisory and surveillance personnel adds to their stress level. Dealers must be tactful when dealing with unruly and frustrated patrons and those who do not know when to stop gambling. They may be exposed to cigarette, cigar, and pipe smoke.

### Earnings and Benefits

Casinos pay dealers a base salary that usually begins at minimum wage. According to the U.S. Bureau of Labour Statistics, the median wage for dealers in 2004 was $14,340 per year; however, dealers earn a substantial portion of their income from tips. Gaming dealers generally prefer weekend, evening, and holiday shifts because those are the busiest times and often bring in the most tips. In some casinos dealers keep the tips they get; in others the tips are shared by all dealers. Casinos usually provide full-time workers with benefits that include health insurance, retirement plans, vacation time, paid sick days, and extra pay for working on holidays.

## HOSPITALITY CASHIER

### Definition and Nature of the Work

Hospitality cashiers are employed in many different establishments, including large resort hotels, restaurants, and small coffee shops. They are also employed in entertainment arenas ranging from Broadway theatres to amusement parks.

Cashiers are responsible for taking payments from customers, making change, and giving receipts. They generally operate a cash register or adding machine. Most modern cash registers automatically add the prices of items, total them, open the cash drawer, and provide a receipt. Some cashiers keep records of business transactions and prepare cash and checks for deposit in banks. Some also prepare sales tax reports.

Hospitality cashiers perform duties that relate directly to the kind of establishment for which they work. Cashiers who work for restaurants are called cashier checkers. They answer telephones, take reservations, and often serve as hosts by seating patrons. In addition, cashier checkers sell candy, cigarettes, and other items displayed at the cash register counter.

Cashiers who work for hotels generally keep track of charges to guests for room service, telephone calls, and valet service. Some sophisticated cash registers are linked to computer systems that can do all these things automatically. Sometimes cashiers assign and take care of safe-deposit boxes in which guests store jewellery and other valuables. They may also have front desk duties such as notifying hotel desk clerks when guests check out.

Those who work for theatres or amusement parks are generally called box office cashiers or ticket sellers. They sell tickets to customers, operate ticket dispensing machines, and answer telephones. In theatres they sometimes handle advance ticket sales and mail-order ticket requests. Cashiers come into contact with many customers throughout the working day. Some establishments, including restaurants and hotels, do a good deal of their business at night; therefore, hospitality cashiers often work evenings. About half of all cashiers work part time. Hospitality cashiers must be pleasant and agreeable and dress neatly. Above all they must be honest and trustworthy, since they often handle large sums of money.

## Education and Training Requirements

Typically an individual needs a high school education to become a cashier. Some employers require that cashiers be at least eighteen years old. In high school prospective cashiers should take courses in business mathematics, bookkeeping, typing, and business machine operation.

Most businesses provide on-the-job training for newly hired cashiers. Large hotels and restaurants may have formal training programs that include classroom instruction. Smaller employers generally train beginners by having experienced cashiers supervise and instruct them.

## Getting the Job

Interested individuals should apply directly to hotels, restaurants, theatres, and other businesses for cashier positions. Jobs are sometimes listed in newspaper want ads or job banks on the Internet. School placement offices may also be able to help candidates find cashiering jobs.

## Advancement Possibilities and Employment Outlook

Cashiers have few opportunities for advancement unless they get additional education or training. Occasionally hotel cashiers advance to become hotel desk clerks. Those who show the ability to handle management responsibilities may be able to enter a management-training program. For example, a cashier in a restaurant may complete training and advance to the position of assistant manager.

The employment outlook for cashiers is mixed. Many hospitality establishments are installing self-service ticketing and checkout systems that eliminate some cashiering positions. Although growth in this field is expected to be slower than average through the year 2014, employee turnover is usually high enough to guarantee a steady number of job openings.

## Working Conditions

Full-time hospitality cashiers generally work a five-day, forty-hour week, but only about half of all cashiers are considered full-time workers. Many work during the evenings and on weekends when the majority of people visit restaurants and movie theatres.

Cashiers often have to work quickly. They are under a great deal of pressure at peak periods of business such as lunch rushes in restaurants. It is important that they are efficient and accurate. Some cashiers have to work in small enclosed spaces such as ticket booths. Depending on where they work, they may have to stand for long periods of time, which can be very tiring.

### Earnings and Benefits

Most cashiers start at minimum wage. Wages vary in different parts of the country. Cashiers typically earn more in the western and northern-central states. According to the U.S. Bureau of Labour Statistics, the median wage for cashiers was $7.81 per hour in 2004. Cashiers who belong to unions often receive higher salaries than non-unionized cashiers. Many full-time cashiers receive benefits such as paid vacations, sick leave, health insurance, and retirement plans.

## HOTEL BELLHOP AND PORTER

### Definition and Nature of the Work

Bellhops and porters usually work in hotels rather than motels. Like all employees in the hospitality industry, their main goal is to make sure that the guests enjoy their stay. In some hotels the duties of bellhops and porters are similar; however, bellhops usually work inside the hotel, whereas porters work outside.

Bellhops carry guests' luggage, show guests to their rooms, and make sure that everything in the room is in order. They check the lights, ventilation, and heating and show guests how to use the air conditioner, television, and telephone. If any equipment is not working properly, bellhops report this to the maintenance department so that it can be repaired as soon as possible. Bellhops may also give guests information about the hotel and local tourist attractions, deliver packages, run errands, and bring food and drink orders to guests' rooms. They also carry luggage for guests who are leaving. In large hotels bellhops are supervised by a bell captain. Bell captains give the bellhops their assignments, train new bellhops, record the bellhops' hours for payroll, and handle complaints made to their department.

Like bellhops, baggage porters handle baggage and suitcases. They deliver luggage to a guest's room on request and, when the guests are prepared to leave, arrange to have the bags shipped and carry them to the loading platform. Porters mail important papers and packages for guests and sometimes run errands that take them away from the hotel-buying tickets to a theater or sporting event, for instance.

Housekeeping porters do heavy work such as arranging furniture and rolling up rugs. They set up displays for conventions and sales meetings, sweep and mop floors, and dispose of trash. The head porter's job is very similar to that of a bell captain. Head porters maintain employees' time records, conduct interviews, and hire and train employees. To ensure that all porters get a fair share of the work, head porters assign the calls equally among the employees.

## Education and Training Requirements

Most employers prefer to hire individuals with a high school education. Beginners usually receive up to one month of on-the-job training. Physical strength is hail cabs, and perform other room service duties. Candidates should be able to get along well with people and take pride in providing services for others. Many bellhops and porters start out as elevator operators. Most large hotels hire only experienced workers. Prospective bellhops and porters can gain that experience by starting out in a small hotel.

## Getting the Job

In the hotel industry promotions usually come from within, meaning existing employees with a good work record have opportunities to advance from entry-level positions. Elevator operators and other entry-level hotel workers are often promoted to the position of bellhop or porter. Interested individuals should apply directly to the manager of a hotel that interests them. State employment offices may also provide job listings for bellhops and porters.

## Advancement Possibilities and Employment Outlook

Bellhops and porters typically start out by working in small hotels to gain experience, then transfer to larger, more luxurious hotels where they will receive better tips. A good work record and a high school education increase the chances of advancing to other jobs within the hotel. Those who have clerical skills may become mail, room, or desk clerks.

A bellhop may become a bell captain, and a porter may advance to the position of head porter. Because there is usually only one bell captain or head porter in a hotel, the chances of becoming a supervisor are limited.

The hotel, motel, and resort industry is expected to grow faster than the average through the year 2014. Motels usually do not employ bellhops or porters; however, a number of large hotels are slated to be built throughout the United States by 2014. These new hotels and the growth in business travel and tourism should create an additional demand for bellhops and porters.

## Working Conditions

The work bellhops and porters do can be exhausting. They must lift and carry heavy luggage, and they are on their feet all day. Bellhops are required to wear uniforms and must be well groomed when they are at work. In some hotels porters wear their own clothes. Bellhops and porters must be helpful and willing to do things for others. Not all hotel guests are easy to please, but bellhops and porters must be able to get along with all kinds of people.

Bellhops and porters usually work eight-hour shifts. Because their services are required twenty-four hours a day, they must be able to work evenings, weekends, and alternating shifts. Many bellhops and porters belong to labour unions.

## Earnings and Benefits

It is difficult to determine how much bellhops and porters earn. Their salaries depend largely on the tips they receive from guests and the geographic location of the establishment in which they work. Those who work in large luxury hotels, including casino hotels and resorts, make more money than those who work in smaller hotels. According to the U.S. Bureau of Labour Statistics, bellhops and porters earn a median salary of $8.69 per hour before tips. Hotels usually offer benefits including insurance plans, paid vacations, and free meals during work hours. Hotels also furnish and maintain uniforms.

## HOTEL HOUSEKEEPER

### Definition and Nature of the Work

Cleanliness is one of the most important features a hotel or motel can offer its guests. Housekeepers, also known as maids, are the staff members who perform cleaning duties in these establishments.

Housekeepers may be assigned specialized cleaning duties. For example, most hotels have laundry facilities for cleaning towels, linen, bedding, and workers' uniforms. Some housekeepers work only in the laundry area, washing, drying, and folding these items and then stocking the linen storage rooms.

Other housekeepers only clean guest rooms. An especially thorough cleaning is done after the occupants of a room check out. Using a large wheeling cart to hold supplies, guest room housekeepers bring clean linen, bedding, cleansers, and all other necessary cleaning equipment to the rooms.

The housekeepers replace soiled linen and towels; restock soap, tissues, and drinking glasses; disinfect bathroom surfaces; dust and polish the furniture; remove all trash; vacuum the carpet; and wash any uncarpeted floors. Before leaving, they check to make sure that the room is spotless and ready for new guests. If housekeepers notice anything in a room that is not working properly, they report it to their supervisor, the executive housekeeper. They also send to the lost-and-found department any articles that previous guests may have left in the rooms when they checked out.

Aside from doing laundry and cleaning guest rooms, housekeepers replace light bulbs, wash windows, empty ashtrays, and clean hallways and stairs. Some housekeepers make sewing repairs or upholster furniture. Others work in lobbies, lounges, and conference and banquet rooms, where they clean carpets and move and set up furniture. In small hotels housekeepers usually perform several of these tasks. Executive housekeepers supervise house workers, purchase supplies and equipment, and prepare budgets for the housekeeping department.

## Education and Training Requirements

A formal education is not required to become a housekeeper, although employers prefer to hire people who have a high school education. Most hotels and motels provide on-the-job training. Hotel housekeepers must be able to work quickly and efficiently without invading their guests' privacy and should have a neat, clean appearance.

## Getting the Job

The best way for prospective hotel housekeepers to find jobs is to apply directly to the hotels and motels in which they would like to work. Newspaper want ads and state employment offices often have listings for hotel housekeepers.

## Advancement Possibilities and Employment Outlook

Housekeepers who have gained experience working in small hotels or motels can apply to luxury hotels that pay higher wages. Housekeepers in a large hotel or resort may be promoted to the position of executive housekeeper; however, since there is only one executive housekeeper in each hotel, advancement possibilities are quite limited. Budgeting, inventory control, and staff selection are among the duties of executive housekeepers. Usually years of experience, a one-year internship, and/or college courses in institutional management, business administration, or hotel services are needed to advance to the executive position. The hotel, motel, and resort industry is expected to grow faster than the average through the year 2014, so the job outlook for housekeepers is good. As more hotels and motels are built to accommodate increased business travel and domestic and foreign tourism, the demand for all hotel workers will rise. Existing hotels and motels are always looking for new members for their cleaning staff, and resort hotels typically hire more housekeepers for the vacation season.

### Working Conditions

Modern hotels and motels have the best cleaning equipment for housekeepers to use; however, the work is demanding. Housekeepers must bend, stoop, climb, and reach to clean in corners and inside closets. Moving heavy equipment and furniture can be exhausting.

Housekeepers typically work forty to forty-eight hours each week. They may rotate from a morning to an evening or night shift and are expected to take their share of weekends and holidays. Most housekeepers wear uniforms. Some employers provide them with uniforms or a uniform allowance; others require housekeepers to purchase their own uniforms.

### Earnings and Benefits

According to the U.S. Bureau of Labour Statistics, hotel housekeepers earned a median annual wage of $16,900 in 2004. Experienced workers may earn more. Executive housekeepers' salaries vary with training, experience, and most importantly the size of the hotel or motel. Their median annual salary in 2004 was $29,640, but some executive housekeepers in large luxury or resort hotels reportedly earned more than $40,000 per year.

Hotel housekeepers sometimes receive tips from guests at the end of their stay and may get free meals during work hours. Most hotels offer full-time housekeepers paid vacations, some paid holidays, health insurance, and retirement benefits.

## LODGING MANAGERS

### Nature of the Work

A comfortable room, good food, and a helpful staff can make being away from home an enjoyable experience for both vacationing families and business travellers. While most lodging managers work in traditional hotels and motels, some work in other lodging establishments, such as camps, inns, boardinghouses, dude ranches, and recreational resorts. In full-service hotels, lodging managers help their guests have a pleasant stay by providing many of the comforts of home, including cable television, fitness equipment, and voice mail, as well as specialized services such as health spas.

For business travellers, lodging managers often schedule available meeting rooms and electronic equipment, including slide projectors and fax machines. Lodging managers are responsible for keeping their establishments efficient and profitable. In a small establishment with a limited staff, the manager may oversee all aspects of operations. However, large hotels may employ hundreds of workers, and the general manager usually is aided by a number of assistant managers assigned to the various departments of the operation. In hotels of every size, managerial duties vary significantly by job title.

General managers have overall responsibility for the operation of the hotel. Within guidelines established by the owners of the hotel or executives of the hotel chain, the general manager sets room rates, allocates funds to departments, approves expenditures, and ensures expected standards for guest service, decor, housekeeping, food quality, and banquet operations. Managers who work for chains also may organize and staff a newly built hotel, refurbish an older hotel, or reorganize a hotel or motel that is not operating successfully. In order to fill entry-level service and clerical jobs in hotels, some managers attend career fairs.

Resident or hotel managers are responsible for the day-to-day operations of the property. In larger properties, more than one of these managers may assist the general manager, frequently dividing responsibilities between the food and beverage operations and the rooms or lodging services. At least one manager, either the general manager or a hotel manager, is on call 24 hours a day to resolve problems or emergencies.

Assistant managers help run the day-to-day operations of the hotel. In large hotels, they may be responsible for activities such as personnel, accounting, office administration, marketing and sales, purchasing, security, maintenance, and pool, spa, or recreational facilities. In smaller hotels, these duties may be combined into one position. Assistant managers may adjust charges on a hotel guest's bill when a manager is unavailable.

An Executive Committee made up of a hotel's senior managers advises the general manager, assists in setting hotel policy, coordinates services that cross departmental boundaries, and collaborates on efforts to ensure consistent and efficient guest services throughout the hotel. The Committee may be comprised of the department heads for housekeeping, front office, food and beverage, security, sales and public relations, meetings and conventions, engineering and building maintenance, and human resources. Executive committee members bring a different perspective of guest service to the total management objective reflecting the unique expertise and training of their positions.

Executive housekeepers ensure that guest rooms, meeting and banquet rooms, and public areas are clean, orderly, and well maintained. They also train, schedule, and supervise the work of housekeepers, inspect rooms, and order cleaning supplies.

Front office managers coordinate reservations and room assignments, as well as train and direct the hotel's front desk staff. They ensure that guests are treated courteously, complaints and problems are resolved, and requests for special services are carried out. Front office managers may adjust charges posted on a customer's bill.

Convention services managers coordinate the activities of various departments in larger hotels to accommodate meetings, conventions, and special events. They meet with representatives of groups or organizations to plan the number of rooms to reserve, the desired configuration of the meeting space, and banquet services. During the meeting or event, they resolve unexpected problems and monitor activities to ensure that hotel operations conform to the expectations of the group.

Food and beverage managers oversee all food service operations maintained by the hotel. They coordinate menus with the Executive Chef for the hotel's restaurants, lounges, and room service operations. They supervise the ordering of food and supplies, direct service and maintenance contracts within the kitchens and dining areas, and manage food service budgets. Catering managers arrange for food service in a hotel's meeting and convention rooms. They coordinate menus and costs for banquets, parties, and events with meeting and convention planners or individual clients. They coordinate staffing needs and arrange schedules with kitchen personnel to ensure appropriate food service.

Sales or marketing directors and public relations directors oversee the advertising and promotion of hotel operations and functions, including lodging and dining specials and special events, such as holiday or seasonal specials. They direct the efforts of their staff to purchase advertising and market their property to organizations or groups seeking a venue for conferences, conventions, business meetings, trade shows, and special events. They also coordinate media relations and answer questions from the press.

Human resources directors manage the personnel functions of a hotel, ensuring that all accounting, payroll, and employee relations matters are handled in compliance with hotel policy and applicable laws. They also oversee hiring practices and standards and ensure that training and promotion programs reflect appropriate employee development guidelines.

Finance (or revenue) directors monitor room sales and reservations. In addition to overseeing accounting and cash-flow matters at the hotel, they also project occupancy levels, decide which rooms to discount and when to offer rate specials.

Computers are used extensively by lodging managers and their assistants to keep track of guests' bills, reservations, room assignments, meetings, and special events. In addition, computers are used to order food, beverages, and supplies, as well as to prepare reports for hotel owners and top-level managers. Managers work with computer specialists to ensure that the hotel's computer system functions properly. Should the hotel's computer system fail, managers must continue to meet the needs of hotel guests and staff.

**Working Conditions**

Because hotels are open around the clock, night and weekend work is common. Many lodging managers work more than 40 hours per week, and may be called back to work at any time. Some managers of resort properties or other hotels where much of the business is seasonal have other duties on the property during the off-season or find work at other hotels or in other areas.

Lodging managers experience the pressures of coordinating a wide range of activities. At larger hotels, they also carry the burden of managing a large staff and finding a way to satisfy guest needs while maintaining positive attitudes and employee morale. Conventions and large groups of tourists may present unusual problems or require extended work hours. Moreover, dealing with irate guests can be stressful. The job can be particularly hectic for front office managers during check-in and check-out times. Computer failures can further complicate processing and add to frustration levels.

## Training, Other Qualifications, and Advancement

Hotels increasingly emphasize specialized training. Postsecondary training in hotel, restaurant, or hospitality management is preferred for most hotel management positions; however, a college liberal arts degree may be sufficient when coupled with related hotel experience or business education. Internships or part-time or summer work experience in a hotel are an asset to students seeking a career in hotel management. The experience gained and the contacts made with employers can greatly benefit students after graduation. Most degree programs include work-study opportunities.

Community colleges, junior colleges, and many universities offer certificate or degree programs in hotel, restaurant, or hospitality management leading to an associate, bachelor, or graduate degree. Technical institutes, vocational and trade schools, and other academic institutions also offer courses leading to formal recognition in hospitality management. In total, more than 800 educational facilities provide academic training for would-be lodging managers. Hotel management programs include instruction in hotel administration, accounting, economics, marketing, housekeeping, food service management and catering, and hotel maintenance engineering.

Computer training also is an integral part of hotel management training, due to the widespread use of computers in reservations, billing, and housekeeping management.

More than 450 high schools in 45 States offer the Lodging Management Program created by the Educational Institute of the American Hotel and Lodging Association. This two-year program offered to high school juniors and seniors teaches management principles and leads to a professional certification called the "Certified Rooms Division Specialist." Many colleges and universities grant participants credit towards a post-secondary degree in hotel management. Lodging managers must be able to get along with many different types of people, even in stressful situations. They must be able to solve problems and concentrate on details. Initiative, self-discipline, effective communication skills, and the ability to organize and direct the work of others also are essential for managers at all levels.

Persons wishing to make a career in the hospitality industry may be promoted into a management trainee position sponsored by the hotel or a hotel chain's corporate parent. Typically, trainees work as assistant managers and may rotate assignments among the hotel's departments—front office, housekeeping, or food and beverage—to gain a wide range of experiences. Relocation to another property may be required to help round out the experience and to help grow a trainee into the position.

Work experience in the hospitality industry at any level or in any segment, including summer jobs or part-time work in a hotel or restaurant, is good background for entering hotel management. Most employers require a bachelor's degree with some education in business and computer literacy, while some prefer a master's degree for hotel management positions. However, employees who demonstrate leadership potential and possess sufficient length or breadth of experience may be invited to participate in a management training program and advance to hotel management positions without the education beyond high school. Large hotel and motel chains may offer better opportunities for advancement than small, independently owned establishments, but relocation every several years often is necessary for advancement. The large chains have more extensive career ladder programs and offer managers the opportunity to transfer to another hotel or motel in the chain or to the central office. Career advancement can be accelerated by the completion of certification programs offered by various associations. These programs usually require a combination of course work, examinations, and experience. For example, outstanding lodging managers may advance to higher level manager positions.

### Employment

Lodging managers held about 58,000 jobs in 2004. Self-employed managers—primarily owners of small hotels, motels, and inns—held about 45 percent of these jobs. Companies that manage hotels and motels under contract employed many managers.

### Job Outlook

Employment of lodging managers is expected to grow about as fast as the average for all occupations through 2014. Additional job openings are expected to occur as experienced managers transfer to other occupations or leave the labour force, in part because of the long hours and stressful working conditions. Job opportunities are expected to be best for persons with college degrees in hotel or hospitality management.

Renewed business travel and domestic and foreign tourism will drive employment growth of lodging managers in full-service hotels. The numbers of economy-class rooms and extended-stay hotels also are expected to increase to accommodate leisure travellers and bargain-conscious guests. An increasing range of lodging accommodations is available to travellers, from economy hotels which offer clean, comfortable rooms and front desk services without costly extras such as restaurants and room service, to luxury and boutique inns that offer sumptuous furnishings and personal services. The accommodation industry is expected to continue to consolidate as lodging chains acquire independently owned establishments or undertake their operation on a contract basis. The increasing number of extended-stay hotels will moderate growth of manager jobs because these properties usually have fewer departments and require fewer managers. Also, these establishments often do not require a manager to be available 24 hours a day, instead assigning front desk clerks on duty at night some of the responsibilities previously reserved for managers.

Additional demand for managers is expected in suite hotels, because some guests—especially business customers—are willing to pay higher prices for rooms with kitchens and suites that provide the space needed to conduct small meetings. In addition, large full-service hotels—offering restaurants, fitness centers, large meeting rooms, and play areas for children, among other amenities—will continue to provide many trainee and managerial opportunities.

### Earnings

Median annual earnings of lodging managers were $37,660 in May 2004. The middle 50 percent earned between $28,640 and $51,030. The lowest 10 percent earned less than $22,680, while the highest 10 percent earned more than $72,160. Median annual earnings for lodging managers in traveler accommodations were $37,420.

Salaries of lodging managers vary greatly according to their responsibilities and the segment of the hotel industry in which they are employed, as well as the location and region where the hotel is located. Managers may earn bonuses of up to 25 percent of their basic salary in some hotels and also may be furnished with meals, parking, laundry, and other services. In addition to providing typical benefits, some hotels offer profit-sharing plans and educational assistance to their employees.

## MOTEL HOTEL AND RESORT DESK CLERK

### Definition and Nature of the Work

Desk clerks, also known as front office clerks or room clerks, are part of the front office staff of hotels, motels, and resorts. They are responsible for checking guests in and out, giving information about rates and the kinds of services their establishment provides, and assigning guests to rooms. Of all lodging employees, desk clerks have the most contact with the public; therefore, it is especially important that they make a good impression and ensure that guests' needs are being met.

There are many kinds of desk clerks in the hospitality industry. Key clerks issue and receive room keys. Reservations clerks handle reservations that guests make by mail, by telephone, or via the Internet and inform the room clerks when the guests plan to arrive. Rack clerks keep track of which rooms are occupied and unoccupied and oversee the work of the housekeepers and maintenance crew. Mail clerks are in charge of the guests' mail and messages. Information clerks tell guests about local places of interest and provide directions. However, only in the very largest hotels are the clerks so specialized. Usually one hotel desk clerk performs several duties such as handling reservations, checking guests in or out, and giving them directions to local sites.

Desk clerks work throughout the country in all kinds of hotels, motels, and resorts. The differences in these types of lodgings lie in their location and needs of their clientele. Hotels are typically found in cities; residential hotels serve people who desire hotel service on a long-term basis. Most motels are located along highways rather than in large urban areas. Because they are designed to serve motorists who are driving a long way, motels are sometimes referred to as motor lodges. Resort hotels are usually located in vacation areas. In addition to providing rooms, many resort hotels provide recreational activities such as horseback riding and swimming.

Most hotels, motels, and resorts are open twenty-four hours every day of the year. There is almost always a desk clerk on duty to take care of the guests' needs. The desk clerk has the most contact with hotel guests. It is important for the desk clerk to be friendly, helpful, and well groomed.

## Education and Training Requirements

Managers of lodging establishments like to hire people who have at least a high school education. Some large hotels prefer hiring individuals with some college experience. On-the-job training is provided. It is helpful to be good at typing, bookkeeping, and office machine and computer operation. Clerks should also have strong interpersonal and problem-solving skills.

Many desk clerks begin as bellhops, switchboard operators, or key clerks. After they gain some experience these workers may be promoted to desk clerk. Desk clerks must have a neat appearance and be able to get along well with people.

### Getting the Job

Prospective desk clerks can learn about job openings from state employment agencies, newspaper want ads, or job banks on the Internet. They can also apply directly to hotels, motels, and resorts in which they want to work. Students attending training schools that specialize in hotel work should check for job listings with the school's placement office.

### Advancement Possibilities and Employment Outlook

Lodging managers generally prefer to promote their employees rather than hire people from outside the staff. Desk clerks who do their jobs well can move up to the position of assistant manager or front office manager. Education beyond high school is useful in getting a promotion. Many colleges and junior colleges now offer courses and programs in hotel management. The hotel, motel, and resort industry is expected to grow faster than the average through the year 2014. An increase in business travel as well as in domestic and foreign tourism will create a demand for all lodging workers. Also, the turnover rate for desk clerks is high so jobs open up regularly.

### Working Conditions

Hotels, motels, and resorts are pleasant places to work. They are usually open seven days a week, twenty-four hours a day. Desk clerks may be asked to work nights, weekends, and holidays. They often put in a five-or six-day forty-to forty-eight-hour week. Employees are usually given extra pay for working irregular hours. Most room clerks rotate their shifts with other workers. Front desks are generally clean and well lighted and the work is not strenuous. However, clerks may be on their feet much of the time, and their work can become quite hectic, especially in busy hotels and resorts; desk clerks in the hospitality industry need to be patient and tolerant even when guests are unreasonable.

## Earnings and Benefits

According to the U.S. Bureau of Labour Statistics, hotel, motel, and resort desk clerks earned a median salary of $17,700 per year in 2004. Those working in large metropolitan areas usually earn more. Benefits for full-time workers include paid vacations and holidays, health insurance, life insurance, and retirement plans. Educational assistance is sometimes available as well.

# MOTION PICTURE PROJECTIONIST

## Definition and Nature of the Work

Motion picture projectionists operate all of the equipment in the projection booths of indoor cinemas and drive-ins. They use movie projectors, audio equipment, and machines that rewind film to provide film entertainment for the theater's customers.

Projectionists must inspect films before they are shown. To do this they place each film reel on a hand rewinding machine and look for holes, worn places, or other defects. If necessary they repair any defects found in the film.

In most cases full-length motion pictures are recorded on several reels of film so projectionists must operate two projectors at a time. When one reel of film is ending, projectionists must have the other projector and film reel ready for showing. Projectionists know when to change projectors by watching for cue marks on the movie screen. When the cue marks appear, they close the shutter of the first projector, open the shutter of the second projector, and then rewind the first reel on a rewinding machine. The first projector is then ready for threading the next reel of film. An average reel runs about twenty minutes. This process is repeated until the entire film is shown. Some projectionists are assisted by a motion picture projectionist's apprentice.

Projectionists also clean and oil the equipment, check for defective parts, and make repairs. For major repairs they are assisted by a service repair worker.

### Education and Training Requirements

There are no specific education requirements for motion picture projectionists, although a few cities and states require that they be licensed. Projectionists must have good mechanical ability because the equipment they use and repair is complex. Excellent hearing, eyesight, and manual dexterity are also important.

Many projectionist jobs are unionized. To qualify as a union projectionist a candidate must serve a one-to two-year apprenticeship and pass a union examination. Apprentices must be at least eighteen years old and have a high school diploma. They learn to operate projectors and other equipment by working on the job with experienced projectionists. Some do not get paid while they are learning; others do and they may also hold other jobs in the theater. Some projectionists learn their skills at vocational or technical schools or on the job at small, nonunion theatres; however, theatres with union contracts will not hire nonunion projectionists.

### Getting the Job

In large cities projectionists who have served an apprenticeship usually find jobs through their union. Nonunion members can apply directly to local nonunion theatres. Projectionist positions are also listed in the want ads of local newspapers.

### Advancement Possibilities and Employment Outlook

Motion picture projectionists who work in large multiscreen theatres may advance to the position of chief operator. Some projectionists become service repair workers who fix sound equipment and projectors. Occasionally an experienced projectionist becomes a theater manager. The job outlook for motion picture projectionists is poor. Although the number of theatres is expected to grow slightly through the year 2014, increasingly sophisticated projection equipment does much of the work automatically. Most openings will occur as workers retire or change jobs.

### Working Conditions

Both indoor and drive-in theatres are usually nice places to work. Most projection rooms are comfortable, clean, well lighted, and well ventilated. Projectionists must be able to work independently and be willing to view movies over and over again. Many motion picture projectionists work part time. Full-time projectionists work forty hours a week, including days and evenings. Their hours may be split over six days of the week instead of five. Some work in more than one theater, especially in multiscreen complexes.

### Earnings and Benefits

Generally theatres in cities pay better wages than suburban or drive-in theatres. According to data from the 2004 Occupational Employment Statistics survey, motion picture projectionists earn a median salary of $8.32 per hour. Benefits for full-time workers may include paid vacations and health insurance as well as retirement plans.

## RESTAURANT HOST OR HOSTESS

### Definition and Nature of the Work

Restaurant hosts and hostesses serve as personal representatives of the restaurant for which they work. They are in charge of making reservations and greeting guests when they arrive at the restaurant. They also seat the guests and make sure that they enjoy their meal.

Hosts and hostesses try to give guests a good impression of the restaurant by greeting them in a warm, friendly manner. If guests have to wait to be seated, hosts and hostesses make them comfortable while they wait. The guests are given an idea of how long they will have to wait and are seated in a waiting area. Sometimes hosts and hostesses suggest that the diners wait at the bar and have a drink. Hosts and hostesses locate a table that is the right size for the guests, take the guests to the table, and give them menus. They may also assist guests in seating small children, or fill their water glasses.

While greeting incoming guests, hosts and hostesses must take care of guests who are leaving. Some hosts and hostesses receive the money for the guests' food and make change. To do this they must know how to operate a cash register. Restaurants sometimes have a candy or cigarette counter. If guests want to buy these items, hosts and hostesses add their cost to the guests' checks. In some restaurants this work is done by a cashier.

At the end of their work shifts, hosts and hostesses record the transactions that have taken place and total all guest checks to determine how much money has been received. These records are used to balance the accounts at the end of the day. The records are then turned in to the restaurant manager for inspection.

The host and hostess stand near the restaurant entrance so they can greet guests as they arrive and then seat them at tables.

## Education and Training Requirements

Individuals interested in becoming a host or hostess should take courses in business, arithmetic, bookkeeping, family and consumer science, and public speaking. Hosts and hostesses should be friendly and outgoing people who can remain calm and courteous during rush periods. They also must be neat and well groomed. Most restaurants prefer to hire people who have a high school education. Some vocational schools have programs in food service that can help prepare students for this kind of work; however, most restaurant hosts and hostesses are trained on the job.

## Getting the Job

Prospective hosts and hostesses should apply directly to restaurants in which they would like to work. Newspaper want ads sometimes have listings for these positions, as do state employment offices. Previous restaurant experience is helpful in landing a hosting job.

## Advancement Possibilities and Employment Outlook

Hosts and hostesses advance by transferring to more expensive restaurants that pay higher salaries. Experienced and responsible restaurant hosts and hostesses may become restaurant managers.

One big trend in the twenty-first century was an increase in the number of Americans dining out. With the restaurant business growing, the job outlook for hosts and hostesses is good, with positions expected to grow about as fast as the average through the year 2014.

## Working Conditions

Because restaurants serve the public, they are usually attractive places in which to work. Expensive restaurants often provide elegant work surroundings. Hosts and hostesses are usually stationed near the restaurant entrance and are on their feet throughout their shifts. They must maintain a neat appearance and always be courteous to guests. Full-time hosts and hostesses work forty hours a week and may rotate shifts, but there are many part-time workers in this field as well. Hosts and hostesses must work their share of weekends, evenings, and holidays. Many of these workers belong to labour unions.

## Earnings and Benefits

Earnings depend on the restaurant, with expensive restaurants generally paying higher salaries. According to the U.S. Bureau of Labour Statistics, hosts and hostesses earned a median wage of $7.52 per hour in 2004. Their wages tend to be higher than that of waitpersons because they usually do not receive tips. (In some restaurants, however, they are included in a tip pool that gives them a small share of the day's tips.) Restaurants often offer full-time employees paid holidays and vacations, health insurance, and retirement plans. Most hosts and hostesses receive free meals when they are at work.

4

# Hotel Staff

## BACKGROUND AND SIGNIFICANCE

This is a pilot study designed to help in the development of a large-scale research project on the future of work in the hospitality industry. The hospitality industry has experienced a wave of restructuring, consolidation, and new practices to cut costs including lean staffing and greater performance demands on the workforce.

The study will explore the impact of these and related changes on the health and quality of life the largest occupational group within the hospitality industry, room cleaners. Jobs in housekeeping (and food and beverage) operations of the hospitality industry represent the future of work in this growing service sector with jobs characterized by increasing repetitive physical workloads, low income, low skill utilization, low job control, and virtually no prospects for training and career advancement.

There is compelling evidence that this kind of low-income jobs result in a disproportionate high burden of illness, injury, and disability. Unlike other services, businesses in the hospitality industry, cannot be moved across the borders but will remain a fast growing sector in industrialized countries, creating increasing societal costs including disproportionate workers' compensation and health care utilization costs. Working conditions in the hospitality industry are representative for a growing number of workers of colour, working women, and former welfare recipients. The hospitality industry has become a major target for welfare-to-work and job training programs in cities throughout the country. An aging workforce is faced with increasing job demands in a competitive industry constantly upgrading services. Few studies have been done on this growing workforce and little is known about their specific working conditions and health risks and how they could be addressed.

This study will take a broad view at physical and psychosocial job factors, health, including general self-rated health, musculoskeletal disorders, work-related injury, and health-related quality of life. Further, this study will investigate which innovative organizational strategies can help to reduce the burden of illness and disability in the service sector by comparing hotels in different market segments, different degrees of unionization, and hotels with innovative joint labour management health and safety programs, negotiated child care/ elder care benefits, and a multi-employer worker training project.

San Francisco is expected to provide several union and non-union cases for comparison to similar cases in low union density markets and to a selected number of additional cases in other high union density markets that highlight organizational innovations (such as training and career laddering in Las Vegas or work redesign in New York to avoid sub-contracting). The pilot study focuses on housekeeping since it is the largest occupational category in the industry and is the central focus of a larger study including hotels in other cities. The study combines qualitative and quantitative research methods and is participatory in design and implementation thereby laying the groundwork for sustainable efforts in understanding and improving health and safety of service workers.

## COOPERATIVE SETTING

The pilot study is administered by the director of the Labour and Occupational Health Program (LOHP) at UC Berkeley Robin Baker, in collaboration with Niklas Krause, physician epidemiologist from the School of Public Health at UC Berkeley. Funding is provided by the United Way of the

Bay Area and Local 2 of the Hotel Employees and Restaurant Employees International Union (HERE).

The level of union density in San Francisco is among the highest in the country. The largest union is HERE Local 2 which represents 8,000 workers or around 70 % of the industry's non-supervisory workforce. In San Francisco the multi-employer bargaining agreement with about 50 hotels in the city has taken wages and benefits out of competition.

The starting wage for non-tipped jobs is $11 per hour plus comprehensive portable benefits. San Francisco presents a special opportunity for comparisons of work conditions in the industry and for future workplace interventions because of a unique partnership with twelve first class hotels that is designed to improve customer service and job quality in the industry.

The San Francisco Hotels Partnership Project has implemented a core-training program throughout much of the industry, and developed pilot projects to resolve conflicts at the lowest possible level within an organization. The parties have also worked to establish joint decision making processes for redesigning work in the food and beverages and housekeeping operations.

## OBJECTIVES

The objectives of the proposed study are:

1. To identify key changes in technology and organization in the hospitality industry that affects the future of work for room cleaners.
2. To explore the impact of industry changes on the health, injury rates, and well being of room cleaners.
3. To develop potential strategies for enhancing the future health and well being of room cleaners.
4. To demonstrate the utility of a participatory research methodology that actively involves room cleaners in every aspect of the study, and that results in the ability of participants to effectively advocate for health-promoting changes in their work.

5. To explore the relevance of the findings to similar low wage populations, particularly in the service sector.
6. To widely disseminate study findings and recommendations to encourage further study and action by academic researchers, labour, management, policy makers, and advocacy groups.

The pilot consists of establishing an advisory group of participants, focus groups with room cleaners, the development and administration of a survey instrument, analysis and discussion of results with participants, and dissemination of results in a final report.

Although designed for comparisons with other cities, the pilot will allow for comparisons between high quality and low quality (in terms of labour relations and customer service) hotels in San Francisco.

In addition, the use of some standardized instruments will enable comparisons of working conditions of housecleaners with jobs in different industries. Finally, future studies are planned to investigate the effects of changes in work conditions and labour-management collaboration on injury incidence, health and functional/quality of life outcomes.

**Progress**

A 30-member advisory group of room cleaners participated in the planning and implementation of this pilot study. Ten focus groups have been conducted with about 20-25 housecleaners at each meeting recruited from different San Francisco hotels.

A survey instrument has been developed and tested in a focus group of 25 roomcleaners. The revised survey has been translated into Spanish and Chinese languages. The survey includes standard instruments such as Karasek's Job Content Questionnaire, Siegrist's effort/reward balance scales including measures of intrinsic and extrinsic effort, SF36 health-related quality of life/functioning, general health status, and specifically developed questions to measure physical workload, musculoskeletal symptoms, work injury, and demographic variables. Depending on reading and language skills it takes 30 to 75 minutes for workers to complete the survey with assistance available from researchers and translators.

139 out of 397 roomcleaners from 4 selected hotels completed the survey during the first wave of data gathering in December 1998.

### Plan

A second wave of data gathering among 258 non-responders is planned for February. Intensive efforts of personal recruitment at the workplace and telephone follow-up is planned for a random 50% sample of 130 non-responders. Data management and basic analyses limited to descriptive statistics and comparisons between four hotels are planned for March and April. A draft report will be prepared for the union by May 15 and will be available for joint labour management focus groups preparing for upcoming bargaining of five-year contracts. Further analyses including comparisons with national survey data, discussions with participants, and a final report will be completed by December 1999. Publications in peer reviewed scientific journals may be prepared simultaneously or thereafter but no funds have been allocated yet for this purpose.

### Specific Aims

(1) Establish cooperative relationships between researchers and stakeholders

(2) Select 2-6 hotels (with a total of about 400 employees) representing "good" and "bad" overall work conditions as perceived by union representatives and key senior employees

(3) Conduct a series of focus groups with room cleaners from different hotels which are not selected into the pilot survey, to (a) gain a detailed understanding of their job tasks, workload, working conditions, and work-related health problems, (b) to discuss the scope and goals of the research project, and (c) to invite further participation in design and execution of the study (e.g. development and administration of survey instrument,

organization of meetings with roomcleaners at participating hotels)

(4) Develop draft survey instrument

(5) Discuss draft survey instrument with union representatives and other key informants

(6) Pre-test survey instrument in focus group with 25 roomcleaners

(7) Revise survey instrument

(8) Translate survey instrument into Spanish and Chinese languages

(9) Obtain names and addresses of current employees at selected hotels

(10) Invite employees of selected hotels by mail to fill out the survey in off-site meetings

(11) Conduct first wave of survey under supervision of University researchers and with assistance of translators at different times and locations in San Francisco

(12) Create database for data entry using Microsoft Access software

(13) Enter data from questionnaires and check for completeness

(14) Follow-up of workers with incomplete responses by telephone in their first language

(15) Update list of employees and draw random 50% sample from survey non-responders

(16) Obtain contact information including telephone numbers for non-responders

(17) Invite all non-responders by mail to fill out the survey in off-site meetings

(18) Invite 50% random sample of non-responders by telephone and/or personal contact to fill out the survey in off-site meetings

(19) Conduct second wave of survey

(20) Provide follow-up meetings with research team for workers willing to participate but unable to attend the pre-scheduled survey meetings

(21) Enter data into database

(22) Check data for missing information and inconsistencies

(23) Prepare final data set with variable labels for all data fields and create scales for work conditions based on theoretical and/or empirical approaches

(24) Analyze survey data and (a) prepare frequency tables for all questionnaire answers and scales stratified by hotels, (b) compare responses of first wave responders with second wave of responders in 50% sample intensively followed up, (c) compare responses between "good" and "bad" hotels, (d) compare work conditions with reports from studies in other industries, (e) investigate the association between work conditions and self-reported general health, musculoskeletal symptoms, quality of life, and work injury

(25) Gather OSHA 200 logs in selected hotels for 1998 and enter in separate database

(26) Replace employee names by ID code in injury data set and merge with survey data

(27) Analyze merged injury (OSHA 200 log) and survey data, and, specifically (a) compare frequency of self-reported and formally reported work injuries, (b) examine self-reported reasons for not reporting a work-related injury, (c) investigate associations between working conditions and both self-reported and OSHA 200 log based injury frequency

(28) Prepared draft report on May 15, 1999

(29) Present report to stakeholders in joint labour management meetings

(30) Prepare final report by December 1999

(31) Prepare peer-reviewed journal article(s)

(32) Integrate results of pilot study into proposed larger study comparing working conditions and health outcomes across different US cities representing different organizational settings and labour markets in the hotel industry

5

# Organising Procedure

A key issue in accomplishing the goals identified in the planning process is structuring the work of the organization. Organizations are groups of people, with ideas and resources, working toward common goals. The purpose of the organizing function is to make the best use of the organization's resources to achieve organizational goals. Organizational structure is the formal decision-making framework by which job tasks are divided, grouped, and coordinated. Formalization is an important aspect of structure. It is the extent to which the units of the organization are explicitly defined and its policies, procedures, and goals are clearly stated. It is the official organizational structure conceived and built by top management. The formal organization can be seen and represented in chart form. An organization chart displays the organizational structure and shows job titles, lines of authority, and relationships between departments.

The informal organization is the network, unrelated to the firm's formal authority structure, of social interactions among its employees. It is the personal and social relationships that arise spontaneously as people associate with one another in the work environment. The supervisor must realize that the informal organization affects the formal organization. The informal organization can pressure group members to conform to the expectations of the informal group that conflict with those of the formal organization. This can result in the generation of false information or rumors and resistance to change desired by management. The supervisor should recognize the existence of information groups, identify the roles member play within these groups, and use knowledge of the groups to work effectively with them. The informal organization can make the formal organization more effective by providing support to management, stability to the environment, and useful communication channels.

## ORGANIZATIONAL STRUCTURE

Even though the differences among organizations are enormous, there are many similarities that enable them to be classified. One widely used classification is the twofold system (mechanistic versus organic forms of organizational structure) developed by Tom Burns and G. M. Stalker in their study of electronics firms in the United Kingdom. (See Burns, Tom and G. M. Stalker, Management of Innovation, London: Tavistock Publications, 1961, p. 19.)

The mechanistic structure is the traditional or classical design, common in many medium-and large-size organizations. Mechanistic organizations are somewhat rigid in that they consist of very clearly delineated jobs, have a well-defined hierarchical structure, and rely heavily on the formal chain of command for control. Bureaucratic organizations, with their emphasis on formalization, are the primary form of mechanistic structures. According to Max Weber, bureaucracy is a form of organization characterized by a rational, goal-directed hierarchy, impersonal decision making, formal controls, and subdivision into managerial positions and specialization of labour. Bureaucratic organizations are tall consisting of hierarchies with many levels of management.

In a tall structure, people become relatively confined to their own area of specialization. Bureaucracies are driven by a top-down or command and control approach in which managers provide considerable direction and have considerable control over others. Other features of the bureaucratic organization include functional division of labour and work specialization.

On the other hand, the organic structure is more flexible, more adaptable to a participative form of management, and less concerned with a clearly defined structure. The organic organization is open to the environment in order to capitalize upon new opportunities.

Organic organizations have a flat structure with only one or two levels of management. Flat organizations emphasize a decentralized approach to management that encourage high employee involvement in decisions. The purpose of this structure is to create independent small businesses or enterprises that can rapidly respond to customers' needs or changes in the business environment. The supervisor tends to have a more personal relationship with his or her employees.

Rensis Likert has conducted extensive research on a non-bureaucratic organization design referred to as System 4 (participative-democratic). Management and employees interact in a friendly environment characterized by mutual confidence and trust.

Contingency organization means that the most appropriate organization structure for each situation depends upon technology, organizational size, goals and strategy, environmental stability, and characteristics of the employees. Mechanistic organizations are best suited to repetitive operations and stable environments, while organic organizations are best suited to an uncertain task and a changing environment.

## ORGANIZATION DESIGN

Designing an organization involves choosing an organizational structure that will enable the company to most effectively achieve its goals. Organization design is the creation of an organization's structure, traditionally functional, divisional, and/or matrix.

Functions or divisions arrange traditional organizations. In a functional organization, authority is determined by the relationships between group functions and activities. Functional structures group similar or related occupational specialties or processes together under the familiar headings of finance, manufacturing, marketing, accounts receivable, research, surgery, and photo finishing. Economy is achieved through specialization. However, the organization risks losing sight of its overall interests as different departments pursue their own goals.

In a divisional organization, corporate divisions operate as relatively autonomous businesses under the larger corporate umbrella. In a conglomerate organization, divisions may be unrelated. Divisional structures are made up of self-contained strategic business units that each produces a single product. For example, General Motors' divisions include Chevrolet, Oldsmobile, Pontiac, and Cadillac. A central headquarters, focusing or results, coordinates and controls the activities, and provides support services between divisions. Functional departments accomplish division goals. A weakness however, is the tendency to duplicate activities among divisions.

In a matrix organization, teams are formed and team members report to two or more managers. Matrix structures utilize functional and divisional chains of command simultaneously in the same part of the organization, commonly for one-of-a-kind projects. It is used to develop a new product, to ensure the continuing success of a product to which several departments directly contribute, and to solve a difficult problem. By superimposing a project structure upon the functional structure, a matrix organization is formed that allows the organization to take advantage of new opportunities. This structure assigns specialists from different functional departments to work on one or more projects being led by project managers. The matrix concept facilitates working on concurrent projects by creating a dual chain of command, the project (program, systems, or product) manager and the functional manager. Project managers have authority over activities geared toward achieving organizational goals while functional managers have authority over promotion decisions and performance reviews. An example is an aerospace firm with a contract from NASA.

Matrix organizations are particularly appealing to firms that want to speed up the decision-making process. However, the matrix organization may not allow long-term working relationships to develop. Furthermore, using multiple managers for one employee may result in confusion as to manager evaluation and accountability. Thus, the matrix system may elevate the conflict between product and functional interests.

Boundaryless organizations are not defined or limited by horizontal, vertical, or external boundaries imposed by a predetermined structure. They share many of the characteristics of flat organizations, with a strong emphasis on teams. Cross-functional teams dissolve horizontal barriers and enable the organization to respond quickly to environmental changes and to spearhead innovation. Boundaryless organizations can form relationships (joint ventures, intellectual property, distribution channels, or financial resources) with customers, suppliers, and/or competitors. Telecommuting, strategic alliances and customer-organization linkages break down external barriers, streamlining work activities. Jack Welch, former CEO of General Electric, to facilitate interactions with customers and suppliers, first used this un-structure.

A boundaryless environment is required by learning organizations to facilitate team collaboration and the sharing of information. When an organization develops the continuous capacity to adapt and survive in an increasingly competitive environment because all members take an active role in identifying and resolving work-related issues, it has developed a learning culture. A learning organization is one that is able to adapt and respond to change. This design empowers employees because they acquire and share knowledge and apply this learning to decision-making. They are pooling collective intelligence and stimulating creative thought to improve performance. Supervisors facilitate learning by sharing and aligning the organization's vision for the future and sustaining a sense of community and strong culture.

## ORGANIZING FUNCTION

The organizing function deals with all those activities that result in the formal assignment of tasks and authority and a coordination of effort. The supervisor staffs the work unit, trains employees, secures resources, and empowers the work group into a productive team. The steps in the organizing process include (1) review plans, (2) list all tasks to be accomplished, (3) divide tasks into groups one person can accomplish-a job, (4) group related jobs together in a logical and efficient manner, (5) assign work to individuals, (6) delegate authority to establish relationships between jobs and groups of jobs.

The nature and scope of the work needed to accomplish the organization's objectives is needed to determine work classification and work unit design. Division of labour, or work specialization, is the degree to which tasks in an organization are divided into separate jobs.

Work process requirements and employee skill level determine the degree of specialization. Placing capable people in each job ties directly with productivity improvement. In order to maximize productivity, supervisors match employee skill level with task requirements.

Supervisors should perform workflow analysis to examine how work creates or adds value to the ongoing processes in an organization. Workflow analysis looks at how work moves from the customer or the demand source through the organization to the point at which the work leaves the organization as a product or service to meet customer demand.

Thus, workflow analysis can be used to tighten the connection between employees' work and customers' needs. Also, it can help to make major performance breakthroughs throughout business process reengineering (BPR), a fundamental rethinking and radical redesign of business processes to achieve dramatic improvements in costs, quality, service, and speed. BPR uses workflow analysis to identify jobs that can be eliminated or recombined to improve company performance.

## DEPARTMENTALIZATION

After reviewing the plans, usually the first step in the organizing process is departmentalization. Once jobs have been classified through work specialization, they are grouped so those common tasks can be coordinated. Departmentalization is the basis on which work or individuals are grouped into manageable units. There are five traditional methods for grouping work activities.

— Departmentalization by function organizes by the functions to be performed. The functions reflect the nature of the business. The advantage of this type of grouping is obtaining efficiencies from consolidating similar specialties and people with common skills, knowledge and orientations together in common units.

— Departmentalization by product assembles all functions needed to make and market a particular product are placed under one executive. For instance, major department stores are structured around product groups such as home accessories, appliances, women's clothing, men's clothing, and children's clothing.

— Departmentalization by geographical regions groups jobs on the basis of territory or geography. For example, Merck, a major pharmaceutical company, has its domestic sales departmentalized by regions such as Northeast, Southeast, Midwest, Southwest, and Northwest.

— Departmentalization by process groups jobs on the basis of product or customer flow. Each process requires particular skills and offers a basis for homogeneous categorizing of work activities. A patient preparing for an operation would first engage in preliminary diagnostic tests, then go through the admitting process, undergo a procedure in surgery, receive post operative care, be discharged and perhaps receive out-patient attention. These services are each administered by different departments.

— Departmentalization by customer groups jobs on the basis of a common set of needs or problems of specific customers. For instance, a plumbing firm may group its work according to whether it is serving private sector, public sector, government, or not-for-profit organizations. A current departmentalization trend is to structure work according to customer, using cross-functional teams. This group is chosen from different functions to work together across various departments to interdependently create new products or services. For example, a cross-functional team consisting of managers from accounting, finance, and marketing is created to prepare a technology plan.

## POWER AND AUTHORITY

Organizational structure is a means of facilitating the achievement of organizational objectives. Such structures are not static, but dynamic. They reorganize in response to changing conditions that occur in the environment, new technology, or organizational growth. Organization structures are dependent upon the employees whose activities they guide. Supervisors rely upon power and authority to ensure that employees get things done.

### Authority

The organizational structure provides the framework for the formal distribution of authority. Formalization is the degree to which tasks are standardized and rules and regulations govern employee behaviour. It influences the amount of discretion an employee has over his or her job. In an organization with high degrees of formalization, job descriptions and policies provide clear direction. Where formalization is low, employees have a great deal of freedom in deciding how thy conduct their work. Within the same organization, different departments may have different degrees of formalization. For example, in a hospital, doctors have freedom in selecting treatments, drugs, and methods for treating patients. However, the hospital physical plant staff has a strict schedule for cleaning buildings, mowing lawns, and maintaining the facilities. Authority is the legitimate power of a supervisor to direct subordinates to take action within the scope of the supervisor's position. Formal authority in the organization can be traced all the way back to the U.S. constitutional right to own property. The owner of the organization has the authority to make decisions. For example, entrepreneurial firms have an informal arrangement of employees and centralization of decision-making authority, the owner.

## Forms of Authority

Three forms of authority are line authority, staff authority, and team authority.

Line authority is direct supervisory authority from superior to subordinate. Authority flows in a direct chain of command from the top of the company to the bottom. Chain of command is an unbroken line of reporting relationships that extends through the entire organization that defines the formal decision-making structure. It helps employees know to whom they are accountable, and whom to go to with a problem. Line departments are directly linked to the production and sales of specific products. Supervisors--in line departments, such as marketing and production--give direct orders, evaluate performance, and reward or punish those employees who work for them. Unity of command within the chain states that each person in an organization should take orders from and reports to only one person. This helps prevent conflicting demands being placed on employees by more than one boss. However, the trend toward employee empowerment, fuelled by advances in technology and changes in design from downsizing and reengineering have tempered the importance of being accountable to only one superior. Span of control refers to the number of employees that should be placed under the direction of one manager. Spans within effective organizations vary greatly. The actual number depends on the amount of complexity and the level of specialization. In general, a wide span of control is possible with better-trained, more experienced, and committed employees.

Staff authority is more limited authority to advise. It is authority that is based on expertise and which usually involves advising line managers. Staff members are advisers and counsellors who aid line departments in making decisions but do not have the authority to make final decisions. Staff supervisors help line departments decide what to do and how to do it. They coordinate and provide technical assistance or advice to all advisors, such as accounting, human resources, information technology, research, advertising, public relations, and legal services.

Team authority is granted to committees or work teams involved in an organization's daily operations. Work teams are groups of operating employees empowered to plan and organize their own work and to perform that work with a minimum of supervision.

Team-Based structures organize separate functions into a group based on one overall objective. Empowered employees create their own schedules, design their own processes, and are held responsible for outcomes. This facilitates efficiencies in work process, and the ability to detect and react to changes in the environment. Employees with the skills and knowledge to manage more than one specialized task are able to promptly provide customers with quality products and services. Cross-functionally training team members allows any member to perform a variety of problem-solving tasks.

Teamwork is an imperative in a flat, boundaryless organizational structure. A team is a small number of people with complementary skills who work toward common goals for which they hold themselves mutually accountable. Self-managed teams are responsible for producing an entire product, a component, or an ongoing service.

In most cases, members are cross-trained on the different tasks assigned to the team. Often, these teams are trained in technical, administrative, and interpersonal skills. Problem-solving teams do not affect an organization's structure because they exist for only a limited period.

They are often used when organizations decide to make improvements in the quality of a product or service. Special-purpose teams consist of members who span functional or organizational boundaries and whose purpose is to examine complex issues such as introducing new technology, improving the quality of work process, or encouraging cooperation between labour and management in a unionized setting.

## Power

In addition to authority, supervisors have more personal sources of power to draw upon for getting things done. Everyone has power in one form or another and it is by exercising this power that organizations get things accomplished. Supervisors who are capable of achieving their objectives independently of others are said to possess strength. When these "strong" supervisors involve and incorporate others into their plans and activities they are making use of power, and in fact increasing the total amount of power available to incorporate into a particular situation or problem. Involving employees in setting objectives and making decisions as it relates to their jobs empowers everyone, and results in greater job satisfaction and commitment, as well as increased productivity. Empowering employees provides them with greater autonomy.

Power is the ability to exert influence in the organization beyond authority, which is derived from position. The supervisor's personal power could include job knowledge, personal influence, interpersonal skills, and ability to get results, empathetic ability, persuasive ability, and physical strength. J.P. French and B. Raven ("The Bases of Social Power" in Studies in Social Power, edited by D. Cartwright, Institute for Social Research, 1959, pp. 150-167) identify six sources of power: legitimate, coercive, reward, expert, referent, and information. Legitimate power is a result of the position a person holds in the organization hierarchy. This position power is broader than the ability to reward and punish, as members need to accept the authority of the position. Coercive power is the threat of sanctions. It is dependent on fear and includes, but is not limited to the ability to dismiss, assign undesirable work, or restriction of movement. Reward power results in people doing what is asked because they desire positive benefits or rewards. Rewards can be anything a person values (praise, raises, and promotions). Expert power comes from expertise, skill, or knowledge. Referent power refers to a person who has desirable resources or personal traits. It results in admiration and the desire to emulate. Information power is based upon the persuasiveness or content of a communication and is independent of the influencing individual. In most instances, supervisors do not need to offer incentives or threaten retribution to get employees to do what they request. They influence employees because the employees want to follow. This power to influence comes from the employee granting authority to the supervisor.

**Centralization versus Decentralization**

Centralization is the degree to which decision-making is concentrated in top management's hands. Decentralization is the extent to which decision-making authority is pushed down the organization structure and shared with many lower-level employees. Centralized organizations have more levels of management with narrow spans of control. Employees are not free to make decisions. Decentralized organizations have fewer levels of management with wide spans of control giving employees more freedom of action. All other things being equal, a wide span of control is more efficient because it requires fewer managers. However, it is important to recognize that, at some point, effectiveness will decline.

The current trend is toward broadening decentralization. As competition intensifies, the need for organizations to be responsive increases. This has made employees, usually those at the lower levels, who are closest to customers extremely important. They are an excellent source of knowledge and implement changes that directly impact performance. Giving this group more input into certain decision-making activities can result in increased firm performance.

Teamwork is an imperative in a flat, boundaryless organizational structure. A team is a small number of people with complementary skills who work toward common goals for which they hold themselves mutually accountable. Self-managed teams are responsible for producing an entire product, a component, or an ongoing service. In most cases, members are cross-trained on the different tasks assigned to the team.

Often, these teams are trained in technical, administrative, and interpersonal skills. Problem-solving teams do not affect an organization's structure because they exist for only a limited period. They are often used when organizations decide to make improvements in the quality of a product or service. Special-purpose teams consist of members who span functional or organizational boundaries and whose purpose is to examine complex issues such as introducing new technology, improving the quality of work process, or encouraging cooperation between labour and management in a unionized setting.

### Power

In addition to authority, supervisors have more personal sources of power to draw upon for getting things done. Everyone has power in one form or another and it is by exercising this power that organizations get things accomplished. Supervisors who are capable of achieving their objectives independently of others are said to possess strength. When these "strong" supervisors involve and incorporate others into their plans and activities they are making use of power, and in fact increasing the total amount of power available to incorporate into a particular situation or problem. Involving employees in setting objectives and making decisions as it relates to their jobs empowers everyone, and results in greater job satisfaction and commitment, as well as increased productivity. Empowering employees provides them with greater autonomy.

Power is the ability to exert influence in the organization beyond authority, which is derived from position. The supervisor's personal power could include job knowledge, personal influence, interpersonal skills, and ability to get results, empathetic ability, persuasive ability, and physical strength. J.P. French and B. Raven ("The Bases of Social Power" in Studies in Social Power, edited by D. Cartwright, Institute for Social Research, 1959, pp. 150-167) identify six sources of power: legitimate, coercive, reward, expert, referent, and information.

Legitimate power is a result of the position a person holds in the organization hierarchy. This position power is broader than the ability to reward and punish, as members need to accept the authority of the position. Coercive power is the threat of sanctions. It is dependent on fear and includes, but is not limited to the ability to dismiss, assign undesirable work, or restriction of movement. Reward power results in people doing what is asked because they desire positive benefits or rewards. Rewards can be anything a person values (praise, raises, and promotions). Expert power comes from expertise, skill, or knowledge. Referent power refers to a person who has desirable resources or personal traits. It results in admiration and the desire to emulate. Information power is based upon the persuasiveness or content of a communication and is independent of the influencing individual.

In most instances, supervisors do not need to offer incentives or threaten retribution to get employees to do what they request. They influence employees because the employees want to follow. This power to influence comes from the employee granting authority to the supervisor.

### Centralization versus Decentralization

Centralization is the degree to which decision-making is concentrated in top management's hands. Decentralization is the extent to which decision-making authority is pushed down the organization structure and shared with many lower-level employees. Centralized organizations have more levels of management with narrow spans of control. Employees are not free to make decisions. Decentralized organizations have fewer levels of management with wide spans of control giving employees more freedom of action. All other things being equal, a wide span of control is more efficient because it requires fewer managers. However, it is important to recognize that, at some point, effectiveness will decline.

The current trend is toward broadening decentralization. As competition intensifies, the need for organizations to be responsive increases. This has made employees, usually those at the lower levels, who are closest to customers extremely important. They are an excellent source of knowledge and implement changes that directly impact performance. Giving this group more input into certain decision-making activities can result in increased firm performance.

It is impractical for the supervisor to handle all of the work of the department directly. In order to meet the organization's goals, focus on objectives, and ensure that all work is accomplished, supervisors must delegate authority. Authority is the legitimate power of a supervisor to direct subordinates to take action within the scope of the supervisor's position. By extension, this power, or a part thereof, is delegated and used in the name of a supervisor. Delegation is the downward transfer of formal authority from superior to subordinate. The employee is empowered to act for the supervisor, while the supervisor remains accountable for the outcome. Delegation of authority is a person-to-person relationship requiring trust, commitment, and contracting between the supervisor and the employee.

The supervisor assists in developing employees in order to strengthen the organization. He or she gives up the authority to make decisions that are best made by subordinates. This means that the supervisor allows subordinates the freedom to make mistakes and learn from them. He or she does not supervise subordinates' decision-making, but allows them the opportunity to develop their own skills. The supervisor lets subordinates know that he or she is willing to help, but not willing to do their jobs for them. The supervisor is not convinced that the best way for employees to learn is by telling them how to solve a problem. This results in those subordinates becoming dependent on the supervisor. The supervisor allows employees the opportunity to achieve and be credited for it.

An organization's most valuable resource is its people. By empowering employees who perform delegated jobs with the authority to manage those jobs, supervisors free themselves to manage more effectively. Successfully training future supervisors means delegating authority. This gives employees the concrete skills, experience, and the resulting confidence to develop themselves for higher positions. Delegation provides better managers and a higher degree of efficiency. Thus, collective effort, resulting in the organization's growth, is dependent on delegation of authority.

## Responsibility and Accountability

Equally important to authority is the idea that when an employee is given responsibility for a job, he or she must also be given the degree of authority necessary to carry it out. Thus, for effective delegation, the authority granted to an employee must equal the assigned responsibility. Upon accepting the delegated task, the employee has incurred an obligation to perform the assigned work and to properly utilize the granted authority. Responsibility is the obligation to do assigned tasks. The individual employee is responsible for being proficient at his or her job. The supervisor is responsible for what employees do or fail to do, as well as for the resources under their control. Thus, responsibility is an integral part of a supervisor's authority.

Responsibilities fall into two categories: individual and organizational. Employees have individual responsibilities to be proficient in their job. They are responsible for their actions. Nobody gives or delegates individual responsibilities. Employees assume them when they accept a position in the organization. Organizational responsibilities refer to collective organizational accountability and include how well departments perform their work. For example, the supervisor is responsible for all the tasks assigned to his or her department, as directed by the manager. When someone is responsible for something, he or she is liable, or accountable to a superior, for the outcome. Thus, accountability flows upward in the organization. All are held accountable for their personal, individual conduct. Accountability is answering for the result of one's actions or omissions. It is the reckoning, wherein one answers for his or her actions and accepts the consequences, good or bad. Accountability establishes reasons, motives and importance for actions in the eyes of managers and employees alike. Accountability is the final act in the establishment of one's credibility. It is important to remember that accountability results in rewards for good performance, as well as discipline for poor performance.

## The Delegation Process

The delegation process has five phases: (1) preparing, (2) planning, (3) discussing, (4) auditing, and (5) appreciating. The first step in delegating is to identify what should and should not be delegated. The supervisor should delegate any task that a subordinate performs better. Tasks least critical to the performance of the supervisor's job can be delegated. Any task that provides valuable experience for subordinates should be delegated. Also, the supervisor can delegate the tasks that he or she dislikes the most. But, the supervisor should not delegate any task that would violate a confidence.

— Preparing includes establishing the objectives of the delegation, specifying the task that needs to be accomplished, and deciding who should accomplish it.

— Planning is meeting with the chosen subordinate to describe the task and to ask the subordinate to devise a plan of action. As Andrew Carnegie once said, "The secret of success is not in doing your own work but in recognizing the right man to do it." Trust between the supervisor and employee-that both will fulfill the commitment-is most important.

— Discussing includes reviewing the objectives of the task as well as the subordinate's plan of action, any potential obstacles, and ways to avoid or deal with these obstacles. The supervisor should clarify and solicit feedback as to the employee's understanding. Clarifications needed for delegation include the desired results (what not how), guidelines, resources available, and consequences (good and bad). Delegation is similar to contracting between the supervisor and employee regarding how and when the work will be completed. The standards and time frames are discussed and agreed upon. The employee should know exactly what is expected and how the task will be evaluated.

— Auditing is monitoring the progress of the delegation and making adjustments in response to unforeseen problems.

— Appreciating is accepting the completed task and acknowledging the subordinate's efforts.

Since motivation influences productivity, supervisors need to understand what motivates employees to reach peak performance. It is not an easy task to increase employee motivation because employees respond in different ways to their jobs and their organization's practices. Motivation is the set of processes that moves a person toward a goal. Thus, motivated behaviours are voluntary choices controlled by the individual employee. The supervisor (motivator) wants to influence the factors that motivate employees to higher levels of productivity.

Factors that affect work motivation include individual differences, job characteristics, and organizational practices. Individual differences are the personal needs, values, and attitudes, interests and abilities that people bring to their jobs. Job characteristics are the aspects of the position that determine its limitations and challenges. Organizational practices are the rules, human resources policies, managerial practices, and rewards systems of an organization. Supervisors must consider how these factors interact to affect employee job performance.

## Simple Model of Motivation

The purpose of behaviour is to satisfy needs. A need is anything that is required, desired, or useful. A want is a conscious recognition of a need. A need arises when there is a difference in self-concept (the way I see myself) and perception (the way I see the world around me). The presence of an active need is expressed as an inner state of tension from which the individual seeks relief.

## Theories of Motivation

Many methods of employee motivation have been developed. The study of work motivation has focused on the motivator (supervisor) as well as the motivatee (employee). Motivation theories are important to supervisors attempting to be effective leaders. Two primary approaches to motivation are content and process.

The content approach to motivation focuses on the assumption that individuals are motivated by the desire to fulfill inner needs. Content theories focus on the needs that motivate people.

Maslow's Hierarchy of Needs identifies five levels of needs, which are best seen as a hierarchy with the most basic need emerging first and the most sophisticated need last. People move up the hierarchy one level at a time. Gratified needs lose their strength and the next level of needs is activated. As basic or lower-level needs are satisfied, higher-level needs become operative. A satisfied need is not a motivator. The most powerful employee need is the one that has not been satisfied. Abraham Maslow first presented the five-tier hierarchy in 1942 to a psychoanalytic society and published it in 1954 in Motivation and Personality (New York: Harper and Row).

**Level I**-Physiological needs are the most basic human needs. They include food, water, and comfort. The organization helps to satisfy employees' physiological needs by a paycheck.

**Level II**-Safety needs are the desires for security and stability, to feel safe from harm. The organization helps to satisfy employees' safety needs by benefits.

**Level III**-Social needs are the desires for affiliation. They include friendship and belonging. The organization helps to satisfy employees' social needs through sports teams, parties, and celebrations. The supervisor can help fulfill social needs by showing direct care and concern for employees.

**Level IV**-Esteem needs are the desires for self-respect and respect or recognition from others. The organization helps to satisfy employees' esteem needs by matching the skills and abilities of the employee to the job. The supervisor can help fulfill esteem needs by showing workers that their work is appreciated.

**Level V**-Self-actualization needs are the desires for self-fulfilment and the realization of the individual's full potential. The supervisor can help fulfill self-actualization needs by assigning tasks that challenge employees' minds while drawing on their aptitude and training.

Alderfer's ERG identified three categories of needs. The most important contribution of the ERG model is the addition of the frustration-regression hypothesis, which holds that when individuals are frustrated in meeting higher level needs, the next lower level needs reemerge. Existence needs are the desires for material and physical well being. These needs are satisfied with food, water, air, shelter, working conditions, pay, and fringe benefits.

Relatedness needs are the desires to establish and maintain interpersonal relationships. These needs are satisfied with relationships with family, friends, supervisors, subordinates, and co-workers.

Growth needs are the desires to be creative, to make useful and productive contributions and to have opportunities for personal development.

McClelland's Learned Needs divides motivation into needs for power, affiliation, and achievement.

Achievement motivated people thrive on pursuing and attaining goals. They like to be able to control the situations in which they are involved. They take moderate risks. They like to get immediate feedback on how they have done. They tend to be preoccupied with a task-orientation towards the job to be done.

Power motivated individuals see almost every situation as an opportunity to seize control or dominate others. They love to influence others. They like to change situations whether or not it is needed. They are willing to assert themselves when a decision needs to be made.

Affiliation motivated people are usually friendly and like to socialize with others. This may distract them from their performance requirements. They will usually respond to an appeal for cooperation.

Herzberg's Two-Factor Theory describes needs in terms of satisfaction and dissatisfaction. Frederick Herzberg examined motivation in the light of job content and contest. Motivating employees is a two-step process. First provide hygienes and then motivators. One continuum ranges from no satisfaction to satisfaction. The other continuum ranges from dissatisfaction to no dissatisfaction. Satisfaction comes from motivators that are intrinsic or job content, such as achievement, recognition, advancement, responsibility, the work itself, and growth possibilities. Herzberg uses the term motivators for job satisfiers since they involve job content and the satisfaction that results from them. Motivators are considered job turn-ons. They are necessary for substantial improvements in work performance and move the employee beyond satisfaction to superior performance. Motivators correspond to Maslow's higher-level needs of esteem and self-actualization.

Dissatisfaction occurs when the following hygiene factors, extrinsic or job context, are not present on the job: pay, status, job security, working conditions, company policy, peer relations, and supervision. Herzberg uses the term hygiene for these factors because they are preventive in nature.

They will not produce motivation, but they can prevent motivation from occurring. Hygiene factors can be considered job stay-ons because they encourage an employee to stay on a job. Once these factors are provided, they do not necessarily promote motivation; but their absence can create employee dissatisfaction. Hygiene factors correspond to Maslow's physiological, safety, and social needs in that they are extrinsic, or peripheral, to the job. They are present in the work environment of job context.

Motivation comes from the employee's feelings of accomplishment or job content rather than from the environmental factors or job context. Motivators encourage an employee to strive to do his or her best. Job enrichment can be used to meet higher-level needs. To enrich a job, a supervisor can introduce new or more difficult tasks, assign individuals specialized tasks that enable them to become experts, or grant additional authority to employees.

The process approach emphasizes how and why people choose certain behaviours in order to meet their personal goals. Process theories focus on external influences or behaviours that people choose to meet their needs. External influences are often readily accessible to supervisors.

Vroom's Expectancy Model suggests that people choose among alternative behaviours because they anticipate that particular behaviours will lead to one or more desired outcomes and that other behaviours will lead to undesirable outcomes. Expectancy is the belief that effort will lead to first-order outcomes, any work-related behaviour that is the direct result of the effort an employee expends on a job.

Equity is the perception of fairness involved in rewards given. A fair or equitable situation is one in which people with similar inputs experience similar outcomes. Employees will compare their rewards with the rewards received by others for their efforts. If employees perceive that an inequity exists, they are likely to withhold some of their contributions, either consciously or unconsciously, to bring a situation into better balance. For example, if someone thinks he or she is not getting enough pay (output) for his or her work (input), he or she will try to get that pay increased or reduce the amount of work he or she is doing. On the other hand, when a worker thinks he or she is being paid too much for the work he or she is doing, he or she tends to increase the amount of work. Not only do workers compare their own inputs and outputs; they compare their input/output ratio with the input/output ratio of other workers. If one work team believes they are doing more work than a similar team for the same pay, their sense of fairness will be violated and they will tend to reduce the amount of work they are doing. It is a normal human inclination to want things to be fair.

Bowditch and Buono note (see Bowditch, James L. and Anthony F. Buono, A Primer on Organizational Behaviour, 4th, John Wiley & Sons, 1997) that while equity theory was originally concerned with differences in pay, it may be applied to other forms of tangible and intangible rewards in the workplace. That is, if any input is not balanced with some fair output, the motivation process will be difficult. Supervisors must manage the perception of fairness in the mind of each employee. If subordinates think they are not being treated fairly, it is difficult to motivate them.

Reinforcement involves four types of consequence. Positive reinforcement creates a pleasant consequence by using rewards to increase the likelihood that a behaviour will be repeated. Negative reinforcement occurs when a person engages in behaviour to avoid unpleasant consequences or to escape from existing unpleasant consequences. Punishment is an attempt to discourage a target behaviour by the application of negative outcomes whenever it is possible. Extinction is the absence of any reinforcement, either positive or negative, following the occurrence of a target behaviour. Employees have questions about their jobs. Can I do what management is asking me to do? If I do thc job, will I be rewarded? Will the reward I receive be satisfactory to me?

Reinforcement is based primarily on the work of B.F. Skinner, a psychologist, who experimented with the theories of operant conditioning. Skinner's work shows that many behaviours can be controlled through the use of rewards. In fact, a person might be influenced to change his or her behaviour by giving him or her rewards.

Employees who do an exceptionally good job on a particular project should be rewarded for that performance. It will motivate them to try to do an exceptional job on their next project. Employees must associate the reward with the behaviour. In other words, the employee must know for what specifically he or she is being rewarded! The reward should come as quickly as possible after the behaviour. The reward can be almost anything, but it must be something desired by the employee. Some of the most powerful rewards are symbolic; things that cost very little but mean a lot to the people who get them. Examples of symbolic rewards are things like plaques or certificates.

## NEW ORGANISING TECHNIQUES

To meet the many demands of performing their functions, managers assume multiple roles. A role is an organized set of behaviours. Henry Mintzberg has identified ten roles common to the work of all managers. The ten roles are divided into three groups: interpersonal, informational, and decisional. The informational roles link all managerial work together. The interpersonal roles ensure that information is provided. The decisional roles make significant use of the information. The performance of managerial roles and the requirements of these roles can be played at different times by the same manager and to different degrees depending on the level and function of management. The ten roles are described individually, but they form an integrated whole.

The three interpersonal roles are primarily concerned with interpersonal relationships. In the figurehead role, the manager represents the organization in all matters of formality. The top level manager represents the company legally and socially to those outside of the organization. The supervisor represents the work group to higher management and higher management to the work group. In the liaison role, the manger interacts with peers and people outside the organization. The top level manager uses the liaison role to gain favours and information, while the supervisor uses it to maintain the routine flow of work. The leader role defines the relationships between the manger and employees.

The direct relationships with people in the interpersonal roles place the manager in a unique position to get information. Thus, the three informational roles are primarily concerned with the information aspects of managerial work. In the monitor role, the manager receives and collects information. In the role of disseminator, the manager transmits special information into the organization. The top level manager receives and transmits more information from people outside the organization than the supervisor. In the role of spokesperson, the manager disseminates the organization's information into its environment. Thus, the top level manager is seen as an industry expert, while the supervisor is seen as a unit or departmental expert.

The unique access to information places the manager at the center of organizational decision making. There are four decisional roles. In the entrepreneur role, the manager initiates change. In the disturbance handler role, the manger deals with threats to the organization. In the resource allocator role, the manager chooses where the organization will expend its efforts. In the negotiator role, the manager negotiates on behalf of the organization. The top level manager makes the decisions about the organization as a whole, while the supervisor makes decisions about his or her particular work unit. The supervisor performs these managerial roles but with different emphasis than higher managers. Supervisory management is more focused and short-term in outlook. Thus, the figurehead role becomes less significant and the disturbance handler and negotiator roles increase in importance for the supervisor. Since leadership permeates all activities, the leader role is among the most important of all roles at all levels of management

In order to perform the functions of management and to assume multiple roles, managers must be skilled. Robert Katz identified three managerial skills that are essential to successful management: technical, human, and conceptual. Technical skill involves process or technique knowledge and proficiency. Managers use the processes, techniques and tools of a specific area. Human skill involves the ability to interact effectively with people. Managers interact and cooperate with employees. Conceptual skill involves the formulation of ideas. Managers understand abstract relationships, develop ideas, and solve problems creatively. Thus, technical skill deals with things, human skill concerns people, and conceptual skill has to do with ideas. A manager's level in the organization determines the relative importance of possessing technical, human, and conceptual skills. Top level managers need conceptual skills in order to view the organization as a whole. Conceptual skills are used in planning and dealing with ideas and abstractions. Supervisors need technical skills to manage their area of specialty. All levels of management need human skills in order to interact and communicate with other people successfully.

As the pace of change accelerates and diverse technologies converge, new global industries are being created (for example, telecommunications). Technological change alters the fundamental structure of firms and calls for new organizational approaches and management skills.

Successful organizations continually innovate and change based upon customer needs and feedback. Values, mission, and vision form the foundation for the execution of the functions of management. They are an organization's guidelines that affect how it will operate. They work only if visible and used in everyday activities and decisions. An organization's values are its beliefs or those qualities that have intrinsic worth and will not be compromised. Its mission is its purpose for existing. The vision is the image of itself in the future.

## Values

Each supervisor's approach to management will reflect his or her values, as well as those of the organization. Building trust starts with creating culture based on shared values. Values are traits or qualities having intrinsic worth, such as courage, respect, responsibility, caring, truthfulness, self-discipline, and fairness. Values serve as a baseline for actions and decision-making and guide employees in the organization's intentions and interests. The values driving behaviour define the organizational culture. A strong value system or clearly defined culture turns beliefs into standards such as best quality, best performance, most reliable, most durable, safest, fastest, best value for the money, least expensive, most prestigious, best designed or styled, easiest to use. If asked, "What do we believe in?" or "List our organization's values" all employees in the organization should write down the same values. For example, McDonald's values were captured in its motto of "Q.S.C. & V." which stands for quality, service, cleanliness, and value.

Supervisors need to appreciate the significance of values and value systems. Values affect how a supervisor views other people and groups, thus influencing interpersonal relationships. Values affect how a supervisor perceives situations and solves problems. Values affect how a supervisor determines what is and is not ethical behaviour. Values affect how a supervisor leads and controls employees. Since employees often base behaviour on perceived values it is critical to ensure their perceptions reflect organizational values. Supervisors must communicate, encourage and reinforce the desired values and related behaviours to integrate them into the organizational culture.

Geert Hofstede identified a work-related value framework that has four dimensions: power distance, uncertainty avoidance, individualism, and polarization. Power distance is the attitude to human inequality and relationships to superiors and inferiors in any hierarchy. Uncertainty avoidance is the tolerance for uncertainty that determines choices and rituals to cope with it in social structures and belief systems. Individualism is the relationship between the individual and the collectivity, especially in the way individuals choose to live and work together. Polarization is the extent to which differences such as masculinity or femininity have implications for social organization and the organizations of beliefs. Every person has a different mental program, based on patterns of thinking, feeling, and acting, which are learned throughout a lifetime. The effects of these differences have many practical implications for those who work or are managers in multinational business and for those involved in international negotiations.

## Mission

A mission is a broad definition of a business that differentiates it from all other organizations. It is the justification for the organization's existence. The mission statement is the "touchstone" by which all offerings are judged. In addition to the organization's purpose other key elements of the mission statement should include whom it serves, how, and why. The most effective mission statements are easily recalled and provide direction and motivation for the organization.

Since an organization exists to accomplish something in the larger environment, its specific mission or purpose provides employees with a shared sense of opportunity, direction, significance, and achievement. An explicit mission guides employees to work independently and yet collectively toward the realization of the organization's potential. Thus, a good mission statement gets the emotional bonding and commitment needed. It allows the individual employee to say; "I know how I should do my job differently." For example, many people might think that The Walt Disney Company's mission is to run theme parks. But, Disney's mission is always moving toward an expanded view. Disney provides entertainment. "Disney's overriding objective is to create shareholder value by continuing to be the world's premier entertainment company from a creative, strategic, and financial standpoint." Also, many people might think that Revlon's mission is to make cosmetics. Yet, Revlon provides glamour, excitement and innovation. Charles Revson, Revlon's founder understood the importance of mission. He said "In the factory, we make cosmetics; in the store, we sell hope."

## Vision

Erich Fromm pointed out; "The best way to predict your future is to create it." A vision might be a picture, image, or description of the preferred future. A visionary has the ability to foresee something and sees the need for change first. He or she challenges the status quo and forces honest assessments of where the industry is headed and how the company can best get there. A visionary is ready with solutions before the problems arise.

A study over the period from 1926 to 1990 found visionary companies that set a purpose beyond making money outperformed other companies in the stock market by more than six to one. (See Gilbert Fuchsberg, "Visioning' Mission Becomes Its Own Mission," The Wall Street Journal, January 7, 1994, B1, 3.) Managers require more vision than ever because change is coming faster than ever. Leaders have the ability to make their vision real by engaging the minds, as well as the hearts of others.

Microsoft's early vision statement was "A Computer on Every Desk and In Every Home." (At approximately the same time, President John Akers said IBM's goal was to become a $100 billion company by then end of the century. At that time IBM sales were $50 billion.) Microsoft's vision has evolved [1998 the "Connected PC and the Connected TV"-the idea of integrating the intelligence and interactivity of PCs with the video and sound of TV] to 2002 "to enable people and businesses throughout the world to realize their full potential."

Life consists in what a man is thinking of all day.--Ralph Waldo Emerson.

A goal is an end that the organization strives to attain. However, the supervisor cannot "do" a goal. Supervisors break down processes, analyze them, set objectives and then drive hard to achieve them. Doing the same thing and expecting different results doesn't work. The supervisor must write an objective for what he or she is trying to accomplish. Thus, an objective is the object or aim of an action. It implies an explicit direction for the action to take and a specific quality of work to be accomplished within a given period of time. Objectives reflect the desired outcomes for individuals, groups and organizations. They provide direction for decision-making and a criterion against which outcomes are measured. Thus, objectives are the foundation of planning.

## MANAGEMENT BY OBJECTIVES

An effective planning tool to help the supervisor set objectives is Management by Objectives (MBO). MBO gained recognition in 1954 with the publication of Peter Drucker's book The Practice of Management. MBO is a collaborative process whereby the manager and each subordinate jointly determine objectives for that subordinate. To be successful MBO programs should include commitment and participation in the MBO process at all levels, from top management to the lowest position in the organization. MBO begins when the supervisor explains the goals for the department in a meeting. The subordinate takes the goals and proposes objectives for his or her particular job. The supervisor meets with the subordinate to approve and, if necessary, modify the individual objectives. Modification of the individual's objectives is accomplished through negotiation since the supervisor has resources to help the subordinate commit to the achievement of the objective. Thus, a set of verifiable objectives for each individual are jointly determined, prioritized, and formalized. The supervisor and the subordinate meet periodically to review the latter's progress. Communication is the key factor in determining MBO's success or failure. The supervisor gives feedback and may authorize modifications to the objectives or their timetables as circumstances dictate. Finally, the employee's performance is measured against his or her objectives, and he or she is rewarded accordingly.

## Steps in MBO Process

Research has demonstrated that when top management is committed and personally involved in implementing MBO programs, they significantly improve performance. This finding is not surprising when one considers that during the MBO process employees determine what they will accomplish. After all, who knows what a person is capable of doing better than the person does him or herself?

Objectives are the driver of planning processes. It is imperative that top managers safeguard the intention of their goals to facilitate middle and lower management's effective translation and implementation of them. Objectives guide managerial activities such as budgeting, the development of action plans, staffing, and the purchasing of equipment. The organization's success ultimately depends on the combined outcomes of its objectives.

## Objectives

Most supervisors set objectives, but not with equal skill. Few, who do not correctly write objectives, will reap MBO's full benefits. An objective is simply a statement of what is to done and should be stated in terms of results. A mnemonic aid to write objectives is SMART (Specific, Measurable, Attainable, Result-oriented, Time-limited).

## Specific

An objective must be specific with a single key result. If more than one result is to be accomplished, more than one objective should be written. Just knowing what is to be accomplished is a big step toward achieving it. What is important to you? Once you clarify what you want to achieve, your attention will be focused on the objective that you deliberately set. You will be doing something important to you.

## Measurable

An objective must be measurable. Only an objective that affects behaviour in a measurable way can be optimally effective. If possible, state the objective as a quantity. Some objectives are more difficult to measure than others are. However, difficulty does not mean that they cannot be measured. Treatment of salespeople might be measured by looking at the absenteeism and turnover rates among the sales force. Also, salespeople could be asked to fill out a behavioural questionnaire anonymously giving their observations of the supervision they receive.

Customer service could be measured by such indices as the number of complaints received, by the number of customers lost, and by customer interviews or responses to questionnaires. Development of subordinates could be measured by determining the number of tasks the subordinate has mastered. Cooperation with other functions could be measured by length of delay in providing requested information, or by peer ratings of degree of cooperation.

Avoid statements of objectives in generalities. Infinitives to avoid include to know, to understand, to enjoy, and to believe. Action verbs are observable and better communicate the intent of what is to be attempted. They include to write, to apply, to recite, to revise, to contrast, to install, to select, to assemble, to compare, to investigate, and to develop.

## Scaling the Progress

### *Attainable*

An objective must be attainable with the resources that are available. It must be realistic. Many objectives are realistic. Yet, the time it takes to achieve them may be unrealistic. For example, it is realistic to want to lose ten pounds. However, it is unrealistic to want to lose ten pounds in one week.

What barriers stand between you and your objective? How will each barrier be overcome and within what time frame?

### Result-oriented

The objective should be central to the goals of the organization. The successful completion of the objective should make a difference. How will this objective help the organization move ahead? Is the objective aligned with the mission of the organization?

### Time-limited

The objective should be traceable. Specific objectives enable time priorities to be set and time to be used on objectives that really matter. Are the time lines you have established realistic? Will other competing demands cause delay? Will you be able to overcome those demands to accomplish the objective you've set in the time frame you've established?

### Write Meaningful Objectives

Although the rules are difficult to establish, the following may be useful when writing an objective.

1. Start with an action or accomplishment verb. (Use the infinitive form of the verb. This means to start the with "to.")
2. Identify a single key result for each objective.
3. Give the date of the estimated completion.
4. Be sure the objective is one you can control.
5. To test for validity of SMART objectives, ask yourself the following questions.
   * S = Exactly what is my objective?
   * M = What would a good job look like?
   * A = Is my objective feasible?
   * R = Is my objective meaningful?
   * T = Is my objective traceable?

The following fill-in-the-blank equation may be useful when writing an objective.

**Objective:** To (+ action verb + single key result + target date)

## ORGANIZING PROCESS

In cases of management transfer, the estalishment process focuses on a level of user organization where no organization presently exists, that is, at a level of the irrigation network previously managed by the government irrigation agency. Typically this entails organizing federations of user groups at the tertiary level under a secondary-canal association. The challenge of creating a new organization of users is perhaps the most central feature of the management transfer process. The act of management transfer from the agency to the users depends upon a user organization that is capable of assuming those management responsibilities.

Before any organizing of the users is carried out, there needs to be a package of incentives in place for both the users and the agency staff whose jobs would be affected by the transfer program. Such incentives are needed both to make the program work, and to maintain credibility with farmers whose long-term support will be required. If organizing is attempted before an adequate incentive structure is established, the transfer program could well collapse, thus setting the entire program back by several years, as well as causing short-term hardships to those concerned. Thus, if the incentives are not clear and attractive to farmers, the organizing process should be delayed until the incentives are clarified.

First determine:

### *Who Will do the Organizing?*

The first step is to decide on the type of organizers who will work directly with farmers in helping establish the organization. [We use the term "water user association" (WUA) to refer to this new organization, although the term, "WUA" can also refer to organizations at the tertiary level of the system which have always been outside the management control of the government irrigation agency.] In the Philippines, a special cadre of social organizers was recruited and trained by the National Irrigation Administration in the late1970s and early 80s. These organizers were mostly social workers or social scientists selected for their ability to work easily with farmers in village conditions. They were trained in irrigation management so they could better understand the technical problems of the farmers they were trying to organize.

The work of the Philippines social organizers was effective, yet this approach has not been widely replicated by irrigation agencies in other countries. The investment and bureaucratic difficulties involved in recruiting new temporary staff from a different discipline has led many irrigation agencies to try other approaches. In Mexico's transfer program, the National Water Commission's own staff were used along with staff from a sister agency, the Institute for Water Technology (IMTA).

In addition, a few consultants were brought in on a case by case basis. In India, some state irrigation departments have relied on extensionists from the Agriculture Department under the Command Area Development Program. Also in India, several NGOs have been involved in organizing, at the request of the irrigation departments. But the organizers of choice, for most irrigation agencies, will be their own field staff. These staff are already within the bureaucratic structure of the agency, so the lines of authority are clear, there is little additional expense involved, and these staff are already familiar with the physical systems and with the local farmers. The problems with using irrigation agency field staff for organizing work, however, are considerable. These staff are not necessarily interested in organizing farmers, They have not received any prior training in social work (in most cases), and their superiors have also no training (nor interest) in these tasks. These would-be organizers must be re-trained for their organizing tasks, and just as importantly, their job assignments need to be re-defined to reflect their new role. In addition, their superiors need to be trained and re-oreinted so they understand and appreciate the new role to be played by their field staff.

### *What Training do the Organizers Need?*

Assuming that agency staff will be used for the organizing, and assuming that their professional training has been in irrigation engineering, they would need to be re-tooled as organizers.

First of all they would need a thorough understanding of the rationale for PIM, so that they can present a clear message both to the farmers and to their own colleagues within the irrigation agency.

Secondly, they will need training in communcation skills (including listening skills) for effective interaction with the users.

Thirdly, they will need training in social analysis, including an understanding of social stratification (by caste, ethnicity, or class), kinship, patron-client relations, labour relations, religious factors, political affiliation, land tenure (tenants, share-croppers, owners), etc. And fourthly, they would need training in methods for gathering information from farmers (e.g., participatory rural appraisal) and in methods for organizing farmers.

### *Who will Provide the Training?*

Irrigation management training institutes?

Universities?

Administrative staff colleges?

NGOs?

What capacity building do these organizations need?

*skills training: TOT course on PIM?*

*structural change in the organization itself? (IMTI case)*

*financing?*

*new or clarified mandate?*

Building support for capacity building may require training and consensus building at political levels, just to provide an enabling environment for the PIM program to get started.

Then,

*Organizing Steps*

**Note:** This assumes there are reasonable incentives for farmers to take over system, and for the government irrigation agency to hand over the system; if not, go back and work on the incentives!

- Organize the organizers: Arrange for supervision/support for the organizers, and clear lines of communication with Departmental staff responsible for the overall project (Ensure that PIM component of program is well integrated with rest of project).
- Meet the farmers and other irrigation stakeholders/ Discuss plans formulated during participatory design phase:

- — village head
- — local administrative officials
- — local political leaders (MLAs/MPs)
- — leaders of other farmer organizations (producer cooperatives)

- Identify key power relations among farmers; develop strategy for organizing
- Establish provisional boundaries of the system (through consultation with key power brokers among the farmers); conduct inventory of potential members; draw map showing command area and irrigation system.
- Arrange series of meetings between farmers and Departmental field staff to discuss improvements that need to be made prior to handover.
  - — arrange canal walk-through to discuss specifics of design/infrastructure improvements
  - — discuss general terms of WUA contracts
- Arrange farmer visits to other associations to discuss with those farmers (and invite those farmers to visit new association).
- Organizational Assistance:
  - — Help prospective WUA leaders arrange farmer meetings to discuss plans
  - — Help formulate/revise by-laws
  - — Advise on elections/selections
  - — Assist with legal registration
  - — Arrange management training for WUA leaders
- Arrange meetings between WUA leaders and Department staff to discuss details of WUA contract and terms of transition phase leading to hand-over;
- Advise on staff recruitment(?)
- Assist with formal hand-over
- Visit periodically to monitor WUA's performance

## ORGANIZING SYSTEMS

One of the main problems that each enterprise faces is to organize the efforts of the people working on common goals. Most of the solutions to this problem originate from the time before computers became available for practically any company. However, it's a general practice even now, that the developers follow the old management scheme when the company is being computerized, whereas modern computers offer unique opportunities for implementing new, far more effective approaches to management. We discovered the limitations of existing management schemes while computerizing a small trading company. Our objective was to develop a system able to assist the office workers in all aspects of their routine work. One of our tasks was a conventional one-to support such activities as taking orders, delivering goods, making a phone call, etc. The other one was more ambitious-to register all completed activities and to help plan new activities based on the completed ones.

We realized very soon that our second objective could not be achieved within the functional management scheme adopted in the company. To cope with our task we started to consider the company's activity as a number of processes (such as "processing an order", "closing a deal") without regard to the way these processes were being managed. As a result a new approach to management was developed which we call a process-oriented management. This approach can be described as a project management without project managers, a project manager's functions, e.g., planning, controlling the execution of activities, etc., being distributed among the workers involved in a particular process.

The main point with the process-oriented management is that it permits a company to gain full control over all the processes within the frame of the existing, often functionally-oriented, organizational structure. This type of management facilitates also the communication between the workers involved in the same process, and it provides them with actual information on the state of the process, as well as on all activities performed and planned.

Below, we present the main ideas of the process-oriented management, and the requirements for a computer system needed to support it. We tried our best to do that in a very informal way to make it easily understood by all concerned. It should also be mentioned that the author is not a specialist in the field of management, but he worked with experts on management throughout the project. The paper reflects a fresh view of an application developer not spoiled by the experience of the pre-computer management era.

The rest of this paper is organized as follows. In section 2, we outline our view on the management of routine work. In section 3, we present the main principles of the process-oriented management. We look at existing approaches to management of the routine work-the function-oriented management and project-oriented management, and then move on to describing the ways of transforming the project-oriented management into the process-oriented one. We discuss the process-oriented management without regards to computer systems, however, this type of management can't be implemented without computers. Requirements for a computer system designed to support the process-oriented management are discussed in section 4. In section 5, we discuss the major issues of the development and implementation of such systems. In section 6, we present a short summary of our practical and research work that lead to the development of a process-oriented approach to management.

## MANAGEMENT OF ROUTINE WORK

It's generally recognized that the main objective of management is to ensure a successful achievement of a company's goals at minimal costs. A company has several different types of goals to achieve at any given moment-long-term, short-term, etc. As we are concerned with the management of routine work, it's the "conventional" everyday goals that are of primary interest to us; we call them "operational" goals. A typical operational goal for a trading company is, for example, to "drive" an incoming order through a delivery to receiving payment within certain time limits. A typical operational goal for a hospital is to administer the appropriate treatment to a patient that would lead to his discharging from the hospital. A typical operational goal for a software development company is to build a software system according to the specifications. But for the section of technical support of such company, a typical operational goal is to process a bug report so that the bug is fixed or/and a work-around solution is found.

Though operational goals may be quite unsophisticated, they, nevertheless, constitute the backbone of any business, as they have to be achieved on a day-to-day basis to ensure the proper functioning of the company. The character of operational goals depends on the type of business, but they have a number of common features:

- operational goals pop up more or less regularly;
- there is, usually, a standard procedure for achieving the operational goals of a given kind, which doesn't mean, of course, that a particular goal can't be approached in a different way if needed;
- there is often a set time limit for achieving an operational goal. If the goal is impossible to achieve within the time limit, it is discarded in a standard way.

To achieve an operational goal, a series of activities should be completed. For example, a series of activities aimed at getting payment for an incoming order includes delivery of goods and sending an invoice to the customer. This series may include more items in certain circumstances, for example, if the ordered goods are out of stock, they should be produced or ordered from the suppliers.

The activities aimed at achieving an operational goal are not, usually, executed immediately one after another, e.g., if the ordered goods are out of stock, it takes some time to get them from the suppliers. The execution of these activities is a process that continues over some period of time. The main objective for management of operational goals is to ensure that this process results in achieving the goal.

Different activities concerning the same goal can be completed by different workers from different divisions. Another objective of management is, therefore, to coordinate the work of all workers participating in the process of achieving an operational goal.

## A RACE TOWARDS A PROCESS-ORIENTED MANAGEMENT

Approaches to management of operational goals may be divided in two types-function-oriented and project-oriented. The function-oriented management (Fn-management) is usually used in the environments where a lot of relatively simple operational goals pop up very frequently. The Fn-management implies that operational goals are handled in a routine manner by the staff where each member has his own function in achieving operational goals. A manager does not coordinate the execution of activities for each goal, workers just react on the incoming documents, phone calls, etc., by completing activities they are assigned, and forwarding the received or newly composed documents further to their colleagues.

The project-oriented management (Pj-management) is usually used with more sophisticated goals such as construction or software projects. The Pj-management implies that a process for a new goal is planned in detail before the work on it starts, and there is someone (e.g., a project manager) who supervises all the work being done.

Fn-management is most cost-effective, but it works poorly when a process of achieving an operational goal deviates from a standard pattern, as it lacks control over individual processes. Pj-management gives full control over an individual process, but it's inefficient when a lot of coexisting processes are involved. There are working environments where one or the other type of management fits well. But in most environments a combination of these two approaches would be the way to obtain both full control over all processes and efficiency.

Below, we discuss our proposals for integration of the Fn- and Pj-managements. The result is a new type of management which we call the process-oriented management, or Pc-management, for short. This name highlights the main objective of the Pc-management-to control the processes, in contrast to

Fn-management that places the emphasis on the execution of activities, and the Pj-management that emphasizes plans. We describe the Pc-management here in the following way. We consider an environment typical for the function-oriented management-a trading company, and try to introduce the project-oriented management in it. The process-oriented management is presented thus as a result of tailoring the project-oriented approach to fit a different kind of environment. We find this way most convenient for discussing our ideas, but it's not, naturally, the only possible one.

The Pc-management is based on the notions of "orgobject", "history" and "dynamic and distributed planning", which we can now turn our attention to.

**Orgobjects**

The Pj-management involves developing a detailed plan for achieving a project's goal before the work on the project can start. This plan is premised on certain assumptions that may turn out wrong after the project is under way. The plan should then be adapted to the changed conditions. For this purpose, a clear picture of the current state of the project is required to figure out what should be done to complete the project.

A project often involves developing some product that is a physical object, e.g. a software system, a building, etc. This product comes into existence in some form already at the earlier stages of the project, e.g. a half-ready software system or a building under construction. This half-ready product serves as a good representation of the current state of the project. As the half-ready product can be studied without regards to how it has been produced, the plan can be revised without going into details of the project's history.

In cases where the Fn-management is involved, there is no half-ready product to represent the current state of achieving an operational goal. A kind of an abstract object that contains all information on the current state of the process would be helpful here. As it would serve as an organizing device for achieving the goal, we call it an "orgobject". For example, an orgobject representing a process of "Get payment for an incoming order" may be a record that contains information on: the name and address of the buyer, a description of each kind of goods ordered, the quantity and price per unit of each kind, the quantities of goods already delivered; the amount of money invoiced; the amount of money received. Having this orgobject, the conditions for the successful achievement of the "get payment" goal could be formulated as follows:

- have the numbers representing the quantities of 'goods ordered' and 'goods delivered' equal for each goods kind,
- have 'money invoiced' equal to the sum of 'ordered' multiplied by 'price•per unit' for all goods kinds, and
- have 'money received' equal to 'money invoiced'.

As the process develops, the corresponding orgobject should change so that it reflects all the time the current state of the process. As soon as some activity is completed, the orgobject representing the process is to be modified.

Thus, in the above example, after the delivery (full or partial), the quantities of the goods delivered are modified; if the customer has changed the order, the types and quantities of the goods ordered are modified, etc. To ensure that the orgobjects are always up-to-date, the routines for every type of activity should list not only the operations required for completing the activity (e.g., packing and shipping for delivery), but also instructions for the appropriate modifications of the relevant orgobjects.

Thus, the current state of an orgobject reflects the overall result of all activities completed earlier, and shows what actions should be taken to achieve the goal. To return to our example, if the quantity of the goods ordered is greater than the quantity of the goods delivered, the missing goods are to be delivered. If, on the other hand, the quantity of the goods ordered is less than the quantity of the goods delivered, then the customer should be asked to return some of the goods. Other examples: if the amount of money invoiced exceeds the payment received, then the customer should pay the difference. If the amount of the money received exceeds that of invoiced, then a credit note should be issued.

## History

The current state of an orgobject contains only the result of the completed activities, but not a list of them, e.g.: the quantity of the goods delivered, but not the number of separate deliveries; the amount of money invoiced, but not the number of separate invoices, etc. This is OK if all goes as it should. But if something goes wrong, e.g., some goods sent off did not arrive, then the information on all activities performed is vital when figuring out what actions should be taken. This information can be collected through logging all the activities completed in the frame of the given process. Let's consider the following logging scheme. Every time a worker executes an activity, he/she doesn't physically change the previous state of the relevant orgobject. He/she makes a new record instead which contain the new state of the orgobject and leaves the former one unchanged. For example, after a delivery, a new record is made containing the same information as the previous one except the information on the quantities of the goods delivered. The latter is updated according to the packing list.

The record on the previous state of an orgobject is placed in a special file containing the history of the given orgobject. The worker who completes an activity composes also a report where he/she records: the kind of activity completed, the name of a person who completed it, the date, time, comments, etc. This report is saved together with the previous state of the orgobject in the history file. Given two consequent states of an orgobject and an activity report, we can reconstruct exactly what happened during the activity execution. For example, in case of delivery, we know exactly by whom and when the goods were delivered, and in what quantities. Thus, our log provides an easy access to the information on both the activity performed, and the state of events before and after it was performed.

## Dynamic and Distributed Planning

As it was mentioned above, the Pj-management involves designing a detailed plan for each new process. If we try to apply the same to a Fn-management environment, two problems would arise:

- as Fn-processes are often trivial, their plans would be trivial too, e.g.: 'delivering goods'-'invoicing the buyer'-'getting payment'. It would be meaningless to record such plan for every process (and there are many in this kind of environments),
- unpredictable external events that often occur in Fn-management environments would demand revising the whole plan, e.g.: a customer has changed his order-additional delivery can be required, an invoice is to be sent later than it was initially planned, etc.

Dynamic planning is our answer to these problems. Dynamic planning involves planning only the first few activities at the first stage. As soon as one or several of these are completed, new activities are planned with regard to the emerging state of the relevant orgobject (and standard routines adopted in the company). For example, after a delivery, another delivery is planned if not all ordered goods have been delivered, or invoicing is planned if all goods have been delivered. The use of dynamic planning is fully beneficial in case of processes that follow a standard pattern. Otherwise, the usual planning is preferable. In case the character of the process (standard/deviating) is difficult to foresee, dynamic planning can be used at first, followed by conventional planning if necessary.

Another poser when trying to introduce the Pj-management in an Fn-environment is how to supervise a process. In cases where the Pj-management is involved, there is usually a project manager who supervises the execution of planned activities, and corrects the plan if needed. In an environment typical for the Fn-management, a project manager supervising each process would result in significant overheads.

A solution to this can be described as "distributed planning". Distributed planning implies that the worker who has completed a planned activity himself plans the subsequent activities. Moreover, he/she can assign these new activities not only to himself, but to other people too. For example, a worker who completes a delivery himself plans invoicing to be completed by another worker.

Distributed planning doesn't exclude the possibility of a centralized supervision of a process. In fact, a supervisor may intervene at any time and correct the plan if needed. Moreover, any member of staff can consult the supervisor in case he/she has some problems with his/her work on a particular process. He/she can do it by planning a special activity, e.g., "asking for help", and assigning his/her supervisor to complete it.

Let's have a look at the issue of implementing dynamic and distributed planning. Above, we considered orgobjects and plans as separate entities. Now, we put a plan inside the orgobject representing the corresponding process. As a result an orgobject besides the information on the current state of the process (e.g., on the customer, goods, delivery and payment) will also include a list of planned activities (e.g., delivery, invoicing, etc.), each of them containing information on what should be done, who's to do that and when.

Thus, a plan becomes part of an orgobject. Consequently, we can treat correction of the plan as one of the operations of changing the orgobject in the course of completing an activity. In section 3.1, we've already mentioned that instructions for modifying orgobjects should be included in the working procedures for each type of activities. To ensure proper dynamic planning, these instructions should embrace modification of the process's plan. In a simple case, a worker who has completed an activity modifies the relevant orgobject by removing this activity from the list of planned activities. In more complex cases, he/she adds new activities to the list, and/or removes some other activities from it.

Being an integral part of the orgobject representing a process, a plan is subjected to the logging we described above. As a result, all acts of replanning are registered in the same way as other modifications of orgobjects. Thus, for example, the name of a person who modified the plan is recorded, which may prove to be useful in case of conflicts.

**Advantages**

The main advantage of the Pc-management is its flexibility. The Pc-management permits to choose the optimum approach to coping with each process, and within the same management scheme. Thus, simple processes that follow a standard pattern are dealt with in a completely decentralized manner, whereas some more sophisticated case will be dealt with by centralized individual planning and supervising. Moreover, the same process may be treated differently at different stages. For example, it may be started as a standard one, but later it can be planned and supervised individually. As a result, full control over all kinds of processes is gained and efficiency is not sacrificed. Another important thing is that the Pc-management is not bound to any particular type of organizational structure. It can be used both in case the same member of staff completes all the activities required for achieving an operational goal, and in case each activity type is assigned to a particular worker. This permits to preserve the same management scheme when the organizational structure is changed, e.g., in case of a company's expansion.

Some other advantages are as follows:

1. Orgobjects provide a perfect insight into the company's state of affairs. The information stored in the orgobjects is of great help to the management staff as it permit to quickly evaluate the state of a process (without going into its history). It also helps to give prompt answers to customers' questions. This kind of information is not easily obtainable when traditional managements schemes are used. Thus, when the Fn-management is used, only the information on the executed activities of a given type is easily accessible, and when the Pj-management is used, only the information on the state of the plans execution is easily accessible.
2. Histories of orgobjects permit to easily trace all the activities completed on a given process, which helps to devise plans for complicated cases. They are also a very important source of data for all kinds of statistical analysis, and other types of information processing required for decision-making.
3. The company's staff becomes goal-and process-conscious, as it is easy for any person to overview all the activities

(one's own and those of others) completed in a process he/she is involved in. The history of old orgobjects is useful for "learning by example", which may help a worker to find solutions in difficult cases. The goal-and process-consciousness isn't easy to acquire with a traditional management scheme. Under the Fn-management, a worker doesn't see how a process he/she's in is accomplished. His/her personal goal becomes to complete as efficient as possible the activities he/she is responsible for. That may result in, e.g., a seller concentrating on making telephone calls most of which don't get him to closing a deal.

4. The Pj-management emphasizes following the schedule, which becomes the main goal of the workers engaged in a project. There is a danger that the workers do not keep their eyes open for changes in the surrounding world, which is, e.g., the main reason why large software projects often produce out-of-day systems.
5. As all the information on the past is being stored, the management staff is in a better position concerning various kinds of conflicts, internal conflicts among workers engaged in the same process, and external ones, e.g., with customers or suppliers.
6. Distributed planning is a very powerful tool for coordinating the work which makes unnecessary the intensive communication (exchanges of documents, phone calls, etc.) among the workers engaged in the same processes. They get the required information from the current states of orgobjects and their histories.

## An Orgsystem Wanted

Let's imagine you are fascinated by the Pc-management and decide to implement it in your company. A lot of orgobjects start circulating around, each accompanied by a huge history file. You don't find the one you need, you never know which of the orgobjects contains the planned activities assigned to you, and when these activities should be completed. You strove for a better order and got yourself into a mess. And, as if that were not enough, you have a lot of extra work to do. You should construct a new state of an orgobject for each completed activity, and remember to put the new activities on the list and assign them to yourself and others. You wanted to improve the efficiency, but it sinks instead.

There is no need to worry, there is a means to restore the order and efficiency, and that's, naturally a computer system. It's primary aim is to make you happy with the Pc-management doing away with the chaos, that's why we call it an "organizing system", or orgsystem for short.

Let's have another look at the Pc-management, this time supported by an orgsystem. Orgobjects do not circulate between various members of the staff who are to work with them, they stay in the same place together with their history and plans, and are easily accessible to all workers involved. All planned activities assigned to a given individual appear immediately in his/her personal calendar, so that each worker knows exactly what activities he/she has to complete and when. An orgsystem provides the means to increase the efficiency by:

- assisting workers in executing each activity,
- providing an extremely user-friendly interface.

These two features are a key to successful implementation of an orgsystem. Without them people would not be motivated to use the system, consequently the Pc-management wouldn't work. Let's look at these features in more detail.

### Level of Help

All operations needed for executing an activity under the Pc-management belong to one of the two groups:

- external operations-operations that affect the "external world", and
- maintaining operations-operations aimed at maintaining orgobjects.

The character of external operation depends on the type of activity, e.g., packing and shipping for delivery, programming and testing for developing a software module, etc. Maintaining operations are the same for all activities. They include:

- updating the information contained in the relevant orgobject,
- correcting the plan,
- logging the preceding state of the orgobject.

An orgsystem assists a worker to complete both the external operations and the maintaining ones.

1. External operations. Level of help which is possible to offer for completing the external operations depends on the type of activity. For example, programming and testing of a software module are usually performed inside the computer, and they are already fully computerized. Here, an orgsystem should just integrate the existing tools for software development, e.g. editors, debuggers, etc., so that a proper tool is invoked when a user chooses to execute these operations. Packing and shipping are not that easily computerized, not now anyway. But even there, an orgsystem can be helpful to some extent by, e.g., making up a packing list. It's important to give a hand in completing the external operations for each kind of activities. There's a risk otherwise. If some activity is left without the orgsystem's assistance, a worker who completes it can easily forget to make the appropriate changes in the orgobject concerned. In that case, the completed activity will still remain on the list of planned activities and the orgsystem will keep reminding the worker to complete it. There is also a danger that the same activity will be completed several times.
2. Updating. Modification of an orgobject can often be done on the basis of the information collected in the process of executing the external operations. For example, an "order" orgobject contains the information on the quantities of the goods already delivered. This information should be updated after each separate delivery. The new quantities can be easily calculated based on the packing list that was made at the previous step, which permits an orgsystem to update the orgobject without assistance from the users.

3. When correcting a plan, a worker is prompted by the system on the appropriate activities to plan next; in simple cases the plan is corrected by the system itself. This is possible, as an orgsystem possesses two type of knowledge:
   - on the working procedures used in the company, which helps to plan new activities, and
   - on division of responsibilities between different divisions, sections, and workers, which permits to correctly assign new activities.
4. Logging includes two operations:
   - saving the old state of the orgobject, and
   - making a report on the activity completed.

Saving the old state of an orgobject is done by an orgsystem without any user assistance, but an activity report needs a human participation. Even there, an orgsystem helps by automatically supplying the information on what activity has been executed, by whom and when. The rest of the report, e.g., comments, is of course the responsibility of the worker.

**User-interface**

Conventional computer systems are designed as a set of functions operating on a common database, the main facility of the user-interface being multilevel menus. This type of the user-interface provides the user with a quick access to a function he/she wants to complete. It reflects the objective of a conventional computer system which is to help workers to cope with single activities like updating information, printing a report, etc. An orgsystem objectives are much wider, which brings about the need for a completely different kind of user-interface. An orgsystem's user-interface permits end-users to freely choose between the object-oriented and activity-oriented way of working with orgobjects, as well as easily switch from one to the other. The object-oriented approach is applied when a user wants to work with a particular orgobject for a longer time. In this case, he/she may need to look at the object's current state and its history, as well as to plan and execute various activities involving the orgobject. The activity-oriented approach is applied when a user wants to complete the same activity for a number of orgobjects. In this case, the dialogue designed for a given activity is repeated for all relevant orgobjects. The object-oriented way is particularly useful when one worker is responsible for many activities involving an orgobject. It is also the way that management staff can use when there is a need to evaluate the state of a particular process and to devise a plan for a difficult case. The activity-oriented approach is preferable if a worker is responsible for only one type of activities. It's also the right approach to completing simple activities that do not require much human assistance, e.g., printing an invoice, etc.

Another distinguishing feature of an orgsystem's user-interface is that it maintains personal calendars. A personal calendar is a list of activities assigned to a particular worker. The point is that these activities are included in different orgobjects and the calendar permits a perfect overview of a persons' many tasks. The orgsystem offers a variety of ways to use the calendar. A user can browse through his/her calendar, or some parts of it, e.g., to see all activities planned for a particular day, all activities of a certain type, etc. When browsing, he/she can start the execution of his/her activities (activity-oriented approach), or move to the orgobject where a particular activity belongs and start working with this orgobject in the object-oriented manner.

To maintain its user-friendly character, an orgsystem's user-interface should satisfy a number of general requirements. Most important are the following two:

- easy access to all information required for working with orgobjects. For example, when working with an orgobject representing an order, a user should have access to all information related to the customer who ordered goods: his address, previous contacts with him, etc.;
- consistency. There should be standard procedures for navigating to an orgobject, for getting information (e.g., a company's address), for planning, for starting the execution of activities, etc. These standard procedures

should be the same for all types of orgobjects and activities.

## Joys and Hardships of an Orgsystems Developer

There are, naturally, technical problems to solve in the development of an orgsystem. The system requirements discussed in the previous section must be met. However, an orgsystem designer's greatest problem is that he starts the development in an environment initially not based on the Pc-management, which makes both design and implementation of an orgsystem far from trivial tasks.

### *Orgsystems Design*

An orgsystem designer should begin with:

- identifying the company's operational goals,
- figuring out what processes are used to achieve them, and
- designing orgobjects to represent these processes.

His/her next task is to review all the working procedures and tailor them to fit the Pc-management scheme (by adding maintaining operations to each activity).

This is often a tough job, as there are seldom some written descriptions of the working procedures, and if they exist, they are far from complete. The only way to cope with the job is to try and get the missing information from the company's workers. The workers would, naturally, know nothing about orgobjects, but they know their job. The conditions in which an orgsystem designer works are similar to those of a linguist who studies a language that exists only in the spoken form. Linguists have special methods permitting them to get the necessary information from the native speakers without teaching them any linguistic notions. Moreover, it's considered a wrong practice to teach informants linguistics, as it may only spoil them.

An orgsystems designer needs similar methods that would permit him to redesign the company's working procedures without introducing the workers into the world of orgobjects, distributed planning, etc. We believe that rapid prototyping is the right method. As soon as a designer has identified the company's operational goals and processes, and designed the orgobjects to represent them, he/she should make a prototype of the system and let the future users test it. To be able to use prototyping, an orgsystem designer needs appropriate application development tools.

These tools should allow him to quickly produce a sketch of the system that has "look-and-feel" of a real system, but lacks processing routines and database access. It's this sketch that we call the prototype of the system. Working with it, a user can navigate among orgobjects in the same way as he would do that when the orgsystem is ready. He can modify existing orgobjects, create new ones, and see how to start different activities.

But he can't save the information or see the results of the completed activities. After the future users have accepted the prototype, the designer can stepwise add database access and processing routines, which would be also done with the help of the above mentioned application development tools.

### *Orgsystems Implementation*

Implementing an orgsystem means introducing the Pc-management in a non-Pc-management environment. This may be achieved in one of two ways:

- by substituting all the old working procedures in the company at once, or
- by gradual introduction of the new working procedures.

The first approach may suit small companies whose workers often switch from one activity type to another. An orgsystem would help to do these switches very quickly, and it would help the workers, who usually have a lot of different things to do, to preserve the order in their affairs. The staff of a small company would easily understand the advantages of using all facilities provided by an orgsystem: object-and activity-oriented ways of working, personal calendars, easy access to the history, etc. However, in case of large companies, the second approach may be the best choice. Large companies usually, have a lot of workers who are involved only in one or several activities for each process. These workers may believe that an orgsystem is too complex for their simple tasks. It would be difficult for them to see the advantages of the object-oriented user-interface, and their earlier experience of traditional computer systems can only make the things worse.

Luckily, an orgsystem provides a means for working in the activity-oriented manner, which would put the workers competing simple activities at ease. There would be no problem to teach them to use the orgsystem in the activity-oriented way, because it resembles their old manner of doing things. Later, the workers could be taught the object-oriented way as well, which would give them better possibilities to take the initiative and find solutions for difficult cases. But even if most of the office workers continue to use the activity-oriented approach, there would always be some key people who benefit from the object-oriented approach, e.g., management staff.

## CONCLUDING REMARKS

### *Orgsystems-What's Been Achieved so Far?*

The notion of the Pc-management came into being when the author together with several colleagues developed an application for supporting sales and marketing activities of a trading company. The system was called "DealDriver" to highlight that it helps the workers to "drive" the deals to the end which is receiving payment. Dealc were thus the first type of orgobjects designed.

The work on the project started in spring 1989, and the first version of DealDriver was ready in summer 1990. Since then, Dealdriver has been successfully used at our home office to support one of IbisSoft's business activities-reselling of professional software.

The DealDriver project, gave us some valuable insights into the problems of orgsystems development which are summarized in our internal reports. We developed also an experimental version of application development tools to support orgsystems development. These tools were later used for building both prototypes and functioning systems in a number of other application fields, e.g., hospital administration.

Next two subsections discuss some theoretical and technical aspects of orgsystems development. The reader who is not interested in such issues is invited to look over these.

### *What are the Related Research Fields?*

Orgsystems development belongs to an application field called groupware. This is a multidisciplinary field where social scientists and computer scientists work together. Some of the computer science fields related to our work are as follows:

- the behaviour of dynamic objects, where the orgobjects belong, is being formalized by the theory of object-oriented systems;
- methods of storing and accessing structured information, which are vital for orgsystems development, are the subject of the database theory. Particularly related to our work are the theories of semantic databases, object-oriented databases, and temporal databases;
- methods of planning for robots are one of AI's (Artificial intelligence) favourite research problems. The results obtained there may in some cases be directly applied to the management field. For example, the difference between classical and reactive planning corresponds to the difference between the pure Pj-and Fn-management.

### *What Makes our Systems Work?*

The main ideas of the Pc-management originate from our previous research work on the CHAOS project (CHAOS stands for Concurrent Human-Assisted Object Systems). The project's objective was to work out a formal model for describing distributed interactive systems. This model is based on the notions of objects and connectors. Objects are used to represent the elements of the "real world", (e.g. people, companies, projects, etc.), whereas connectors are the active elements of the system whose task is to make changes in the objects. A connector may be thought of as a little computer connected to one or several objects. As soon as some of these objects change, the connector changes all the other objects to restore the consistency of the system.

Thus defined, our model has a purely reactive nature, i.e. changes in objects are made as a reaction to changes in other objects. But objects in our model can be complex, i.e. they themselves can contain connectors, which means that a reaction can result in adjusting the system configuration to changes in the environment.

The CHAOS model fitted the management field so well that all we had to do was to use another set of terms. Thus, complex objects became orgobjects, connectors became planned activities, and the principle of reactive reconfiguration of the system was called dynamic and distributed planning. Some of the results of applying the CHAOS model to management field were virtually the same as those from the research works based on the theory of planning. However, being more general than the theory of planning, our model provides a better framework for management automation as it covers all aspects of management not only the issues of planning.

The CHAOS model is abstract, but the approach taken in the DealDriver project was very pragmatic. The objective of the project was to create a working system, not to speculate on the management automation issues. This project differs in many ways from similar research projects. Below we list the most important differences:

1. Computer environment. We worked with PC computers under MS DOS in stand-alone and network versions, whereas research projects are often completed on Unix-based workstations. We used text-based terminals, not a graphic-based windowing environment with a mouse, icons, etc. This environment was chosen because it was the one an average company could easily afford.
2. Development tools. Research workers often choose programming languages popular among computer scientists like Lisp, Prolog, Smalltalk, etc. These languages have a sound theoretical basis (e.g., function theory, logic, etc.), but require a lot of programming

when they are used for the development of an application. We made a point of getting the maximum available help with programming by employing commercially available application development tools. We chose JAM from JYACC as a front-end tool, and Btrieve from Novell as a record manager. These tools were of great help to us, as we had limited resources for completing the project (in terms of time and manpower).

3. Design principles. Researchers are often far too interested in the technical issues, such as methods of software design and programming, etc. We concentrated on user-interface issues instead. Our only principle of programming was: a program should work and permit to easily make necessary changes. All programming was done in C-language, and though our system was object-oriented in a very high degree, we didn't use any object-oriented extension to C.

Thus, two factors contributed to the successful completion of the DealDriver project:

- the use of a powerful abstract model, and
- a pragmatic approach to system development, and we strongly believe that both of them are obligatory for the development of a computer system of a totally new kind.

We are also convinced that there is no need to wait 10-20 years, which it usually takes for new research ideas to be implemented in application systems. New ideas can be implemented today and with the means available now.

6

# Hotel Environment Management

The Caribbean hotel industry is positioned to reinvent itself in a way that improves profitability, enhances guest relations, builds bridges into the local communities, and preserves the Caribbean's natural beauty.

Over the past 2 years, this trend has been translated into results in Jamaica in the form of the Environmental Audits for Sustainable Tourism (EAST) project, sponsored by the Jamaica Hotel and Tourist Association and funded by the United States Agency for International Development (USAID).

This paper presents a case study of the USAID/Jamaica EAST project demonstrating the power of becoming an environmentally friendly hotel through the adoption of an environmental management system (EMS), a comprehensive organizational approach designed to achieve environmental care in all aspects of operations.

Partnering environmental protection with cost-saving environmental improvements and best practices, the EAST project is a model for the hotels and tourism destinations in the Caribbean region and beyond for environmental assessments and actions, as well as voluntary environmental audits that can lead to the GREEN GLOBE International Certification.

## INTRODUCTION

A "quiet revolution" is taking place in the Caribbean-one less visible than the construction of new hotels and the building of new cruise ships. Nevertheless, its advent is profoundly changing the nature and shape of the tourism and hospitality industry, in every hotel guestroom, housekeeping, laundry or maintenance facility, and in every tourism destination that elects voluntarily to join the environmental movement. This revolution is environmentally sustainable tourism. The Caribbean hotel industry, particularly, is positioned to reinvent itself in a way that improves profitability, enhances guest relations, builds bridges into the local communities, and preserves the Caribbean's natural beauty.

Over the past 2 years, this trend has been translated into results in Jamaica in the form of the Environmental Audits for Sustainable Tourism (EAST) project, sponsored by the Jamaica Hotel and Tourist Association and funded by the United States Agency for International Development (USAID).

### USAID/Jamaica EAST Project Description

In 1997, the Jamaica Hotel and Tourist Association, Government of Jamaica, Jamaica Manufacturers Association, and a number of tourism-related public and private-sector industry organizations committed to undertake the Environmental Audits for Sustainable Tourism (EAST) project. With funding from the U.S. Agency for International Development, Hagler Bailly implemented a program of environmental audits within a corporate environmental management system aimed at the tourism and hospitality industry in Negril, with a smaller component focused on manufacturing industries in Kingston and St. Andrews.

The project is a model for environmental action and voluntary audits for the tourism sector, combining promotion and outreach, training, audits, and investment.

The objectives of the EAST program are:

- to develop greater awareness and understanding of the benefits of environmental systems and audits among hotel and restaurant owners and allied tourism businesses;
- to upgrade the technical skills of Jamaicans who are expected to conduct the audits and advise on environmental management systems;

- to assist a select, representative number of tourism-related establishments in carrying out environmental audits, and
- to help finance in the tourism industry, on a cost-sharing basis, selected audit recommendations in order to demonstrate the financial benefits of the systematic application of environmentally friendly practices and, thereby, encourage others in the tourism industry to do likewise.

The activities of the EAST project include:

- institutionalizing environmental management in the tourism industry;
- performance monitoring of EAST demonstration hotels;
- environmental assessments, audits, and certification; environmental awareness and training; regulatory assistance in environmental licensing;
- audits and technical assistance in the manufacturing industry;
- targeted environmental investment fund feasibility and financing; performance awards programs, and international human resources exchange programs.

An important next step for Jamaica is to sustain and expand this improved level of environmental management among government and private-sector organizations.

## EAST FINDINGS AND RESULTS

The following is a discussion of some of the EAST findings and results. When Hagler Bailly began in June of 1997, the awareness was quite high in Negril (the target area for the EAST project) due primarily to the influx of questionnaires and surveys sent by European tour operators such as Tui and British Airways Holidays. These inquiries were from European markets interested in buying the export products, e.g., traveling to destinations supporting environmental best policies and management practices. Hagler Bailly started with a survey of hotels in Negril to ask hoteliers why they choose to become "environmentally friendly." The results showed a genuine concern about the impact their operations have on the physical environment and an appreciation for how this can be translated into cost savings. Interestingly, the government's enforcement of environmental laws and standards ranked lowest. This told us that hoteliers were interested in measurable results and that they would respond better to incentives than to government intervention. Initially, however, when we asked individual hoteliers what they thought "going green" implied, the most common answer was to replace plastic straws with paper straws. The obvious next question, since none of the respondents had achieved the "environmentally friendly" status, was what are the perceived barriers to becoming a green hotel. The results pointed to the up-front cost of learning how to make the transition, and then to the financing to implement it.

## HOTEL ENVIRONMENTAL MANAGEMENT SYSTEM

One of the most critical elements of becoming an environmentally friendly hotel is the adoption of a new culture that extends throughout the hotel organization, and between the hotel and its guest, local community, and even its vendors. We call this an environmental management system (EMS).

An EMS is defined as a comprehensive organizational approach designed to achieve environmental care in all aspects of operations. The International Standards Organization (ISO) 14000 series is an international standard for EMS. The World Travel and Tourism Council's GREEN GLOBE international certification has developed an EMS standard specifically for the travel and tourism industry.

An effective EMS can help a hotel assure its guests of its commitment to environmental management as partners in programs such as recycling, linen and towel reuse, etc. It can set specific and realistic performance objectives and targets, and allow the hotel to monitor to see if the objectives and targets are being met. As mentioned earlier, it can enhance a hotel's image in the marketplace and help reach nearly 43 million Americans, as well as hundreds of thousands of environmentally aware tourists from Europe and elsewhere interested in visiting environmentally friendly destinations and staying in accommodations with environmental policies and programs in place.

Most importantly, an EMS can improve efficiency and reduce operating costs. In fact, the savings alone should be sufficient for any hotel to commit to implementing an EMS.

Few hotels today have what we would consider an EMS. This is not to say that there are no hotels implementing environmental programs such as water conservation and composting, but it is typically not done as part of a larger management system, nor is it integrated with other environmental programs.

There is a growing demand to have an EMS that meets international standards such as ISO 14001 and GREEN GLOBE. An EMS evaluation, because of its broad-reaching implications, will begin to encompass other concerns such as health, safety, and security, emergency preparedness, compliance with discharge and emissions standards, and employee training.

What constitutes an EMS? The principal components of an EMS, as defined by GREEN GLOBE, include the following: an environmental policy that clearly communicates the organization's commitment to maintaining the social, cultural and physical environment; an action plan to guide the property's actions and expenditure of resources; the implementation or operations of the EMS that encompasses all of the property's actions relative to the environment, including awareness and training, staff procedures, incentive programs, and community outreach among other things; corrective action or monitoring to ensure that the EMS performs as expected, allowing for responsive actions to capture things such as leaking toilets and chemical spills and review, typically by senior management, to determined how to improve the EMS and the level of compliance with the hotel's environmental policy.

## EMS AND ENVIRONMENTAL PROGRAMS

Many will say, we already have hotels in the Caribbean that are operating in an environmentally responsible manner.

That is to say that the hotel is currently composting much of its organic solid wastes, or that guestrooms have low flow showerheads installed.

We call these environmental programs. An EMS is the integration of those programs under a comprehensive organizational system. An EMS takes the following approach to addressing its environmental issues (or aspects as they are referred to in the standards).

- First, an assessment is done to determine what improvements can be made, how much they cost, and what types of changes in consumption or waste generation can be expected. The assessment also allows you to establish a baseline against which change can be measured.
- Next, the hotel sets objectives such as to reduce water consumption for the entire property by 10%. Each objective is supported by a set of specific targets, such as introduce towel and linen reuse program by June 31st, or install low-flow showerheads in guest rooms and staff locker rooms by August 1st.
- The individuals, or departments, responsible for achieving the targets are identified in an action plan. It is important to remember that the greatest improvements are made through changes in staff procedures.
- Finally, the impact or results, in terms of changes from the baseline, must be measured and documented. This provides the necessary feedback to determine whether the EMS is working.

The EMS can be viewed as the integration of multiple environmental programs. Environmental programs are typically designed to address a specific environmental problem or issue such as recycling or composting solid waste; or are focused on a specific department such as a linen reuse program in housekeeping and laundry. In some instances, particularly for smaller hotels, environmental programs may involve multiple properties, such as sharing the cost of a bottle crusher for glass recycling

**East Environmental Management Audit Findings**

Hagler Bailly designed a specific audit protocol that combines the attributes of an energy audit, an environmental audit, and a management audit —the EAST Environmental Management Audit. We tested the audit protocol on the full range of hotel properties, from 15 rooms to over 200 rooms. The audits covered the following areas energy use, water use, wastewater generation and disposal, solid waste generation and disposal, use of chemicals, and management and staff practices. Summarized below are some of the general findings of the EAST audits.

**Inefficient use of Water:** Leaking toilets accounted for 40% of the daily water use in one 35-room hotel. The cost of the leaks was US$600 per month. In another property, a defective drain valve on a washing machine increased laundry water use by more than 1 million gallons per year equivalent to US$6,000 of wasted water.

**Inefficient use of Energy**: Loose louvers and doors and poor insulation force air conditioners to work continuously in order to keep guest rooms cool. This mode of operation increases energy consumption and shortens the air conditioner's service life.

**Excessive and Unnecessary use of Chemicals**: Instead of manually cleaning the kitchen grease trap, a property used 420 gallons/year of sulfuric acid (or Drano) to do the job. This cost of this dangerous habit exceeded US$6,000 per year.

**Excessive Solid Waste Generation**: A 25-room property spent US$1,700 per year to purchase large plastic trash bags. Many properties place all yard waste in plastic bags and pay to send this material to the dump. Organic wastes from kitchen and landscaping accounts for up to 50% of a property's solid waste and can be easily composted.

**Staff not Participating in Environmental Programs**: In 90% of cases, housekeepers automatically replace all used guest towels in properties that have towel reuse programs.

**Poor (or no) Monitoring**: Approximately 70% of audited properties had no effective utilities monitoring program. Water and electricity bills are simply received and paid. A 20,000-gallon per day leak went undetected for more than a week because the property didn't check the water meter daily. There was considerable variation in water use among 14 properties we audited ranging from 15 to 70 rooms. To provide a common base for comparison, we calculated each hotel's consumption in terms of Imperial gallons per guest night. The results are shown in table below. The most efficient of the hotels used just one-third the water per guest night of the least efficient.

***Water Use in Properties Audited by EAST Imperial gallons/Guest Night***

| | |
|---|---|
| Most Efficient Hotel | 116 |
| Average Efficient | 216 |
| Least Efficient | 351 |

A similar comparison was also done among audited properties for electricity consumption. The results are shown in table below. Again, the most efficient hotel used only one-quarter of the electricity per guest night of that of the least efficient hotel.

***Electricity Use in Properties Audited by EAST KWH/ Guest Night***

| | |
|---|---|
| Most Efficient Hotel | 8.7 |
| Average Efficient | 21.4 |
| Least Efficient | 32.9 |

## Detailed Analysis of Efficiency Improvements in the EAST Demonstration Hotels

The water and energy use indices of a hotel are affected by occupancy rates as well as by its conservation efforts and investments in efficient technologies. As a general rule, water and energy indices rise during low occupancy months and drop during high occupancy months. Given the influence of occupancy and conservation efforts on efficiency, the monitoring data collected from the properties should be analyzed in greater detail to ensure that efficiency gains result from improved environmental practices rather than better occupancy rates. This higher scrutiny is particularly important, for example, in the case of a hotel that reduced its water and electricity use indices by more than 25% while simultaneously increasing its occupancy by 16%.

Figures below present the result of a more rigorous data analysis, and show how the hotel's monthly water and electricity use indices varied with respect to occupancy before and after its involvement with the EAST project. Since the water and electricity use indices are consistently lower "after" the EAST audit, regardless of the actual occupancy levels, these graphs prove that the property's water and electricity savings are due to improved conservation practices rather than higher occupancy rates. The vertical distance separating the "before EAST" and "after EAST" trend lines represents the actual water and electricity savings achieved through the property's conservation efforts at any given occupancy level.

## RECOMMENDATIONS FOR IMPROVEMENT

So what did it take to improve performance in a typical Jamaican hotel?

Most of the recommendations made in the EAST Audit reports have the following characteristics. They have low implementation costs, rapid payback periods, and they are relatively simple and easy to implement.

The EAST auditors also found that the greatest environmen-tal and financial benefits can be achieved by improving: frequent monitoring, particularly utility bills; management supervision, oversight to ensure that programs are operating effectively; staff practices, training, and providing incentives for staff to implement programs, and preventive and routine maintenance, particularly of energy-and water-using equipment. In the breakdown of EAST audit recommendations for a typical hotel, the following was evident. Over three-quarters of the recommen-dations cost less than US$10/guest room, 19% of the recommendations cost between US$10-50 per guest room and only 3% cost more than US$50 per guestroom.

Payback period is defined as the length of time required before the savings from a measure equal the cost to implement the measure. In terms of payback period for EAST audit recommendations: 62% of the recommendations had a payback of less than 2 months, another 36% had payback periods of between 2 months and 1 year, and only 2% had payback of greater than 1 year. Another way to break down the EAST audit recommendations is by area of activity (or department) in the hotel. Our auditors identified that the largest, by far, can be found in the maintenance and engineering department. We should note that more often than not, the problems lie in insufficient resources resulting in shortages of staff, parts, and supplies, and unwillingness to pay repair bills to fix a problem properly. Guest rooms (or housekeeping department) and restaurant and bar (or food and beverage department) accounted for 15 and 16 percent of the recommended actions, respectively. This is mainly due to the high degree of energy and water used in these areas.

## ADVANTAGES OF A "GREEN HOTEL"

During our visits to Jamaica, we became aware of one small hotel in Port Antonio-Hotel Mocking Bird Hill-that has made considerable strides in improving environmental performance. For purposes of the following example, we will refer to Mocking Bird Hill's consumption levels as that of a "green hotel." Using the average from the 14 EAST hotels audited for both water and electricity; we show the difference relative to the "green hotel."

Looking now at an illustration of the cost advantages of a green hotel, let's assume a 50-room hotel, with 60% occupancy, and 2 guest per room. Over the course of a year, the water savings are over 3.6 million gallons, or savings of US$21,829 in water bills. The electricity savings are 186,000 kWh per year, or savings of US$23,886 in electricity bills. Total savings, for both water and electricity amounts to US$45,715 per year.

The savings can greatly improve a hotel's profitability. For example, if it takes US$10 of revenue to generate US$1 of profit, savings of US$45,715 in utility costs would have an impact equivalent to US$457,150 in additional revenue. Assuming average revenue of US$100 per guest night, the savings represent the equivalent to additional 4,571 guest nights worth of revenue.

## Cash Flow Associated with "Going Green"

So how would the investment and savings look over an extended period of time? Most of the costs are incurred in the first 9 months. These include the cost of an external audit, energy and water savings equipment, and training of key staff. After the first year, the costs are only associated with preventative maintenance and preparing for the annual GREEN GLOBE certification. Over a 3-year period, the initial investment of US$40,000 will yield approximately US$112,000 in savings, or a net profit of about US$70,000.

## Implications for the Jamaican Hotel Industry

Just to illustrate the point further, we asked the question: "What would becoming a green hotel mean for Jamaica as a whole?" Here we have used the Jamaican Tourist Product Development Company (TPDCo) hotel data for 1996, assumed 60% occupancy and 2 guests per room like the earlier example. Obviously, this over-simplifies the hotel industry, but the point is valid.

For all of Jamaica, the difference between an industry comprised of green hotels and one comprised of average hotels is over 930 million gallons of water per year. The green hotel industry will use 77% less water than the average, and 86% less than the inefficient hotel industry.

The reductions in water consumption also translate directly to the volume of wastewater coming from the hotel industry. We can do the same simulation for energy or specifically electricity consumption. For all of Jamaica, the difference between green hotels and the average hotel industry is over 47 million kilowatt-hours per year.

The green hotel industry will use a third less electricity than the average, and two-thirds less electricity than the inefficient hotel industry.

## CONCLUSION

So what does this all mean to the Caribbean hotel industry? First, it is a "win-win" proposition. You can improve your market share while reducing your operating costs. Second, it is neither rocket science nor is it untried or untested. The audit recommendations are relatively simple and proven to work right here in the Caribbean. Third, you have no choice.

Resorts throughout the Caribbean countries and hotels all over the world have recognized the advantages of going green. International certification programs like GREEN GLOBE are driving the industry toward improved performance. This means that instead of getting the marketing advantage of being a leader, those that fail to make the transition may soon be termed as "brown hotels." Know anyone who would prefer to stay in a brown hotel rather than in a green one?

We should also look at what it means to different stakeholders such as the government and local communities across the Caribbean. The reduced water, wastewater, and energy consumption levels of a green hotel industry translate directly to reduced shortages and lowered needs for infrastructure in water supply, wastewater treatment plants, and power plants. The same holds true for solid waste and the need for sanitary landfills.

So the more important question becomes, what are the hotels waiting for? Governments should begin laying out the necessary incentives and standards to move the industry in this direction. Banks should open special lines of credit to finance the improvements. And Caribbean Hotel Association, Caribbean Tourism Organization, and the tourist board of each island should find ways to link the marketing of Caribbean hotels directly to the computers of those millions of so-called "eco-tourists" in the U.S. and Europe who are beginning to plan their next family vacations.

7

# Employee Recognition and Motivation

## INTRODUCTION

The foundation of recognition and motivation is that people need and want Acceptance, Approval and Appreciation. Almost all positive motivation is based on these needs. People want to know that what they do makes a difference. Just recognizing the staff is the most important step one can take. You may want to count the number of "we's that are said instead of "I's in order to assess the extent to which your staff feels part of the team and part of the business' future. One saying is, "Powerlessness corrupts, absolute powerlessness corrupts absolutely."

These nine actions will help immensely to give your staff what they need: Communicate, Communicate, Communicate, Recognize, Recognize, Recognize, Thank, Thank, and Thank! From various sources, Vicki developed a list of ideas for ongoing weekly or monthly programs to keep employees connected to the hotel or restaurant emotionally, to create excitement and to make your business unique relative to your nearby competitors for employees. Remember, the competition for staff may be from other industries such as retail, manufacturing, etc. Pick a few and try them for a while; but, you must give them a chance, one time will not do it. The staff will see right through you.

- Gift certificate for the most challenging question posed to the President

- Money or chocolates or lottery ticket to a spouse with a note thanking for his/her support during overtime
- Thumbs-up certificates redeemable for merchandise
- Soda, fruit, snacks to housekeeping staff all the time
- When anyone makes a negative comment, put $0.25 or $0.50 into a pot and use the money for a Fun Committee
- Bring Polaroid camera to work occasionally and take candids of staff and post pictures on a bulletin board for all to enjoy
- Selection of employee of the month/quarter/year by peers not just management
- When he/she is employee of the month, give him/her a special name tag highlighting that status
- Points given out at any time for anything, good attendance, helping out a guest, etc., and are redeemable for prizes
- When you reach a certain level in revenues, give all staff a reward, being sure to give them the goal in advance
- Spontaneous calls from corporate to line staff saying how they are appreciated
- Allow line workers to participate in all personnel function decisions, hiring, training, evaluating, firing, schedules
- Fine those who arrive late to a meeting and distribute the money to those who were there on time
- Create a symbol of the team, maybe just property logo but put it on T-shirts, mugs, caps
- Certificate of achievement, lunch, and mug for perfect attendance, gift certificate to the one with longest perfect attendance
- Allow those with perfect attendance record to enter a lottery to get a $100 or $200 gift certificate
- Quarterly teleconference with all employees and support staff, especially CEO
- Family orientation for new employees with slide show or video program with refreshments

- Several line staff call new hire to welcome him/her to the team the day before he/she starts
- Toll-free hot line to President where they can leave any question, suggestion, etc. and will get a response
- Hold a regular meeting to tell staff what is going on and how they are doing
- Always hang charts, graphs, etc. to depict regularly how the property is doing
- Full page ad in newspaper once a year thanking employees and name all individually
- Public praising of an individual at a department or hotel meeting
- Make sure all rewards, praise, bonuses, etc. are in public
- Have the General Manager spend at least an hour with every new employee
- Golden Broom Award to all (excluding housekeeping staff) who are seen picking up trash-after two, they can redeem them for a gift
- Pick a trophy that is passed from rewardee to rewardee so it is much desired, it does not matter what it is and actually the odder the better so it is fun
- Pre-printed "you done good" or "a pat on the back" or "bravo" note cards to have management inscribe whenever appropriate spontaneously
- Praise immediately and tell them specifically what they did right and how it helps the company
- Always find ways to get staff's input into the operation-just simple suggestion box works great
- Work hard at finding a way to implement each suggestion and give a clear explanation why it cannot be used if that is the case
- Acknowledge all suggestions, even if not implemented, express appreciation perhaps also a small reward If you implement an idea, give a reward, and widely publicize it

- Pins for uniforms that say "The guest comes first" or "I will do my best" or "We're glad you're here" or something similar
- Periodically hold contests like a TV game show where employees answer questions about the property hotel, perhaps in teams
- Use an 800# service which employees call periodically to be given randomly selected test questions and win a prize if they get them all correct
- Give a small gift on the date of their anniversary
- Hold an annual banquet for those with more than a certain number of years of service
- Give every employee printed business cards
- At Ritz Carlton, all employees throughout the hotel are authorized to spend up to $2,000 each incident to resolve a guest's complaint, but few spend anywhere near that amount
- Ask employees regularly what else we can do for them to enable them to do a good job
- Tell employees regularly what else they can do for management to enable you to do a good job
- Hold weekly meetings with small groups of employees to discuss anything, serve food
- Hold a weekly 20 minute meeting with one employee to discuss anything
- Make it personal, people naturally commit themselves to other people, not to organizations
- Hold monthly employee meetings at which the financial performance of the previous month and other goals are discussed in specific
- Distribute daily reports of revenue performance last night and month-to-date
- Send employees and family to a competitive property and have them write a report
- Send employees and family to your property and have them write a report

- Imprint the hotel's four key business goals on T-shirts
- Include career development discussion in all performance reviews
- Send line staff to schools to do recruiting and interviewing
- Tell staff that if they achieve x,y,z, etc., you will call their mothers and tell them how great their child is and actually do it
- Always make sure their work environment is positive, attractive, and reflective of your goals and values
- Ideas for back-of-the-house areas: plants, framed art (let them choose), clean unworn carpets, adequate ventilation, natural light, meeting space, adequate work-space, well-functioning equipment, attractive break facilities
- Form a recreation committee to plan monthly activities
- Regular employee newsletter
- Ask for input on cost-cutting programs during times of low demand
- Implement management reviews where line staff assess management's performance

These are only a few of the infinite number of ideas to keep good staff members and motivate them to work hard toward common goals. Whatever you choose to do, keep doing it consistently and make sure that you are sincere. Good luck on making your hotel or restaurant a unique and rewarding place to work.

# 8

# Organisation and Operation

Meetings are a crucial part of an organization's overall strategy, and planning them requires special skills and tools. This article describes how to get the job done and where to turn for help.

## INTRODUCTION

So you've been handed the responsibility of organizing an off-premises meeting. Welcome to a task that isn't as easy as it seems. Before long, you'll be making decisions and following up on all manner of details. You may find yourself searching madly for reference materials or interviewing professionals to help you organize . Don't worry, there's no shortage of either.

## MEASURING VALUE

The best meetings support an organization's business objectives and help convey its overall message to those attending. The best meeting planners actively participate in honing the content to ensure that the meeting furthers the goals of the organization and is consistent with its mission. To measure the meeting's effectiveness, they are prepared to demonstrate its return on investment (ROI) to management.

Through ROI, organizations justify the dollars spent on meetings by measuring desired criteria, i.e., the knowledge gained by attendees or the increase in sales directly attributable to their participation. Determining ROI is accomplished through a variety of means, such as feedback from management, post-meeting evaluations, and surveys.

## QUESTIONS TO ASK

When handed the task of planning a meeting, first ask yourself whether there are alternatives to having a meeting at all. Is there a less costly way to communicate with this group, say, with videoconferencing or computer conferencing? Chances are your organization will decide there is no substitute for a face-to-face gathering, so two other questions are in order:

- What is the objective of this meeting?
- Who will attend?

The answers to these questions will form the basis of all logistical decisions to come, such as where the meeting is to be held, the size of the budget, what type of hotel or other facility you will use, the content of the agenda, what type of recreation will be called for, and even how the chairs in the meeting room will be set up. The importance of these early steps cannot be overemphasized, in particular the question: "Why are we having this meeting?" An incentive meeting held as a reward for salespeople, for example, will likely be held in an upscale resort hotel with recreation as part of the program. On the other hand, a short, hastily called brainstorming meeting is best staged at a business hotel, perhaps one located near an airport so that attendees can get in and out quickly. Obviously, fancy meals and recreation will not be necessary. And a meeting called to teach salespeople a new skill will best fit in a conference center that specializes in training and team-building programs. There, some form of recreation may provide a welcome break.

## VENUE SELECTION

Only after you are sure of the nature of the meeting and what type of hotel or facility you will use, can you go about selecting a venue. For openers:

- Contact the convention and visitors bureau in the destination you are considering. The bureau will send you literature that describes local hotels .
- Consult a hotel directory, such as SourceBook, a special issue of Successful Meetings magazine, Gavel, a special issue of Meetings & Conventions magazine, or the

Official Meetings & Facilities Guide, a web-based facility guide. (For details, see Publications.)

- Contact the sales offices of major hotel chains for directories of their properties.

After compiling a list of possible venues, send the sales department of each a request for proposal (RFP) outlining the requirements of your meeting. (If you're contacting several hotels in a destination, the convention and visitors bureau may serve as a middleman). The RFP should include such information as the preferred dates for your meeting, the number and type of sleeping rooms you require, the range of acceptable room rates, food and beverage requirements, a tentative agenda, and the amount and type of meeting space needed. This information will help the hotel decide whether it is able to host the meeting according to your specifications. Based on the hotels' responses to your RFP, narrow down the field and arrange to inspect the hotel or hotels you're considering. Things to consider during a site inspection: overall appearance of the hotel and its guest rooms, lobby, and meeting space; proximity to the airport and availability of shuttle services; attitude of the service staff; whether meeting rooms have obstructions, such as pillars or overhangs, that interfere with audiovisual presentations; accessibility for people with disabilities. If you cannot inspect the site in person, a detailed questionnaire will suffice. Also, many hotels have Web sites that include layouts of their meeting space.

## NEGOTIATING A CONTRACT

By now, you should be ready to accept a letter of agreement from one property. This outlines the space reserved for your group. You can begin to negotiate with the salesperson from the property on the terms of the contract that will eventually be signed. If you've held a similar meeting before, you may strengthen your bargaining position by mentioning how much was spent on basic items.

Nearly everything is negotiable: the sleeping room rate; the meeting room rental, which may be waived if the group generates sufficient guest-room and food and beverage revenue;

upgrades to suite accommodations; meeting room equipment; and the complimentary room ratio (typically, hotels "comp" one room for every 50 booked).

Negotiating with a conference center is simpler, because such properties offer a complete meeting package (CMP). This provides a per-person cost for everything from sleeping rooms and meals to conference space and audiovisual needs. Regardless of the venue, make sure you have a written contract that outlines the guest room commitment, room rate, complimentary accommodations, reservation and deposit procedures, method of payment, meeting space, banquet space, and cancellation policy.

Before the contract is signed, however, you might want to include special provisions that could be difficult to add later on. For instance, you could insert a clause stipulating that certain organizations, such as a competing company, may not meet in the hotel at the same time.

Or you could provide for financial relief in the event that the hotel is double-booked and can't honour its commitments.Keep in mind that you have the option of outsourcing your meeting to meeting specialists who will undertake all logistics (or only those elements you wish to outsource) from site selection to on-site management of the meeting. This company need not be based in the city where you hold the meeting.

## Details

After the contract is signed, your meeting file will be turned over to the property's convention services manager. Think of this person as your in-house meeting planner, the person who, from now until your meeting ends, will coordinate all your needs and serve as a liaison between you and other departments within the property. Leading up to the meeting, you will be confronted with countless details (meeting publications often publish diagrams showing what must be done and when). Among the critical details:

- *Transportation:* Will flights be booked by your organization's in-house travel department or an outside agency? Airlines have special departments that handle groups. They offer discounted fares and cargo rates, complimentary tickets (depending on the number of seats booked), and special ticketing and billing. How will attendees get from the airport to the meeting property? Taxi? Hotel shuttle? If you're expecting high-level executives or other VIPs, you'll have to arrange limousine transfers.

- *Check-in:* To expedite check-in, the property will need to be briefed on the arrival pattern of attendees.
- *Agenda:* As the meeting nears, a schedule of meeting-related activities and food-and-beverage functions should be drafted and shared with the convention services manager.
- Meeting-room setup depends on the nature of the sessions. Use an auditorium-style setup when a speaker is addressing the group. Arrange tables in a U for sessions where attendees will be interacting.
- *Audiovisual:* Well before the meeting, talk to the convention services manager about your requirements and how the equipment should be set up. Bear in mind that some rooms have structural elements that are not conducive to audiovisual presentations.
- *Food and Beverage:* Menus should be discussed and confirmed with the convention services manager and with the catering department.
- Recreation and special events. The convention services manager can assist in setting up recreational programs on the property, such as a golf tournament. Off-site events, such as dinners and outings, are best arranged through a destination management company (DMC), a type of tour operator that focuses on groups. Production companies can assist you with organizing themed banquets, Broadway-style shows, or multimedia presentations. Ask the local convention and visitors bureau for a list of such companies.

## MAKING THE MEETING INTERACTIVE

Interactive technology provides ways to improve understanding and learning at your meeting, then measure the progress. It gives planners a more precise and immediate system for evaluating the results of a meeting. A key interactive element is the audience response system, which enables a presenter to ask questions and have the answers displayed instantly on a large screen in front of the audience. (Questions and answers can also be printed out and distributed after the meeting.)

Attendees are each given a wireless keypad with which they answer questions. They can pick Yes or No or punch in a number that corresponds to a multiple-choice answer. Answers are tabulated by an on-site computer, then displayed on the screen in various formats, such as bar graphs or pie charts. Besides getting people involved in the learning process, the system makes it possible to obtain immediate feedback. That makes it especially useful for business meetings, media testing, and focus groups. Often, the audience is divided into teams that compete for the best score. Audience response systems can be used at virtually any meeting facility, whether in-house, off-site, or at several remote sites linked by videoconferencing.

Setup time is nominal. A 500-pad meeting can be set up in an hour and a half. The price varies, depending on the size and duration of the meeting and the amount of customization required.

### On Site/Aftermath

Ideally, the meeting planner should arrive at least a day before the attendees. At that time, the meeting planner, the convention services manager, and the appropriate department heads can discuss last-minute needs. Some form of post-meeting evaluation is necessary to determine the meeting's ROI. Example: a questionnaire distributed to attendees plus follow-up interviews with attendees and managers.

# 9
# Future Trends

## BRANDING AND CERTIFICATION PROGRAM

The HTNG Branding and Certification Program is formally launched at HITEC 2005 with the publication of the HTNG Certification Policy. Four months in the making, this document was the result of a collaborative effort between an HTNG Board Committee and The Open Group. The Open Group is one of the world's leading practitioners of certification programs, and serves as the certification authority for the Common Operating Environment (COE) Platform, CORBA, LDAP, Linux Standard Base (LSB), POSIX, UNIX, the Wireless Application Protocol (WAP), and numerous other specifications and standards bodies.

"Certification and branding provides important benefits to both buyers and sellers of technology," said Douglas Rice, Executive Director of HTNG. "The 'HTNG Certified' label will provide assurance to buyers that a particular technology product will deliver a minimum level of interoperability with other products." Through the certification process, technology vendors can apply to use that trademark for their products. They must show that the products meet the specifications at the outset, and agree to quickly rectify any deficiencies that appear later on.

Technology vendors who implement open HTNG specifications benefit from being able to advertise their compliance. Buyers who are HTNG members will benefit from access to the certified product register, which identifies precisely which products, versions, and configurations meet a product specification, and which optional features of that specification they implement.

"Unlike self-policed compliance claims, the 'HTNG Certified' label will be protected by trademark law," says Rice. "This means that vendors who complete the effort to become certified can be confident that their legitimate claims of compliance will not be lost among false claims by companies that have not met the same requirements."

The next step in the process will be for HTNG workgroups to identify the specifications that they believe would benefit from certification. The program is designed to be able to accommodate any workgroup specifications, but there is no requirement that every specification be submitted to the certification process. The participants in each workgroup can determine which specifications would benefit from certification. It is anticipated that workgroups will begin submitting specifications to become part of the certification program over the next few months.

The costs of certification will vary depending on the specifications involved, and the means of verifying compliance with each one. Initially, HTNG anticipates that compliance with most specifications will be based on self-certification by the vendor. Under this approach, providers will need to complete a certification checklist and provide evidence (such as testing results) that their product is compliant. "We believe that this approach is the right starting point, as it minimizes the costs of administering the certification program, and will help keep certification fees low" said Rice. "Our industry depends on many small technology companies, and we think it is critical that the cost of certification not impose a financial burden on the industry innovators. If third-party testing programs prove necessary for some specifications, we can always implement them later, on a selective basis."

## IN-ROOM TECHNOLOGY WORKGROUP WHITE PAPERS

The HTNG In-Room Technology Workgroup released the first two of a series of groundbreaking White Papers, representing hundreds of hours of contributions from some of the best hotel, engineering, and marketing minds in the business.

The first White Paper, "Convergence: Hotel Technology for Today and Tomorrow," addresses the issue of network infrastructure in hotels. For years, hotels have been built with separate networks to support different applications, including in-room entertainment systems, telephony, high-speed Internet, building control systems, and administrative systems. The hotel CIO/CTO community has known for years that the redundancy in cabling is costly, and that the historical approach made it difficult to get these different systems to work cooperatively. This White Paper makes the business case for migrating hotels to a single converged network; identifies the alternative infrastructures that should be the targets; and considers the key applications that need to coexist-entertainment, Internet access, telephony, and room controls.

"If you want to future-proof your technology investments, this is the one document you can't afford not to read," said Nick Price, Chief Technology Officer of Mandarin Oriental Hotel Group and President of HTNG.

The Infrastructure White Paper reflects design work from top engineers at leading technology companies in all major guest-room application areas, as well as critical input from participating hospitality companies, including Ginn Clubs & Resorts, The Kor Group, Mandarin Oriental, Marriott International, The Peninsula Group, and Royal Caribbean. The paper was developed by a team chaired by Angela Landon of Cisco Systems; was edited by Donald C. Wynes, PMP, of Lorica Solutions; and included significant contributions from engineers and executives at Cisco Systems, Datanamics, Ginn Clubs & Resorts, Heckaman Group, LodgeNet Entertainment Corporation, Lorica Solutions, Mitel, Mandarin Oriental Hotel Group, Paradyne, Royal Caribbean, and SolutionInc Limited.

The second White Paper, "The Guest of the Future: In-Room Technology Preferences Today and Tomorrow" represents an amazing view into the needs of tomorrow's guests, and what it will take to satisfy them. Hotel rooms being built today will, over the course of their lifetime, be occupied mostly by people who are still under 30, or even 20. Their expectations will not be the same as today's travellers, and if the hospitality industry is to succeed at meeting those expectations, it needs to understand how the expectations of younger generations differ from those of older ones-and how they are likely to continue to evolve over time.

This White Paper was authored by the Center for Marketing Effectiveness (CeME), with significant input from executives at Guest-Tek, Mandarin Oriental, Marriott International, Mitel, The Peninsula Group, and SolutionInc Limited.

A third White Paper, which covers the need for and design for an "all in one" guestroom device to control all technologies, is still under development and will be published for HTNG member comment in the near future. This device, modelled after the traditional cable-TV "Set-Top Box," does not yet exist in the marketplace. Once the design is complete, the workgroup will seek to engage manufacturers to create this "smart" terminating point for the IP network within the room, which will allow coordinated, guest-centric control of all in-room technologies and devices.

The full White Papers are available online to HTNG members at no charge. They will be released to the general public when the In-Room Technology Workgroup completes its mission and ceases to exist in approximately 12 months.

## ABOUT HOTEL TECHNOLOGY NEXT GENERATION

The premier technology solutions association in the hospitality industry, HTNG is a self-funded, non-profit organization with members from hotel and hospitality companies, technology vendors to hospitality, and other industry members including consultants, media, and academic experts. HTNG's members participate in focused workgroups to bring open solution-sets addressing specific business problems to the hospitality market.

Membership in HTNG is open to hotel and hospitality companies, technology vendors to hospitality, consultants, academics, press and others. Currently more than 200 companies and individuals from across this spectrum are active HTNG members. Workgroup proceedings, drafts, and specifications are published for all HTNG members as soon as they are created, encouraging rapid and broad adoption.

## RENAISSANCE HOTELS AND RESORTS

Renaissance Hotels & Resorts are a stylish division of Marriott Hotels, offering distinctive accommodations, expressive decors, imaginative dining and attentive personal service. In each city you visit, wherever you may travel, you will immerse yourself in the unique experiences only Renaissance Hotels deliver.

Renaissance Hotels & Resorts are a division of Marriott Hotels, one of the world's strongest hotel chains. Renaissance Hotels offer distinctive accommodations, exacting attention to detail and attentive personal service in more than 100 great destinations around the globe. Stylish decors and imaginative dining create an ambiance of a boutique; brand signatures include interior design, a "street" restaurant and savvy service.

The personalized service style of Renaissance Hotels enhances your well-being. You will feel special and recognized at Renaissance. You will experience comfort, warmth, and quality in a stylish and sophisticated ambience.

The decor of Renaissance is imbued with imagination and flair. The atmosphere is residential, personal, unique, and distinctly tied to the local character. When you stay at Renaissance, you will know what city you are visiting because you will feel it all around you. There is a sense of place at Renaissance Hotels. Dining at Renaissance Hotels is also a unique experience.

Well-defined restaurants feature delightfully imaginative menus, environments are inviting and alive, and-as always-service is as savvy and sophisticated. The unique ambiance of Renaissance is always grounded in the practicality of a full-service hotel, allowing you the flexibility to be both productive and comfortable.

The work space in each room has all the essentials: high-speed Internet access; a spacious desk and comfortable, ergonomic chair; easily accessed data ports; power outlets at desk level; 2 telephones (1 cordless); and voice mail. In your room, you'll find individual room temperature controls, a comfortable relaxation chair, a 25" TV with remote control, a radio, and an alarm clock. Renaissance Hotels are great for meetings, adding a touch of understated sophistication and inspired personalization to events of any kind and size. Each hotel has a business center with a sizeable library and outstanding conference and banquet facilities.

You can also let the stress roll away any time of the day at the fitness center with a swimming pool. Renaissance Hotels & Resorts boast 130 properties world-wide, 64 US, 66 international. In each city you visit, wherever you may travel, you will immerse yourself in the unique experiences only Renaissance Hotels deliver.

Renaissance Hotels delight your senses and inspire your imagination. Its distinctive & individualistic style is a blend of attentive service, expressive decor, luxurious bedding and imaginative dining. Stay interesting with Renaissance Hotels.

## WESTIN HOTELS

Westin Hotels & Resorts redefine efficient service with an effortless style and gracious attitude that ensures a truly unforgettable experience. Every Westin Hotel-and there are more than 120, including 30 of the world's finest resorts-is a haven of serenity and a distinctive alternative for those who appreciate a higher standard.

Welcoming yet never overwhelming, each Westin Hotel is architecturally inspiring, thoughtfully designed and located in the world's most exciting cities and sumptuous resort destinations. From business travellers to those travelling with small children, any Westin Hotel offers special services and exclusive amenities: the Heavenly Bed, the Heavenly Shower, WestinWORKOUT powered by Reebok Gym to help you to keep yourself fit, Westin Kids Club, offering fun activities, essential amenities and helpful services for children under 13,

Westin One Call, Designed to organize and facilitate every detail of your meeting or event and Westin Technical Concierge, an around the clock tech assistance that assures trouble-free connectivity.

The Heavenly Bed is a Westin hotel signature innovation, winning glowing reviews and loyal fans since its introduction in 1999. Sumptuous and stylish, the all-white Heavenly Bed is made up of a custom designed pillow-top mattress set, a cozy down blanket, three crisp sheets ranging in thread count from 180 to 250, a comforter, duvet and five plush pillows. The Heavenly Bath offers guests a fully customizable shower experience via exclusive dual showerhead configuration and a revolutionary curved shower rod affording eight additional inches of elbowroom. Indulgent signature spa amenities, Brazilian combed cotton bath sheets and custom-designed velour bathrobes complete this lavish picture and add even more incentive to get out of bed. For those traveling with kids Westin created a special kids program. Beyond the basic babysitting services and children's menus, Westin Kids Club delivers services, furnishings and amenities geared for kids of all ages, including infants. With a Westin Hotel traveling is safe and enjoyable for families.

For businessmen Westin's Guest Office offers the option of staying in rooms that double as offices for just $20 above the standard room rate. Developed to meet the increasing needs of business travellers, Westin's Guest Office combines the efficiency and technology of an office with the unsurpassed comfort and luxury of a private guest room. A Guest Office room at each Westin Hotel includes a comfortable work area complete with an ergonomically-designed chair, multi-function laser printer/fax/copier, speakerphone with data port, printer cables, voice messaging and free, unlimited local calls and long distance access. Westin's Guest Office also includes convenient late checkout privileges. All Westin meeting rooms are equipped for high speed Internet access and feature extensive VPN capabilities, allowing guests secure, instant access to e-mail and corporate networks. Multimedia presentations featuring live web content can be easily delivered to large or small audiences, as can online product demonstrations, training sessions, video conferences and webcasting. Whether it's a small gathering of executives, a corporate retreat or an annual conference with the entire company, you can count on a Westin Hotel to make your meeting a success. With Westin One Call, a toll-free number available in the United States and Canada, you can "delegate" the planning responsibilities to a Westin meetings expert, who will schedule, organize, price and manage every detail of your function.

Above all, Westin guests can enjoy the convenience of Express Checkout with approved billing using a major credit card. No matter what time of day or night, guests may bypass the front desk for checkout and drop their hotel bill in a strategically located Express Checkout box. Billing receipts are mailed to guests within 24 hours.

In 2005, Westin Hotels & Resorts celebrates its 75th birthday, proving that exceptional service and luxurious comfort are never out of style. Starting with issuing the first guest credit card to the creation of the Heavenly line of services and amenities, Westin has built a tradition of anticipating needs and satisfying them-effortlessly, efficiently and with gracious aplomb.

**RADISSON HOTELS**

Radisson Hotels & Resorts is a leading, global hotel company that provides genuine hospitality at every point of guest contact in 435 hotels, representing more than 102,000 guest rooms in 61 countries. With headquarters in Minneapolis, Minn., Radisson Hotels & Resorts is one of the lodging brands of Carlson Hotels Worldwide, one of America's largest privately-owned hotel companies.

Radisson has grown from its home country of the United States to become a global leader in the hospitality industry by entering into management agreements, licensing and through embracing partnerships with existing hotel companies. Examples of the company's highly successful partnerships include Rezidor SAS Hospitality's development of Radisson SAS hotels and Radisson Edwardian Hotels in the United

Kingdom. Radisson opened the American-managed hotel in Moscow in 1991 and today has several locations throughout Eastern Europe. Radisson's entry into the United Arab Emirates, Lebanon and Saudi Arabia in December 2002, expanded the brand's global presence to 61 countries.

Radisson hotels have achieved a global presence by expanding into new markets around the world and by focusing on total guest satisfaction, industry-leading loyalty programs and extensive customer relationship programs. In order to provide personalized comfort, Radisson hotels have elaborated Select Comfort program. Sleep Number Bed by Select Comfort is a unique air technology that allows you to adjust the level of firmness to ensure a great night's sleep. Sleep Number beds are available at a growing number of Radisson hotels.

Existing Gold Rewards program offers guests the opportunity to earn and redeem Gold Points within an exclusive network of leading brands. Members can earn Gold Points and redeem the points for free night stays, airline miles, luxury cruises, merchandise, meals, and more. Currently, Gold Points are earned at all Radisson hotels in the United States, Canada, the Caribbean, Mexico, Central and South America. Residents of these countries can earn points at Radisson SAS and Radisson Edwardian hotels in Europe as well. Members of Radisson Gold Rewards earn 1,000 Gold Points per night, up to 10,000 points per stay.

Faced with today's new business environment, accelerated industry consolidation and changing customer expectations, the leadership of Radisson re-examined everything it does. From its franchise partners and strategic allies, to every manager and employee at every hotel, the Radisson organization is committed to providing personalized, professional guest service. Radisson hotels are named after the famous French explorer, Pierre Esprit Radisson, who visited many parts of the Upper Midwest and Canada during the 17th century. Global presence and expansion into new markets is a key part of Radisson's heritage. Radisson Hotels is a recognized and trusted brand, this trust being maintained through a consistent, quality and personalized guest service.

## CROWNE PLAZA HOTELS

Crowne Plaza is an upscale hotel brand with assets in key cities world-wide. Launched in 1994, Crowne Plaza is the preferred hotel brand of the world's business. A part of InterContinental Hotels Group, Crowne Plaza hotels were set up to move the group into the upscale market. With its wide variety of premium services and amenities, including fully-appointed guest rooms with ample work space, full complement of business services, excellent dining choices, quality fitness facilities and comprehensive meeting capabilities, Crowne Plaza hotels exceed guest expectations by providing the right room, the right technology and the right service. Recognizing the importance of getting a great night's sleep when traveling, Crowne Plaza hotels have developed the Crowne Plaza Sleep Advantage program. The program includes comfortable new beds, guaranteed wake-up calls and also sleep CDs and relaxation tips. Crowne Plaza presents a wide variety of meeting venues-from comfortable and practical to luxurious. In the frame of innovative Meeting Success program, Crowne Plaza hotels provide tailored food and beverage options for meetings.

The first is Lunching In, a menu for time-conscious delegates, who need to work through lunch, offering a variety of shared table meals, developed to keep them stimulated and engaged. Crowne Plaza hotels also offer Snack Attack, an all-day snack bar within the meeting room, stocked with a range of snack options from nuts, chocolate and soft drinks through to muffins, energy bars, fruit, juices as well as tea and coffee.

Perfect for interactive meetings such as training sessions or workshops, Snack Attack ensures that meetings can run uninterrupted, while still providing opportunities for short working refreshment breaks. As not all meetings are held in formal environments, Crowne Plaza hotels have introduced Meet and Eat for informal sessions.

Meet and Eat is a menu of easy-to-eat snacks and lunches, s well as essential business products such as business services and stationary items for people holding meetings in lobby or lounge areas. With Meet & Eat, Crowne Plaza hotels show understanding of a wide range of meeting needs. Crowne Plaza hotels make every stay relaxing, invigorating, stimulating and filled with positive interactions. Whether it's a group meeting in the hotel, a one-on-one meeting with a colleague or clients, or a getaway with a loved one or friends, Crowne Plaza is the hotel for people who value the energy and positive interactions that take place when people come together. In virtually every major business center across North America and in 40 countries around the world, Crowne Plaza is the place to meet.

## PARK HOTELS

Located far enough to avoid street noise, park hotels are a bit like your Granny's house. Very quiet and peaceful places, they are laced with warmth and hospitality. Park hotels offer you the charm of the garden, elegant styling and general attention to detail. You can have an appetizing snack in a park bar or restaurant, smell the over powering scent of flowers, listen to the birds signing, have a look at some exotic animals, or simply take a walk and enjoy the nature.

There is a large number of hotels, adjacent to world famous parks. With stunning views over Hyde Park and Kensington Gardens, the Hilton Hyde Park Hotel is a beautiful 129 bedroom town house hotel, conveniently situated in central London.

The Hilton Hyde Park Hotel is almost opposite Hyde Park and is close to Queensway with many recreational amenities within the Queensway area. The Darlington Hyde Park Hotel is also not far from the eminent park. Located in Sussex Gardens, the traditional and elegant facade of this London hotel encompasses a professional yet friendly atmosphere. It is one of the only London hotels near Hyde Park that is also 5 minutes walk from the Heathrow Express Terminal.

The country that boats a collection of outstanding theme parks is USA. The theme park revolution was begun by Walt Disney at Disneyland. It is now a 47 square miles destination resort, filled with four theme parks, two water parks, 30 resort hotels, six golf courses and two shopping-dining-entertainment complexes.

You can choose deluxe resorts, such as Animal Kingdom Longe that feature balconies overlooking 33-acre tropical savannah, a home to more than 200 mammals and birds, including giraffe, zebra, thomsons gazelle, ostrich and sacred ibis. Value park hotels are also available. Quite moderate in price, All Star Movies Resort has giant icons from Favourite Disney Movies including 101 Dalmatians, Toy Story, Fantasia and The Mighty Ducks. Along with theme parks, US also hides a treasure of outstanding ornamental gardens. In North Louisiana southern growing season is mild and extended, allowing a wide variety of plants to be grown. The most popular garden in North Louisiana is located near Shreveport-it is The American Rose Center, outstanding demonstration garden containing over 20,000 rose bushes. In all, these bushes represent over 650 rose varieties.

The Best Western Chateau Suite Hotel is in a short drive away from The American Rose Center. It offers oversized standard and deluxe rooms as well as spacious two-room suites, which include a kitchenette and are perfect for families or extended stays. The Best Western Richmond Suites Hotel in Shreveport is also not far from the prominent garden. The hotel is great for corporate travellers and has free high-speed Internet in the rooms, a hot buffet breakfast served every morning, an oversized fitness center and business center. No matter what kind of park hotels you choose, a small quite one, or located in the busy area of Disneyland, it will be an absolutely healthy decision. Parks awaken your senses and take you away from stresses of modern life. Gardens nourish the soul with their lush greenery and beautiful bloom. Should you happen to change across a fragrant blossom, you won't probably be able to stop yourself from bending over to take a deeper whiff of the natural perfume that so readily tantalizes the nose.

## MACDONALD HOTELS

Macdonald Hotels & Resorts operates about 65 luxury hotels and resorts throughout the UK. Founded in 1990 by chairman Donald Macdonald, Macdonald Hotels is a unique brand of hospitality, offering spa and beauty breaks, romance packages and an unrivalled range of outdoor activities. Each of Macdonald Hotels has its own special charm and character and many of them are set in some of the country's most beautiful locations, from dramatic loch sides and peaceful countryside to vibrant and historic city centres.

At Macdonald Hotels you will discover the friendly atmosphere and enjoy the finest of local produce in award-winning restaurants, relax and unwind in one of the excellent leisure clubs and spas you'll find at many of Macdonald Hotels. Some of Macdonald Hotels also have their own championship-standard golf course, or a golf round can be arranged at a club nearby. Historic locations, beautiful landscapes and the diverse culture of Britain make Macdonald Hotels the great place for the game of golf. Besides golf, a wide range of leisure activities is offered, from clay pigeon shooting to quad biking. However you choose to spend your break, you can be as active or relaxed as you like.

Also at a number of hotels you'll be surprised to find the perfect antidote to the stresses of modern life: Vital Health, Fitness and Beauty Club-are the special revitalizing breaks for both mind & body. You can work out in a fully equipped gym, or play it cool in an indoor swimming pool. Soothe in a sauna or steam room, or just lie back in a jacuzzi and let the world go by. At Macdonald Hotels you can massage away your troubles and enjoy a selection of the finest treatments. An expert therapist will help find the perfect solution, for both women & men. At Macdonald Hotels attention to detail is demonstrated through impeccable service, promise of 'on time, every time' and award winning cuisine with the use of only the finest and freshest ingredients. And of course, this is complemented by carefully designed and thoughtfully furnished bedrooms providing a comfortable haven that is perfect for work and for relaxation. Spacious lounge, dining area, comfortable bedrooms and fully equipped modern kitchen are features of most lodges, chalets, bungalows and apartments-some even have two bathrooms and a sauna.

Macdonald Hotels & Resorts have an outstanding collection of properties in great locations across the UK, from elegant manor house retreats set in extensive grounds, to modern and contemporary hotels in city centre locations. Whether you are looking for a wedding location, leisure break or the little extra's like Romantic Breaks, Spa Breaks, Golfing Breaks & Live Music you are sure to discover the perfect setting at Macdonald Hotels.

## MARRIOTT HOTELS

With over 2,600 lodging properties world-wide, Marriott Hotels make every business trip a pleasure and every vacation the trip of a lifetime. Marriott offers a complete family of hotels to please all tastes, from luxurious full-service hotels and resorts to affordable lodging along the way. Marriott hotels' chain embrace such well-known brands as Marriott Hotels & Resorts, JW Marriott Hotels & Resorts, Renaissance Hotels & Resorts, Courtyard, Residence Inn, Fairfield Inn, TownePlace Suites, The Ritz-Carlton and others. Marriott Hotels & Resorts is the most trusted name in hotels; renowned for its "spirit to serve," its consistent quality and its genuine care. Marriott Hotels & Resorts business centers, concierge, room service for business, leisure and group events.

JW Marriott Hotels & Resorts is the most elegant and luxurious Marriott brand with exquisite architectural detail, the finest dining, and gracious sophistication. It offers business and leisure travellers a deluxe level of comfort and personal service. Another popular brand, Renaissance Hotels & Resorts provides distinctive decors, imaginative dining, and attentive service in fantastic destinations around the world.

In 1998 Marriott purchased The Ritz-Carlton, worldwide symbol of the finest accommodations, dining, and service. In the heart of the world's most picturesque cities and resort destinations, the Ritz-Carlton creates a warm atmosphere and a unique ambience of the local culture. However, not all the Marriott hotels are luxurious. Courtyard is a moderately priced lodging brand, designed for business travellers. It offers all the essential services and amenities for you to stay productive while on the road: helpful staff, high-speed Internet access, ergonomic work spaces, business libraries, 24-hour access to food, and hot breakfast buffets. Fairfield Inn is also a reasonably priced brand, offering a consistent, quality lodging. It's the most affordable of all Marriott hotels. Marriott also offers extended-stay brands, such as Residence Inn and TownePlace Suites. Residence Inn was designed as "home away from home" for travellers staying 5 or more nights. TownePlace Suites is more a residential community than a hotel, designed for travellers for weeks at a time on the road. Here you can rearrange the furniture, bring your favourite recliner, or your beloved dog. When you need extra space to spread out, SpringHill Suites is the perfect choice. At this moderately priced, all-suite lodging brand, guest suites are up to 25% larger than standard hotel rooms.

Whichever Marriott brand you choose, you can always count on Marriott's unique blend of quality, consistency and personalized service. As one of the world's strongest brands, Marriott enjoys outstanding consumer recognition, customer preference, unprecedented international distribution and a reputation for operational excellence.

## LUXURY HOTELS

"Making guests feel at home" has long been the main objective of the hotel industry. At the most basic level this means offering a clean room with a comfortable bed. Yet, as our lives have evolved to include more comforts, hotel services have improved, and luxury hotels have appeared. Elegantly styled, luxury hotels have unique amenities that often include king-sized beds piled high with pillows, CD players, telephones and TVs in the bathroom, and even spas in some of locations. The most famous chains of luxury hotels are The Four Seasons Hotels and The Ritz-Carlton.

Founded in 1960, Four Seasons invented luxury for the modern traveler. Spacious rooms, beautiful flowers, award-winning cuisine, spa escapes, resourceful assistance of the multilingual Concierge,-these are the temptations of Four Seasons. You may also count on high-speed Internet access and expert communications support, with in-room convenience from speakerphones to data ports. The concept of The Ritz-Carlton hotels is elegant lifestyle. At The Ritz-Carton the guests are treated with respect and dignity, following the motto: "We are Ladies and Gentlemen serving Ladies and Gentlemen." The company has grown a collection of luxury hotels around the world, located in the most picturesque cities and resort destinations. Several of these hotels are historic landmarks, as The Ritz-Carlton Hotel Company is committed to preserve architecturally important buildings. Some examples are The Ritz-Carlton, San Francisco; The Ritz-Carlton, Philadelphia; The Ritz-Carlton, New Orleans; and The Ritz-Carlton, Huntington Hotel & Spa. While The Ritz-Carton hotels are chic, stylish and very successful, their appeal is targeted more to a hip, affluent clientele. Four Seasons, on the other hand, try to bridge the gap by being stylish as well as providing the businessperson with the traditional requirements of meeting space and business centers.

Other chains of luxury hotels are Crowne Plaza Hotels, Embassy Suites, Staybridge Suites, W Hotels and others. Although being quite different in style, they all have meticulous personal approach and high-class service. Independent luxury hotels and resorts can compete now with well-known luxury hotel chains, providing intimacy of a smaller property. The hotel personnel, not constrained by corporate policies, has the freedom to act according to the demands of each situation. Besides, independent luxury hotels offer special amenities and services sometimes not found at the name brand hotels. At the Elan Hotel Modern in LA, each guestroom is handsomely appointed with a complimentary assortment of thoughtful amenities you'd expect to pay extra for, including an extensive video library, 200 thread Egyptian Cotton bedding and two phones with remote voice message pickup. In Scottsdale, the Hotel Waterfront Ivy is not a typical luxury hotel either. Starbucks Coffee, cotton robes and natural bath products are just a few of the in-room standard amenities.

Luxury hotels are constantly upgrading the amenities. Trying to assess the needs of the future guests, hoteliers tend to build large spas. Owners of luxury hotels understand that modern travellers become better educated about the importance of health and are willing to incorporate the spa experience as an important component of both their vacation and business trips. Small Luxury Hotels, the exclusive hotel brand featuring over 329 independently-owned, luxury hotels, recognized the growth in consumer demand for luxurious spa experiences and has extended their brand power and expertise in the form of the Spa Book. The book is a complete guide to spa experiences, selecting some of the best spas around the world. With or without spa, luxury hotels create an elegant warm ambience, where luxurious comfort soothes body and soul.

## INTER CONTINENTAL HOTELS

Inter Continental Hotels Group PLC is the world's most global hotel company and the largest by number of rooms. The Group has more than 3,500 owned, leased, managed and franchised hotels and approximately 535,000 guest rooms across nearly 100 countries and territories. Every year more than 120 million people find a welcome at one of the InterContinental Hotels lodging brands. InterContinental Hotels Corporation was founded by Pan-American World Airlines in 1946. It served not only as a quality hotel brand, meeting the international travellers' needs, but also taking care of the 40,000 airline crew and staff as they flew the airlines' routes.

Today, InterContinental Hotels are the part of InterContinental Hotels Group PLC that owns also a portfolio of such well-recognized and respected brands, as Crowne Plaza Hotels & Resorts, Hotel Indigo, Holiday Inn, Holiday Inn Express, Staybridge Suites and Candlewood Suites. Crowne Plaza is an upscale hotel brand with assets in key cities world-wide. Crowne Plaza and InterContinental Hotels are the preferred hotel brands of the world's business.

At InterContinental Hotels and Resorts guests can enjoy 24 hour services, from Business Centers that will open in the middle of the night to expert InsiderTM Concierges, who can help guests to get the most from a city. Upscale Staybridge Suites and mid-scale Candlewood Suite brands cater for comfortable and complete extended stay in the U.S. The Hotels Group has also leading positions for mid-scale brands-Holiday

Inn and Holiday Inn Express in key countries including the US, the UK and China.

Due to its large network, the InterContinental Hotels Group has access to considerable funds to promote and support its brands. These funds, known as 'system funds', represent a stable financial source used to support marketing activities, special programmes, relationship marketing and system infrastructure. The global nature and scale of the InterContinental Hotels Group enables it to drive growth and profitability while reducing operating costs. InterContinental Hotels have important global position. Encompassing mid-scale and upscale markets, the Group enjoys a worldwide reputation for exceptional facilities and personal attention.

## HOLIDAY INN HOTELS

No matter where you're traveling, you'll find a familiar place to stay at Holiday Inn hotels. With more than 1,500 Holiday Inn full-service hotels around the world, you will be sure to find a convenient location offering many features to make your stay more enjoyable, including comfortable guest rooms equipped with coffeemakers, hair dryers and irons. Today Holiday Inn hotels offer travellers full-service amenities such as restaurants and room service, a relaxing lounge, swimming pool and fitness center and, for the business traveler, Holiday Inn hotels provide 24-hour business services, meeting facilities and the Holiday Inn Meeting Promise.

For over 50 years Holiday Inn hotels have been the reassuring choice for business and leisure travellers where guests receive the famous warm welcome and friendly service. Holiday Inn was founded in 1952 by Kemmons Wilson in Memphis, Tennessee to cater for the travel needs of US families. With continued investment Holiday Inn grew internationally and other brands were developed to expand the portfolio and build on its strong infrastructure. In 1995 Holiday Inn Worldwide became the first hotel company to offer direct booking capability.

Together with Holiday Inn Select, Holiday Inn SunSpree Resorts, Holiday Inn Express, Holiday Inn Garden Court and some other brands, Holiday Inn hotels are the part of InterContinental Hotels Group. InterContinental Hotels and Resorts is the leading international hotel company that has more than 3,500 properties around the world. Holiday Inn Select is the hotel brand for individuals with a passion for business and an appreciation of value. Located throughout North and South America near business centers and airports, Holiday Inn Select hotels feature business class rooms, 24-hours business services, comprehensive meeting facilities and services.

Holiday Inn SunSpree Resorts have casual atmosphere and modern facilities. Whether traveling to a tropical escape or a mountain getaway, it is easy for the entire family to have fun together.

Holiday Inn SunSpree Resorts offer all of the conveniences you're looking for, like a great restaurant, in-room refrigerator, laundry facility, expansive pool area, and a variety of recreational facilities. Friendly staff and trained Activities Coordinators schedule numerous adult events and supervise children's activities as well.

For value-oriented guests, Holiday Inn Express is a fresh, clean, and uncomplicated choice, offering a free breakfast bar featuring fresh fruit, cereals and pastries, as well as free local calls within the U.S. There are over 1000 locations around the globe, and it is growing fast. Holiday Inn Express is the fastest growing hotel brand in the industry, opening on average two hotels a week. Holiday Inn Garden Court hotels, located in Europe and South Africa, have a style and character unique to its location.

Each Holiday Inn Garden Court hotel offers quality guest rooms, meeting and leisure facilities, as well as a number of other services and amenities. Holiday Inn hotels offer contemporary business and leisure travellers dependability, friendly service and modern attractive facilities at an excellent price. You'll find them throughout the world-in small towns and major cities, along quiet roadways and near bustling airports-because full-service Holiday Inn hotels are always conveniently located.

## GAY HOTELS

The hotel business seems to get more and more aware of the gay public. Major companies in the travel industry have aligned themselves with gay tourism campaigns. Gay hotels offer the opportunity to socialize with other gays, and the feeling that one can relax safely among other gay people.

The hotel business seems to get more and more aware of the gay public. Major companies in the travel industry have aligned themselves with gay tourism campaigns. Gay hotels offer the opportunity to socialize with other gays, and the feeling that one can relax safely among other gay people.

Often gay-owned or managed, gay hotels have permissive or liberal attitudes towards gays and feature a prominent gay infrastructure (bars, businesses, restaurants, nightlife, entertainment, media, organisations, etc.). Gay travel destinations are usually large cities, Amsterdam being the most famous place in Europe. This old city with historic houses is considered to be "gay-friendly". Amsterdam has a lot of gay hotels, and it is illegal for any hotel in Amsterdam to refuse a gay couple. Other popular destinations in Europe include Barcelona, Berlin, Copenhagen, Ibiza, London, Munich and Paris. But the most important source of gay and lesbian tourists is the U.S. market. North America has numerous gay-friendly locations. Philadelphia is running the USA's largest gay tourism marketing campaign "Get your history straight and your nightlife gay".

Other popular gay tourism places are gay neighbourhoods, or gay villages. Such areas represent gay-friendly oases in otherwise hostile cities, or simply have high concentrations of gay residents or businesses. They contain a number of gay-oriented establishments, such as gay hotels, bars, pubs, nightclubs, bathhouses, restaurants, bookstores, and other businesses. Manhattan is the site of gay villages Christopher Street, the birthplace of the gay liberation movement, Greenwich Village and Chelsea. Vancouver is the site of gay village Davie Village, home of Davie Street Festival which is held in conjunction with Vancouver's annual Gay Pride Parade. Gay tourism often coincide with special gay events such as annual gay pride parades, gay neighbourhood festivals and such gay community gatherings as gay chorus festivals and concerts, gay square dancing conventions, gay sports meets like Gay Games, World Outgames or Eurogames and conferences of national and international gay organisations. Manhattan holds enormous annual gay pride parade. Chicago has large gay pride parade in June, gay neighbourhood festival in August and hosts Gay Games in summer 2006. San Francisco has an enormous gay pride parade in June and such world-famous street festivals as the Folsom Street Fair, the Castro Street Fair and the Halloween festivities in the Castro. The Castro is the street in San Francisco, which is best known for being the heart of San Francisco's gay community. Mexican coastal city Cancun holds annual Cancun International Gay Festival in May. Travel analysts state that the existence of a core gay friendly population is often the primary catalyst for the development of gay hotels. According to Tourism Intelligence International, some 10% of international tourists are gay or lesbians, accounting for more than 70 million arrivals worldwide. This important market segment is expected to continue to grow as a result of a change in a world-wide attitude to homosexuality. American gay and lesbian tourists are estimated to generate $54.1 bn a year-about 10% of the total US travel industry. Travel companies have become aware of the substantial money produced by this marketing niche, and have started to introduce new gay tourism campaigns.

## FAMILY HOTELS

If you are the parents of young children, planning a holiday for you inevitably means putting the kids' needs first and your own desires second. Nowadays, however, it is not always so. There are plenty of family hotels and resorts that provide comfortable rest for every member of the family.

If you are the parents of young children, planning a holiday for you inevitably means putting the kids' needs first and your own desires second. Nowadays, however, it is not always so. There are plenty of family hotels and resorts that provide comfortable rest for every member of the family. Family hotels and resorts have a variety of amenities which might include supervised, planned activities; fun activities like theme parks and attractions nearby; larger or themed rooms that accommodate families; or special rates and meals for kids.

There exist several hotel brands that cater for family trips. Four Seasons Hotels have locations throughout the world with amenities just for the kids. Restaurants have children's menus. The "Kids For All Seasons" program provides supervised activities which vary at each property. Most resorts have children's swimming pools and play areas. Some have cribs, roll-away beds and amenities like baby soap.

Children can really have fun at a place like Walt Disney World. It's a safe place to assert some independence from parents. When traveling to Disney World, you are sure to find plenty of family hotels nearby. With Disney World Hotels and Resorts both you and your children will have an exiting rest. Wilderness Lodge and Animal Kingdom have rooms with bunk beds available. The All-Star Resorts and Pop Century feature larger-than-life icons like 101 Dalmations and Mr. Potato Head that will delight younger children. Polynesian, Contemporary and Grand Floridian are a short monorail ride away from the Magic Kingdom.

Another popular chain of family hotels is Kimpton. These are stylish boutique hotels in metropolitan areas. Most offer family vacations that vary with the hotel. For example, the Hotel Marlow in Cambridge offers "Museum of Science" family vacations that include four VIP passes to the museum and mountain bikes. The Hotel Monaco in Denver offers "Monaco Munchkins" family vacations that include four passes to Six Flags (or to the IMAX, the Denver Zoo and the Museum of Nature & Science), a $25 gift certificate to Johnny Rockets, snacks and morning coffee. Most hotels have special programs for children.

The "Loews Loves Kids" program at the Loews hotel was developed in conjunction with Parenting magazine. Family amenities vary by hotel, but generally include children's menus, board game and video libraries, welcome gifts and supervised children's programs. Ritz-Carlton, worldwide luxury hotel chain has an extensive "Ritz Kids" program that caters to family vacations. Amenities vary at each hotel. Babies in Hong Kong can enjoy a butler-drawn bath, while families vacationing in Cancun can request quiet suites with phones that light up instead of ringing. Kids in Grand Cayman kayak and snorkel, while in Orlando families enjoy dive-in movies and take golf lessons. Most locations have creative "Healthy Taste" children's menus, and some have special kid suites.

Other family hotel brands include Hilton, Hyatt, Westin, Radisson and Marriott. You might not necessarily choose these chains, but before booking a hotel for family vacation, you should consider the possibilities offered for your kid. Inquire about the supervised activities provided for your children's age-group, what they include and if they cost extra. You might also need to know if a hotel has a baby-sitting service and an on-site doctor or registered nurse. Most hotels have a swimming pool, but ask if there is a shallow end for children or separate toddler's pool.

Thankfully more and more resorts now have websites, so you can often preview rooms as well as the pool and the resort itself. Bear in mind that if you are a family with three or more kids many family travel arrangements-such as 'kids stay and eat free'-are restricted to one child per paying adult. Bear in mind, too, that sometimes a maximum of four individuals are allowed per room. Many family resorts have family suites or cottages that can accommodate a larger family, but expect to pay extra money. Finally, remember it's not just the facilities that matter, but a relaxed, kid-friendly atmosphere of family hotels which can make all the difference.

## DOUBLETREE HOTELS

With a growing collection of upscale accommodations in more than 150 gateway cities, metropolitan areas and vacation destinations throughout the U.S., Canada and Latin America, Doubletree Hotel chain features distinctively designed properties that provide true comfort to today's business and leisure travellers. With a growing collection of upscale accommodations in more than 150 gateway cities, metropolitan areas and vacation destinations throughout the U.S., Canada and Latin America, Doubletree Hotel chain features distinctively designed properties that provide true comfort to today's business and leisure travellers.

The first Doubletree Hotel was opened in 1969, and then Doubletree Corporation was formed in 1994, following the merger of Guest Quarters Suites Hotels and Doubletree Hotels. Since 1999 Doubletree Hotel is a part of Hilton Hotels Corporation. Now Doubletree Hotel brand has rapidly expanded in such cities as Dallas, Chicago, Atlanta and Toronto. These properties offer unique, contemporary upscale accommodations and full-service facilities and amenities, including restaurants and lounges, room service, health clubs, business centers and extensive meeting and banquet space. At Doubletree, "service" is more than just giving guests a quick and efficient check-in and a clean room. Doubletree is committed to providing more than what guests when staying at any of the brand's 160 properties in the US, Canada and Latin America.

Doubletree Hotel CARE program is the key to developing relationship with guests and obtaining their loyalty. CARE stands for Caring, Attentive, Responsive, and Empowered. The CARE concept grew out of the belief that if you treat guests and team members with CARE they'll stay with you. At check in already each guest is presented with chocolate chip cookie that is baked fresh daily at each property. Synonymous with Doubletree hospitality, the cookie has played a starring role in differentiating the Doubletree Hotel brand from its competition. The chain is constantly improving the service and a new Sweet Dreams program has been introduced recently. At Doubletree, old beds are moving out and new luxurious beds are on their way in. New beds are beautiful with elegant decorative bedcovers and also have plush top-mattresses for a comfortable rest.

Each Doubletree Hotel offers not only a comfortable stay, but also great opportunities for those traveling on business. It has a nationwide collection of conference centers that meet the stringent standards of the International Association of Conference Centers (IACC). These dedicated small-to-medium-sized meeting facilities are custom-built to meet all IACC specifications for the most productive meetings, training sessions, corporate retreats and much more. Every Doubletree Hotel has an innovative guest technology package that includes high-speed Internet access and printing service. All Doubletree Hotels in North America have high-speed Internet access available in all guestrooms. Several Doubletree Hotels in major metropolitan areas across the U.S. have wireless high-speed Internet access.

Today's Doubletree Hotel brand is experiencing an incredible resurgence in growth. With 15 new hotels joining the brand in 2005 and an additional 25 Doubletree deals in various stages of planning and/or development, Doubletree has set an aggressive goal to increase their current hotel portfolio to 200 full-service hotels throughout North America and Latin America by 2008. Doubletree's success is measured by customer loyalty, which includes three key dimensions that work together to build commitment to the Doubletree brand: customer satisfaction with products and services, willingness to return and willingness to recommend Doubletree Hotel to others.

## COUNTRY HOTELS

Country hotels are gaining popularity as people are becoming tired of noisy cities and are willing to enjoy healthy and harmonious atmosphere of the country. Fresh air, beautiful surroundings, spa and sport facilities together with country hospitality guarantee comfortable rest in any season.

Country hotels are gaining popularity as people are becoming tired of noisy cities and are willing to enjoy healthy and harmonious atmosphere of the country. Fresh air, beautiful surroundings, spa and sport facilities together with country hospitality guarantee comfortable rest in any season. Country hotels offer five star luxury and service, including superb cuisine. Warm decor and cozy rooms will make you feel right at home.

It is an ideal place to relax, to forget about your troubles and sorrows, to feel at peace with yourself. You'll be greeted by a friendly staff, who is always eager to meet your individual requirements. Country hotels are perfect for leisure, as have spa and outdoor facilities; the latter may include a swimming pool, golf courses, rugby, fishing and so on. Country hotels are also great for conferences and meetings of any kind. A business meeting in the natural healthy environment is sure to produce more efficient ideas and solutions than an ordinary office discussion. Most country hotels have meeting rooms for that purpose. However, country hotels do not specialize mostly on business travellers. They provide ideal venues for weddings and ceremonies. A romantic countryside location will emphasize the beauty and glamour of the party. Besides, country hotels are a good issue for elderly people, who obviously want a quiet, peaceful rest, far away from bustling towns.

Country hotels are common in Europe, North and South America, Africa, Middle East and some other places. But it goes without saying that the key provider of country hotels is Great Britain. Probably, because of outstanding landscapes, or, may be, well-established traditions of gardening. In general, the British have greater experience of living in the country than other people. New country hotels start to appear in UK, marrying modern style with luxury and spa facilities. Hotel spas offer the chance to have a relaxing treatment, or even just a soothing swim. In these hotels, the accent is made on soft, fluffy beds, indulgent food, fantastic wines and lots of lounging around on plump sofas in front of open fires or beautiful views-you can call it a spa treatment or all-round sensuous experience.

The world famous chain of country hotels is Country Inns & Suites By Carlson, part of Carlson Hotels Worldwide. Founded in 1987, this lodging concept consists of over 320 locations all around the world in the U.S., Canada, Germany, Austria, England, France, Indonesia, India, Mexico and Panama. Country hotels are luxurious places to stay; therefore the prices are quite high. It is a considerably new type of accommodation that is developing rapidly. Perhaps, country hotels with warm atmosphere and all the amenities of five star hotels will be the number one in hotel business in future.

## AIRPORT HOTELS

People who worry about traveling and spending time in public places might be relieved to learn that most airport hotels are pretty safe places to be, offering almost the same quality of service as city hotels.

People who worry about traveling and spending time in public places might be relieved to learn that most airport hotels are pretty safe places to be, offering almost the same quality of service as city hotels. Airport hotels can be a good way out for businessmen, coming to international meetings from all parts of the world. In particular, airport hotels work best for short duration meetings-boards, executive councils, committees and training sessions.

The members can fly in, take a shuttle to an airport hotel and leave the same way. It is really very practical, especially in some places like Northern California, where the lack of public transportation makes airport hotels with courtesy shuttles very desirable for such kinds of meetings. The company doesn't have to rent a car to take members to the hotel in that case. Airport hotels lessen corporate costs. Accommodation at airport hotels is cheaper, compared to their city counterparts. That's due to far fewer amenities, from stylish rooms to choice of dining and shopping experiences. But if you're flying in to work, that shouldn't be a drawback. All you need is to stay in a well-maintained hotel and have a brief meal off the airport grounds.

However, airport hotels are popular not only with business travellers, but with leisure travellers as well. If you have a morning flight, you can book a room at an airport hotel with several days parking. That's much better than rising in the middle of the night, driving to the airport in the dark, and boarding your plane already near exhaustion. You can stay at the airport hotel the night before travel, sleep much later than you would otherwise, and walk out the door of their hotel to board the hotel shuttle right to the terminal. On return, you take the same hotel shuttle back to the hotel parking, get in your car, and head for home. Although extra money will be spent on parking, for those who can afford it, it's really very convenient.

According to PKF Consulting, an American consulting company, airport hotels nationwide have had even higher occupancy levels in recent years than their city counterparts. That's not surprising, as airport hotels seem to be very competitive, offer good service for a less price. Another plus is convenient location, within easy reach of an airport. Take into consideration the increasing number of short international meetings, and you'll understand why airport hotels are so popular. They may not be glamorous, but very functional indeed!

## IRC Americas Program Investigative Series

The concept of city has traditionally been assumed to be synonymous with progress, with new and better job opportunities, and therefore with economic well-being and a "modern" lifestyle. In addition, voices questioning urban sprawl have usually been accused of being enemies of progress and change, derided as being enamoured of the status quo, and demonized before the public, all while the cities are circled by shantytowns and plagued by growing unemployment, the spread of the informal sector, and inadequate medical, educational, and recreational services. Things are turning out differently in Loreto, Baja California Sur, which the National Tourism Promotion Fund (Fonatur), a federal agency, plans to turn into a large international-class tourist attraction by building hotels, condominiums, marinas, and villas, mainly for U.S. and Canadian tourists. This could lead to a tenfold increase in the town's population by 2025. Fonatur's plans were backed by the municipal government through its proposed "Subregional Urban Development Program for the Loreto-Nopolo-Notri-Puerto Escondido-Ligüi-Ensenada Blanca region."

The program was met by a united response from loretanos, academics, services providers, and social organizations. After numerous meetings, including at the regional level and with outside participants, most notably from Harvard University, these stakeholders drafted an alternative growth plan and a series of proposals that are currently being analyzed by the town council. They oppose following in the footsteps of San José del Cabo and Cabo San Lucas, better known as "Los Cabos," once quiet fishing villages whose physiognomy and customs have changed at a dizzying pace. Indeed, Los Cabos have now emerged as Baja California's leading international destination for sand and sun, sportfishing, and adventure tourism.

Loretanos have also kept a close eye on events in the state capital, La Paz, where urban growth has led to the building of shopping malls, hotels, and marinas for yachts, mostly from the United States, on what used to be public beaches. Urban growth has destroyed the flora and fauna, while coastal fishermen point to that growth as one, but not the only, reason for the dwindling number of fish species. At the same time, there is growing social discontent because the construction projects prevent local residents from using paths that are now exclusively for the new owners. The citizen-participation process and the outcome of this process in Loreto will provide lessons for those in other parts of Mexico facing the challenge of unbridled urban growth at the expense of the destruction of natural resources and a lower quality of life. The experience has required resorting to legal resources and planning instruments available to the federal, state, and municipal governments; alternative forms of organizing, which allow for consensus-building among stakeholders as different as business people and residents who depend on the ocean for their livelihood; as well as international and local organizations. All of the stakeholders come together in meetings to take part in decisions on projects that affect the environment and pose a menace to future generations.

Whether by air, land, or sea, the view upon arriving at the town of Loreto is spectacular. Loreto is bordered on one side by the Sea of Cortez, with its range of blue hues and island-dotted waters; on the other, by the Giganta mountain range. The town boasts a history that goes back to pre-Hispanic times and a great wealth of terrestrial and marine natural resources. Most of this peaceful town's 15,000 residents are services providers and fishers. Loreto, Ixtapa-Zihuatanejo, Los Cabos, and Cancun were Mexico's emblematic tourism projects in the 1970s. Plans for Loreto stalled because of its remoteness from central Mexico and the paucity of public and private investment. As far back as 1976, Fonatur planned Loreto as the main residential area for the local population, Nopolo as the hotel, tourist and real-estate area, and Puerto Escondido as the harbour.

**No Limits and in a Hurry**

The "Subregional Urban Development Program for the Loreto-Nopolo-Notri-Puerto Escondido-Ligüi-Ensenada Blanca Region" picks up where that original plan left off. Of several possible scenarios proposed for 2025, the one that was selected purports to allow for "balanced and decentralized growth, with support villages, creating attractive areas for urban development outside of Loreto and Nopolo, locating new infrastructure in those areas to meet the needs of the population in Ensenada Blanca, Ligüi, Puerto Escondido and Notri." The program calls for the construction of 13,000 tourism-related rooms in three stages. These rooms are expected to attract 126,561 new inhabitants, that is, nearly 10 for each new room, including labourers and their family members and other in-migrants.

This ambitious plan sparked a controversy, which heated up further when Harvard University released the results of a study titled Alternative Futures for the Region of Loreto, Baja California Sur, Mexico, written in conjunction with researchers from the Autonomous University of Baja California Sur, the University of Arizona, the Centro de Investigaciones del Noroeste, San Diego State University, and other institutions.

In the opinion of Sergio Morales Polo, leader of Grupo Ecologista Antares, the new drive to develop Loreto comes from the fact that the federal government's proposed Escalera Nautica project has not produced the desired outcomes. "We thought their project was too big and, in addition, they wanted to submit a single environmental impact statement for the 27 marinas, but we succeeded in having them commit to submit one for each one and to reduce the number of marinas." Morales Polo says that the project "gradually lost steam, and the financial backing was to come from private investors, but given the country's economic conditions, they are unlikely to come onboard." More than 300 years after being founded, the municipality of Loreto is home to some 15,000 people. The program proposes a tenfold growth in just 20 years.

"The truth is, the project scared us," says Rodolfo Palacios, of Loreto 2025, a citizens' organization made up of owners of hotels, restaurants, and vehicle-rental agencies; academics; fishers; and services providers. Loreto 2025 and the Loreto Hotel Association submitted observations on the Subregional Program at the public-comment consultation held by the municipal government.

"The municipal government is now analyzing the proposals and will have to explain why it did or did not decide to take them into consideration," Palacios says. The report coordinated by Harvard argues that the Program's projected population growth, based on the number of rooms, falls short, since experiences in other tourist destinations assume a population-to-room ratio of 15 to 1, rather than the 10 to 1 assumption used in the municipal government's document. If the number of rooms is assumed to be 12,000, that is, 1,000 fewer than in the original proposal, and the ratio of population to residents is 20 to 1, Loreto's population will grow to 240,000. This is equivalent to an average annual growth rate of 14.9%. Local residents reject such a future and find it unimaginable.

Richard Kiy, president of the International Community Foundation, which sponsored the Alternative Futures report, is categorical: "You don't go from 15,000 to 240,000 people overnight without regretting the consequences." He adds that he hopes the report will serve as an instrument for the people of Loreto to think about the long-term growth of the region, because the growth called for in government plans will have a "tsunami effect."

In the least drastic scenario described in the report-2,000 new rooms and 15 residents per room-the population will double in 20 years, for an average annual growth rate of 3.5%. An adage rooted in popular wisdom advises "paso a paso se llega mas lejos" (roughly, "slow and steady wins the race"), and this adage could well be applied to urban-growth planning.

## The Water Limit

The main constraint on the region's development is the lack of water. Residents now get their water from an aquifer

30 km. away, in San Juan Londo. Pumping already outstrips recharge, and the aquifer is under additional strain to meet demand for new livestock projects. Alternative Futures states that "any future development must find an alternative water source for that development and the associated growth in supporting population." But, as often occurs in many parts of Mexico, events on the ground have overtaken the plans: The Loreto Bay Company is already constructing, as stated in its plans, 6,000 villas for the Canadian and U.S. market, on 3,200 hectares of land. Also planned are two 18-hole golf courses, a tennis center, a marina, a sportfishing center, a beach club, restaurants, boutiques, art galleries, and a market. The company says it agrees with "environmental conservation, job creation, and the commitment to devote a portion of proceeds from home sales to developing the community of Loreto, in addition to setting aside 2,000 hectares as a natural reserve. Being a sustainable community also means producing more drinking water than we consume, which will enrich existing streams and marshes and encourage the biodiversity of the land on which the villas sit"-according to the company's website.

Several groups believe the Loreto Bay project is too big and will have disastrous consequences. "Each [tourism-related] room generates 20 new residents, consisting of five employees plus three relatives each; that makes 15, and the remaining five might be unplanned in-migrants, seeking adventure. The intention is to construct 6,000 villas, each one with two dwellings, which adds up to 12,000 rooms, and [multiplying this] by 20 persons results in 240,000 new residents, yet Loreto only has water for 60,000 people," argues Morales Polo, whose Loreto-based group belongs to the Network of Environmental Organizations of Baja California Sur (Rocas).

Loretanos ask that the number of rooms be reduced from 6,000 to 2,000, since not only Nopolo but also the surrounding areas are slated for development. "We are pressuring the town council to scale it down and put very tight locks on the development plan and reduce the number of rooms per hectare. They are now constructing an Infonavit [National Fund for Worker Housing] complex, but a deluxe one; they try to use land to the utmost and they ruin the landscape. That is going to lead to overcrowding," says Morales Polo, adding that it is unclear how Loreto Bay is going to solve issues such as garbage, water, or electricity. "At the beginning, about two years ago, we did not have a clear idea of the magnitude of the project, but in the last year we have seen that this was going to be serious and that was when we decided to participate," he says.

Nevertheless, mayor Rodolfo Davis Osuna believes that the Subregional Program is viable since it has a very low density and impact. "If in this tourist corridor in Loreto, we were to copy a Cancun-, Los Cabos-, or Ixtapa-style development, for example, we would have 45,000 more rooms and more than 450,000 residents. That's not what we are doing," he said at a forum on funding drinking water and other critical infrastructure projects in Baja California Sur, last October.

The previous mayor also ignored Alternative Futures estimates on water availability, which were based on mathematical models and geographic information system data, among others. "He has told us that there is no water. Very knowledgeable voices from outside, with every intention to help, tell us that our main source of water, San Juan Londo, can only sustain 20,000 residents. They tell us that to grow more would mean depleting that aquifer sooner or later," the former mayor said at that time, claiming that Loreto pumps 9.7 million liters of water from the aquifer, of which a large quantity is wasted due to inefficient management. He also claimed that a modern, efficient system would provide water for 35,000 residents without pumping one more cubic meter from San Juan Londo, and he asked for financing for this purpose.

What is clear, as Kiy notes, is that "It is irresponsible to plan a large-scale development without determining where the water and energy will come from," and he explains that those are the reasons for which Loreto has not seen much development. The water situation in Loreto is uncertain and the only point nearly all stakeholders agree on is that there is not enough of it. The Loreto Hotel Association, in one of the proposals submitted at the public consultation on the Subregional

Program, is emphatic on this point: " Because of the high degree of uncertainty on the amount of water available, we propose strictly limiting the number of hotel rooms to 3,500, which implies a population of 59,500 ." The Association also advises that development be gradual until conclusive studies have been completed.

The Association points out, moreover, that the estimated figure of 10 million cubic meters of annual recharge given in the 1986 geohydrological study of the San Juan Londo basin by the National Autonomous University of Mexico (UNAM) is impossible, since, according to the National Water Commission, average annual precipitation is 5.9 million cubic meters. The Association adds that the mathematical model used by the University of Arizona estimates a maximum annual recharge of two million cubic meters. Currently, three million cubic meters are being pumped for Loreto and four million cubic meters for the agricultural area of San Juan Londo. Hence, based on per-inhabitant consumption data, in the best case scenario, water availability limits growth to 30,000 residents, while in the worse case scenario, the aquifer is currently being overpumped and will experience saline intrusion between 2015 and 2025, even without population growth.

**New Types of Constraints**

In addition to the Loreto Hotel Association, Loreto 2025, and Antares, the Niparaja civic organization and the director of the Loreto Bay National Park also submitted observations and recommendations. In general, they agree on the need for reasonable growth and on making water the priority for any scenario. At the same time, they stress various issues that illustrate the value locals place on factors such as landscape, marine fauna, wetlands, and the poor example they believe is being set by the explosive growth of the Los Cabos region in recent years. "In Cabo San Lucas you go to the beaches and you find all kinds of trash-diapers, plastic, bottles, and now street vendors are proliferating. It seems that residents are bewildered by the change to the city, they still haven't grasped how ugly it has become, there are many complaints over the lack of services. Fifteen years ago, the town was not half what it is now," says Jorge Luis Diaz Calderon, an employee at the Cabo San Lucas Marina, who prefers going for walks on the beaches in La Paz.

Another of the constraints referred to by the members of Hotel Association is the need to avoid the destruction of wetlands proposed in the Subregional Program. They see a contradiction between the intention to channel the streams and dry the wetlands and that of using the land for the real-estate industry. The criticism leveled by the hotel industry extends to the government's plans to locate tourist facilities on property facing the most popular beaches of the region, Chuenque and La Salinita. "Nothing should allow them to be above the collective interest of our town, which seeks to protect its identity, conserve its quality of life, and preserve the ecological wealth of our environment and the harmonious growth of the city," the Association said in a document delivered to the municipal authorities and signed by its president, Gilberto Amador Davis.

Niparaja is opposed to the Subregional Program being accepted in its current form-among other reasons, because it is not based on a comprehensive environmental assessment and it proposes land-use density policies that disregard the natural potential and attributes of the sites. Niparaja recommends exercising caution and immediately initiating a comprehensive water management master plan, and says the town council should set up an information system comprised of a property registry, and data on and water, ecology, and municipal services.

Regarding Loreto Bay National Park, Niparaja's proposal, delivered to the mayor's office and signed by Gabriela Anaya Reyna, the organization's executive director, asks that development modalities and projections be reconsidered once the park's carrying capacity is known. To determine its carrying capacity, Niparaja suggests drafting a technical study to determine the impact of the desalination plants, compiling an inventory of the main point and non-point sources of pollution in the coastal area, as well as monitoring the quality of the seawater and the accumulation of toxins in marine species as bioindicators of contamination. For its part, Grupo Antares demands the inclusion of subprograms designed to take each community's specific characteristics into account. This would add San Nicolas, Juncalito, and San Bruno-El Mango to the communities already included (Loreto, Nopolo, Notri, Ensenada Blanca, Puerto Escondido, Ligüi, and El Bajo-San Basilio). The group also asks that important areas overlooked by the Subregional Program be addressed, including oases, estuaries, wetlands, mangroves, streams, and reefs. It notes that the number of green areas is insufficient and asks that the municipal landfill be relocated once the required technical study has been conducted.

The office in charge of Loreto Bay National Park, headed by Roberto Lopez Espinosa de los Monteros, is concerned by the Subregional Program, "because it lacks a sustainable and comprehensive vision of the development of Loreto and, consequently, of the national park." Among other objections, park officials point out that the program overlooks potential impacts on or changes in the park resulting from population growth. Lopez Espinosa recognizes that failing to take these impacts into account will put ecosystems and species at irreversible risk by giving massive numbers of visitors access to island ecosystems, beaches, diving sites, bird breeding colonies, sea lion resting sites, and the feeding and breeding grounds and migratory routes of various marine mammals that pass through the park. In addition, he warns of a possible collapse of the stocks of commercial and sport fish. Like the civic organizations, the park directors request new studies on the water situation and a reduction in population growth projections. According to Kiy, the challenge is to preserve such a sensitive ecosystem, which has remained undisturbed for thousands of years. Unlike Los Cabos, Loreto's appeal is ecotourism, the beauty of the landscape, sportfishing, Concepcion Bay, and the Giganta mountain range. "The risk of developing too quickly is that you kill the goose that laid the golden egg," Kiy says, adding that, in any event, "the entire area of the Sea of Cortez is going to change."

10

# Uniform Conditions

The Uniform Conditions for the Hotel and Catering Industry (UVH) are the terms and conditions on which catering establishments set up in the Netherlands, such as hotels, restaurants, bars and related businesses (including catering firms, party service firms, etc.), provide catering services and enter into catering agreements. The UVH are registered with the District Court and the Chamber of Commerce and Industry in The Hague.

**DEFINITIONS**

In the UVH and in the offers and agreements to which the UVH applies, the words below shall have the meanings assigned to them in this clause.

*1.1 Catering Establishment*

The natural person or legal entity or partnership which is in the business of providing hotel and/or catering services and is a member of Koninklijk Horeca Nederland (Dutch trade association for hotel and catering industry).

*1.2 Host*

Whoever represents a Catering Establishment in entering into and carrying out catering agreements.

*1.3 Provision of Catering Services*

The provision by a Catering Establishment of accommodation and/or food and/or drink and/or the supplying of halls and/or rooms and/or grounds, all these with all the associated work and services, and all in the broadest sense of the word.

*1.4 Customer*

The natural person or legal entity or partnership which has entered into an agreement with a Catering Establishment.

*1.5 Guest*

The natural person(s) entitled to one or more Catering Services based on a catering agreement entered into with the Customer. Wherever the UVH speak of Guest, or Customer, this refers to both Guest and Customer, unless it is clear from the content and implication of the clause that only one of the two can be intended.

*1.6 Catering Agreement*

An agreement between a Catering Establishment and a Customer involving one or more Catering Services to be provided by the Catering Establishment at a price to be paid by the Customer. The term Reservation is sometimes used in place of the term Catering Agreement.

*1.7 Hotel Establishment*

The Catering Establishment where the provision of Catering Services consists mainly or exclusively of supplying accommodation.

*1.8 Restaurant Establishment*

The Catering Establishment where the provision of Catering Services consists mainly or exclusively of supplying food and accompanying drink.

*1.9 Bar Establishment*

The Catering Establishment where the provision of Catering Services consists mainly or exclusively of supplying drink.

*1.10 Room Rental Establishment*

The Catering Establishment where the provision of Catering Services consists mainly or exclusively of providing rooms or halls.

*1.11 Reservation Value (the value of the Catering Agreement)*

The total expected turnover of the Catering Establishment including service charges, (tourist tax) and VAT relating to a

Catering Agreement concluded with a Customer, which expected turnover is based on the averages applicable to that Catering Establishment.

*1.12 Koninklijk Horeca Nederland*

Het Koninklijk Verbond van Ondernemers in het Horeca- en Aanverwante Bedrijf (The Royal Association of Businesses in the Catering and Related Industries) known as "Horeca Nederland" or any legal successor to this.

*1.13 Cancellation*

The written notice by the Customer to the Catering Establishment that one or more of the agreed Catering Services is no longer required in part or in full, or the written notice by the Catering Establishment to the Customer that one or more of the agreed Catering Services shall no longer be provided in part or in full.

*1.14 No-show*

The failure of a Guest, without prior Cancellation, to make use of one of the Catering Services provided on the basis of a Catering Agreement.

*1.15 Group*

A group of 10 or more persons entitled to one or more Catering Services from a Catering Establishment under the terms of a Catering Agreement or more than one agreement regarded as connected.

*1.16 Individual*

Every person that does not form part of a Group as defined above.

*1.17 Goods*

All Goods, including money, valuables and papers of value.

*1.18 Corkage*

The price charged when drink not provided by a Catering Establishment is consumed on the premises of that Catering Establishment.

*1.19 Food Charge*

The price charged when food not provided by a Catering Establishment is consumed on the premises of that Catering Establishment.

*1.20 Turnover Guarantee*

A written declaration from the Customer that the Catering Establishment will realise a certain minimum turnover from one or more Catering Agreements.

Clause headings are used exclusively for reference purposes. No rights may be derived from these.

**SCOPE**

2.1 The UVH apply to the making and content of all Catering Agreements, as well as all offers relating to the making of such Catering Agreements, to the exclusion of all other general terms and conditions. If other general terms and conditions besides these are actually in force, the UVH shall prevail where any conflict arises.

2.2 Departure from the UVH is only possible if set down in writing and on a case by case basis.

2.3 The UVH also cover all natural persons and legal entities which the Catering Establishment uses or has used in concluding and/or carrying out a Catering Agreement or a different agreement or in running the Catering Establishment.

2.4 Once the UVH have been declared legally applicable to a certain Catering Agreement, then the latest valid version of the UVH is considered to apply to all subsequent Catering Agreements between the same parties, unless agreed otherwise in writing.

**THE MAKING OF CATERING AGREEMENTS**

3.1 A Catering Establishment can at any time and for any reason refuse to enter into a Catering Agreement, except where such a refusal is based purely on one or more of the grounds specified in Clause 429 of the Criminal Code (discrimination).

3.2 All offers presented by a Catering Establishment in connection with the making of a Catering Agreement are without obligation and conditional "on the supply (or capacity) being adequate". If the Catering Establishment invokes the said restriction within a period which can be considered reasonable in the circumstances following the Customer's acceptance of the offer then the intended Catering Agreement shall be considered not to be made.

3.3 If the Catering Establishment has granted the Customer (option holder) a right of first refusal, this right cannot be revoked, except if and insofar as another potential Customer makes an offer to the Catering Establishment to enter into a Catering Agreement concerning all or part of the Catering Services due in the option. In that case the option holder must be informed of this offer by the Catering Establishment, whereupon the option holder must state whether or not he wishes to take up the right of first refusal.

If the option holder does not give notice that he wishes to take up the right of first refusal then this right shall lapse. A right of first refusal can only be granted in writing.

3.4 Catering Agreements for one or more Guests entered into by intermediaries (shipbrokers, travel agencies, other Catering Establishments, etc.), whether or not in the name of their business connection(s), shall be considered to be concluded partly for account and risk of this intermediary. The Catering Establishment shall not owe any commission or percentage, by whatever name, to the intermediary unless specifically agreed otherwise in writing. Payment by the Guest of the whole or part of the amount due shall release the intermediary to the same extent.

## GENERAL OBLIGATIONS OF THE CATERING ESTABLISHMENT

4.1 The obligations specified in this clause apply to every Catering Establishment. All obligations arising from the special nature of the Catering Establishment and the type of Catering Services to be performed are contained in the following clauses.

4.2 In the event that the special regulation referred to in Clauses 5 et seq. is at variance with a general stipulation in subclauses 4.3-4.7, the special regulation shall apply.

4.3 Under the terms of the Catering Agreement, the Catering Establishment is, without prejudice to the stipulations in the following clauses, bound to provide the agreed Catering Services at the agreed times in the manner customary in that Catering Establishment.

4.4 The obligation mentioned in Clause 4.3 does not apply:

1. in the event of force majeure on the side of the Catering Establishment as defined in Clause 15;
2. if the Guest fails to arrive or arrives more than half an hour late;
3. if the Customer's payment of the guarantee deposit/ interim payment referred to in Clause 10 is not made in good time;
4. if the Customer fails to provide a Turnover Guarantee in good time, despite a request to do so;
5. if the Customer in any other way fails to fulfil all his obligations towards the Catering Establishment in whatever respect.

4.5 The Catering Establishment is not obliged to accept and/or take into safe keeping any property of the Guest.

4.6 If the Catering Establishment makes any charge to the Guest for accepting Goods and/or taking Goods into safe keeping, the Catering Establishment is obliged to take reasonable care of those Goods, without prejudice to the stipulations in Clause 12.

4.7 The Catering Establishment is never obliged to admit any domestic animal belonging to the Guest and may attach conditions to such admission.

## OBLIGATIONS OF THE HOTEL ESTABLISHMENT

5.1 The Hotel Establishment is during the agreed period obliged to provide the Guest with accommodation of the standard customary in that hotel, subject to the stipulations in the third subclause.

5.2 The Hotel Establishment must also be able to provide the associated Catering Services customary in that hotel and to supply the facilities customary there.

5.3 The accommodation should be available to the Guest from 14.00 hours on the day of arrival until 12 noon on the day of departure.

5.4 The Hotel Establishment should hang or affix or deposit the house rules in a clearly visible place for the information of the Guest, or hand over the house rules in writing to the Guest. The Guest is obliged to observe the house rules.

5.5 The Hotel Establishment is entitled to terminate the provision of Catering Services to a Guest at any time without prior notice if the Guest repeatedly breaks the house rules, or otherwise behaves in such a way that the order and peace and quiet in the Catering Establishment and/or the normal running of the place may be or is disturbed. In that case the Guest must leave the hotel at the first request. The Hotel Establishment may only exercise this right if the nature and seriousness of the breaches of the house rules by the guest give sufficient cause, in the reasonable opinion of the Hotel Establishment.

5.6 Unless otherwise agreed, the Hotel Establishment is entitled to regard the reservation as cancelled if the Guest has not checked in on the first day of the reservation by 18.00 hours, without prejudice to the stipulations in Clause 9.

5.7 The Hotel Establishment is entitled to ask the Guest to accept accommodation that differs from what is described in the Catering Agreement, except if such a request is clearly unreasonable and must be considered obviously too inconvenient for the Guest. In the latter case, the Guest/Customer has the right to cancel the Catering Agreement to which the aforementioned request of the Catering Establishment applies, with immediate effect, without prejudice to his obligations based on other Catering Agreements.

If the Catering Establishment saves money in the above circumstances by providing accommodation that differs from what is described in the Catering Agreement, the Guest and/ or Customer is entitled to the amount that is saved. Beyond that the Catering Establishment shall never be obliged to pay any compensation.

## OBLIGATIONS OF THE RESTAURANT ESTABLISHMENT

6.1 The Restaurant Establishment is obliged to provide the Guest with the agreed facilities at the agreed time and to supply the agreed food and drink in the quantity, quality and in the manner customary in that restaurant.

6.2 If no food and drink are agreed in advance then the Restaurant Establishment shall on request provide whatever food and drink is available at that moment, without prejudice to the other stipulations in Clause 6.1.

6.3 The Restaurant Establishment is entitled to refrain from providing Catering Services or to terminate these at any time if the Guest does not behave in a way that is fitting to the class and operation of that restaurant. The Restaurant Establishment may, among other things, lay down rules concerning the outward appearance of the Guest. The Guest must leave the restaurant at the first request.

6.4 If the Guest has not arrived by half an hour after the reserved time, the Restaurant Establishment may consider the reservation cancelled, without prejudice to the stipulations in Clause 9.

## OBLIGATIONS OF THE BAR ESTABLISHMENT

7.1 The Bar Establishment is obliged on request to provide the Guest with the drinks which it has in stock. In addition the Bar Establishment must be able to provide the Catering Services customary in that establishment.

7.2 The Bar Establishment is entitled to refrain from providing Catering Services or to terminate these at any time if the Guest does not behave in a way that is fitting to the class and operation of that bar. The Bar Establishment may, among other things, lay down rules concerning the outward appearance of the Guest. The Guest must leave the bar at the first request.

## OBLIGATIONS OF THE CATERING ESTABLISHMENT CONCERNING ROOM RENTAL

8.1 The Catering Establishment is entitled to provide rooms that differ from what is described in the Catering Agreement, except if such a request is clearly unreasonable and must be considered obviously too inconvenient for the Guest. In the latter case, the Guest/Customer has the right to cancel the Catering Agreement to which the aforementioned request of the Catering Establishment applies, with immediate effect, without prejudice to his obligations based on other Catering Agreements. If the Catering Establishment saves money in the above circumstances by providing rooms that differ from what is described in the Catering Agreement, the Guest and/or Customer is entitled to the amount that is saved. Beyond that the Catering Establishment shall never be obliged to pay any compensation.

8.2 The Catering Establishment must in addition be able to provide the Guests with the Catering Services customary in that establishment.

8.3 The Catering Establishment is entitled to refrain from providing Catering Services or to terminate these at any time if the Guest does not behave in a way that is fitting to the class and operation of that Catering Establishment. The Catering Establishment may, among other things, lay down rules concerning the outward appearance of the Guest. The Guest must leave the Catering Establishment at the first request.

8.4 The Catering Establishment is entitled, after consultation with the competent authorities locally, to cancel the Catering Agreement on the grounds of justifiable fear that the public order may be disturbed. If the Catering Establishment makes use of this power, then the Catering Establishment shall not be liable to pay any compensation.

## CANCELLATIONS

9.1 Cancellation by Customers, general

9.1.1 The Customer is not entitled to cancel a Catering Agreement, unless he at the same time makes a binding offer to pay the amounts fixed below. Every Cancellation is considered to include such an offer. Such an offer is considered to be accepted if the Catering Establishment does not reject the offer forthwith.

Cancellation should take place in writing and be dated. The Customer cannot derive any rights from a verbal Cancellation. The stipulations in Clause 9 apply without prejudice to the stipulations in other clauses.

9.1.2 The Catering Establishment may inform the Customer at the latest one month before the first Catering Service based on the relevant Catering Agreement is due to be provided that it will regard certain Individuals as a Group. In that case all the conditions for Groups apply to those persons.

9.1.3 The stipulations in Clauses 13.1 and 14.6 also apply to Cancellations.

9.1.4 In the event of No-show, the Customer is in all cases required to pay the Reservation Value.

9.1.5 In the event that not all the agreed Catering Services are cancelled, the conditions below apply pro rata to the Catering Services that are cancelled.

9.1.6 If one or more agreed Catering Services are completely or partly cancelled, the periods in the following clauses shall be increased by 4 months, if the Reservation Value of the cancelled Catering Services amounts to more than the correspondingly calculated value of the other Catering Services that the Catering Establishment could have provided during the period in which the cancelled Catering Services were to have been provided.

9.1.7 Any amounts which the Catering Establishment already owes to third parties at the time of Cancellation based on the cancelled Catering Agreement must at all times be fully reimbursed by the Customer to the Catering Establishment, provided the Catering Establishment has not acted unreasonably in entering into the commitments in question. The amounts involved shall go towards a reduction of the Reservation Value referred to in the following clauses.

9.2 Cancellation of hotel accommodation/lodgings

9.2.1 Groups

If a reservation for only hotel accommodation is made, either with or without breakfast, for a Group then the following applies to the Cancellation of this reservation.

1. In case of Cancellation more than 3 months before the time when the first Catering Service should be provided under the terms of the Catering Agreement, hereinafter called "the Commencement Date", the Customer is not obliged to make any payment to the Hotel Establishment.
2. In case of Cancellation more than 2 months before the Commencement Date, the Customer is obliged to pay 15% of the Reservation Value to the Hotel Establishment.
3. In case of Cancellation more than 1 month before the Commencement Date, the Customer is obliged to pay 35% of the Reservation Value to the Hotel Establishment.
4. In case of Cancellation more than 14 days before the Commencement Date, the Customer is obliged to pay 60% of the Reservation Value to the Hotel Establishment.
5. In case of Cancellation more than 7 days before the Commencement Date, the Customer is obliged to pay 85% of the Reservation Value to the Hotel Establishment.
6. In case of Cancellation 7 days or less before the Commencement Date, the Customer is obliged to pay 100% of the Reservation Value to the Hotel Establishment.

9.2.2 Individuals

If a reservation for only hotel accommodation is made, either with or without breakfast, for a one or more Individuals then the following applies to the Cancellation of this reservation.

1. In case of Cancellation more than 1 month before the Commencement Date, the Customer is not obliged to pay any money to Hotel Establishment.
2. In case of Cancellation more than 14 days before the Commencement Date, the Customer is obliged

to pay 15% of the Reservation Value to the Hotel Establishment.

3. In case of Cancellation more than 7 days before the Commencement Date, the Customer is obliged to pay 35% of the Reservation Value to the Hotel Establishment.
4. In case of Cancellation more than 3 days before the Commencement Date, the Customer is obliged to pay 60% of the Reservation Value to the Hotel Establishment.
5. In case of Cancellation more than 24 hours before the Commencement Date, the Customer is obliged to pay 85% of the Reservation Value to the Hotel Establishment.
6. In case of Cancellation 24 hours or less before the Commencement Date, the Customer is obliged to pay 100% of the Reservation Value to the Hotel Establishment.

9.3 Cancellation of restaurant/table reservation

9.3.1 Groups

If a reservation for only a restaurant (table reservation) is made for a Group then the following applies to the Cancellation of that reservation:

1. if a menu has been agreed:
    1. in case of Cancellation more than 14 days before the reserved time no payment is due;
    2. in case of Cancellation 14 days or less but more than 7 days before the reserved time the Customer shall pay 25% of the Reservation Value;
    3. in case of Cancellation 7 days or less before the reserved time the Customer shall pay 50% of the Reservation Value;
    4. in case of Cancellation 3 days or less before the reserved time the Customer shall pay 75% of the Reservation Value.
2. if no menu has been agreed:
    1. in case of Cancellation more than twice 24 hours before the reserved time no payment is due;

2. in case of Cancellation twice 24 hours or less before the reserved time the Customer shall pay 50% of the Reservation Value.

9.3.2 Individuals

If a reservation for only a restaurant (table reservation) is made for one or more Individuals then the following applies to the Cancellation of that reservation:

1. if a menu has been agreed:
    1. in case of Cancellation more than four times 24 hours before the reserved time no payment is due;
    2. in case of Cancellation four times 24 hours or less before the reserved time the Customer shall pay 50% of the Reservation Value.
2. if no menu has been agreed:
    1. in case of Cancellation more than twice 24 hours before the reserved time no payment is due;
    2. in case of Cancellation twice 24 hours or less before the reserved time the Customer shall pay 50% of the Reservation Value.

9.4 Cancellation of other Catering Agreements

9.4.1 The following shall apply to the Cancellation of any reservations not covered by Clauses 9.2 and 9.3.

9.4.2 The Cancellation of a Reservation made for a group shall be subject to the following.

1. In case of Cancellation more than 6 months before the time when under the terms of the Catering Agreement the first Catering Service should be provided, the Customer is not obliged to make any payment to the Catering Establishment.
2. In case of Cancellation more than 3 months before the said time, the Customer is obliged to pay 10% of the Reservation Value to the Catering Establishment.
3. In case of Cancellation more than 2 months before the said time, the Customer is obliged to pay 15% of the Reservation Value to the Catering Establishment.

4. In case of Cancellation more than 1 month before the said time, the Customer is obliged to pay 35% of the Reservation Value to the Catering Establishment.
5. In case of Cancellation more than 14 days before the said time, the Customer is obliged to pay 60% of the Reservation Value to the Catering Establishment.
6. In case of Cancellation more than 7 days before the said time, the Customer is obliged to pay 85% of the Reservation Value to the Catering Establishment.
7. In case of Cancellation 7 days or less before the said time, the Customer is obliged to pay 100% of the Reservation Value to the Catering Establishment.

9.4.3 The Cancellation of a Reservation made for one or more individuals shall be subject tc the following.

1. In case of Cancellation more than 1 month before the time when under the terms of the Catering Agreement the first Catering Service should be provided, the Customer is not obliged to make any payment to the Catering Establishment.
2. In case of Cancellation more than 14 days before the said time, the Customer is obliged to pay 15% of the Reservation Value to the Catering Establishment.
3. In case of Cancellation more than 7 days before the said time, the Customer is obliged to pay 35% of the Reservation Value to the Catering Establishment.
4. In case of Cancellation more than 3 days before the said time, the Customer is obliged to pay 60% of the Reservation Value to the Catering Establishment.
5. In case of Cancellation more than 24 hours before the said time, the Customer is obliged to pay 85% of the Reservation Value to the Catering Establishment.
6. In case of Cancellation 24 hours or less before the said time, the Customer is obliged to pay 100% of the Reservation Value to the Catering Establishment.

9.5 Cancellation by the Catering Establishment

9.5.1 The Catering Establishment is entitled to cancel a Catering Agreement subject to the following, unless the Customer has given written notice within seven days after the signing of the said Catering Agreement requiring the Catering Establishment to waive its powers to cancel the agreement, provided that the Customer at the same time clearly states that he is also waiving his own powers to cancel the agreement.

9.5.2 If the Catering Establishment cancels a Catering Agreement to provide food and accompanying drink, the Clauses 9.1.1 and 9.3.2 apply correspondingly, transposing Customer and Catering Establishment.

9.5.3 If the Catering Establishment cancels a Catering Agreement other than the one referred to in Clause 9.5.2, then Clauses 9.1.1 and 9.2.2 apply correspondingly, transposing Customer and Catering Establishment.

9.5.4 The Catering Establishment is at all times entitled to cancel a Catering Agreement, without being obliged to pay the aforementioned amounts, if there are sufficient indications that the gathering to be held in the Catering Establishment on the grounds of the Catering Agreement is of such a different character from what might have been expected on the grounds of the Customer's statement or on the grounds of the capacity of the Customer or Guests, that the Catering Establishment would not have concluded the agreement, if it had been aware of the actual nature of the gathering. If the Catering Establishment exercises this right after the gathering in question has started, the Customer shall be obliged to pay for the Catering Services provided up to that point in time, but the Customer's obligation to pay for the rest shall cease to apply. In such an event, the payment for the Catering Services provided shall be calculated in proportion to the time the gathering was due to last.

9.5.5 Instead of exercising its right referred to in 9.5.4, the Catering Establishment is entitled to set additional requirements for the course of the gathering in question. If there are sufficient indications that these requirements are not being (or will not be) fulfilled, the Catering Establishment shall still be entitled to exercise the right referred to in 9.5.4.

9.5.6 If and insofar as the Catering Establishment also acts as a tour operator in the legal sense, the following shall apply with regard to travel agreements in the legal sense. The Catering Establishment may change an essential point in the travel agreement, owing to important circumstances that are immediately reported to the Customer. The Catering Establishment may also change a non-essential point in the travel agreement, owing to important circumstances that are immediately reported to the Customer. Up to twenty days before the commencement of travel, the Catering Establishment may increase the cost of the trip in connection with changes in the cost of transport, including fuel costs, the levies that are due, or the applicable exchange rates. If the traveller refuses to accept any such change, the Catering Establishment may cancel the travel agreement.

## GUARANTEE DEPOSIT AND INTERIM PAYMENT

10.1 The Catering Establishment can at any time require the Customer to deposit or arrange to have deposited with the Catering Establishment a guarantee deposit amounting at most to the Reservation Value less any interim payments already made. Guarantee deposits received shall be subject to proper accounting procedures, shall serve exclusively as security for the Catering Establishment and definitely do not count as already realised turnover.

10.2 The Catering Establishment can in each case ask for an interim payment for Catering Services already provided.

10.3 The Catering Establishment may recover all sums owed by the Customer on any account out of the amount deposited in accordance with the previous clauses. The balance must be repaid to the Customer by the Catering Establishment immediately.

## TURNOVER GUARANTEE

11.1 If a Turnover Guarantee is issued, the Customer is obliged to pay the Catering Establishment at least the sum determined in the Turnover Guarantee in respect of the Catering Agreements concerned.

## LIABILITY OF THE CATERING ESTABLISHMENT

12.1 The exclusion of liability in this clause does not apply insofar as the Catering Establishment has received a payment from an insurance company or from another third party relating to the risk that has materialised.

12.2 Without prejudice to the conditions in Clause 4.6, the Hotel Establishment is not liable for damage or loss of Goods which have been brought into the hotel by a Guest who is staying there. The Customer indemnifies the Hotel Establishment against claims from Guests in this respect. These stipulations do not apply insofar as the damage or loss is caused intentionally or the hotel is grossly at fault.

12.3 Without prejudice to the conditions in Clauses 12.7 and 12.8, the Catering Establishment is never liable for any damage whatsoever suffered by the Customer, the Guest and/or third parties unless the damage is caused intentionally or the Catering Establishment is grossly at fault. This liability exclusion also applies in particular to damage resulting from consuming foods prepared or served by the Catering Establishment, and to damage resulting from computer-related problems. If imperative law only permits a less extensive liability restriction, that less extensive restriction shall apply.

12.4 In no case is the Catering Establishment obliged to pay a higher sum in compensation than:

1. the Reservation Value or, if that is more,
2. (1) the amount paid out by the Catering Establishment's insurer to the Catering Establishment for the damage, or (2) the compensation for the damage received from another third party.

12.5 The Catering Establishment is never liable for damage to or caused by vehicles of the Guest, except if and insofar as the damage is caused intentionally or the Catering Establishment is grossly at fault.

12.6 The Catering Establishment is never liable for damage caused directly or indirectly to any persons or property as a direct or indirect result of any defect or any feature or circumstance on or in any moveable or immoveable property which the Catering Establishment is looking after, holding on a long or short lease, hiring or which it owns or which is in any other way at the disposal of the Catering Establishment, except if and insofar as the damage is caused intentionally or the Catering Establishment is grossly at fault.

12.7 If the Guest finds there has been any damage to the Goods placed in safe keeping, in exchange for payment as referred to in Clause 4.6, the Catering Establishment is obliged to make good the damage to these Goods resulting from their being damaged or lost. Compensation is never due in connection with other Goods contained inside the Goods which are handed in.

12.8 If the Catering Establishment accepts Goods or if Goods are deposited, left in safe keeping and/or left behind in any way, anywhere or by anyone without the Catering Establishment charging any money for this, then the Catering Establishment is never liable for damage to or in connection with those Goods however this may arise unless the Catering Establishment deliberately caused this damage, or the Catering Establishment is grossly to blame for the damage.

12.9 The Customer (not being a natural person who is not acting in the exercise of a profession or business) indemnifies the Catering Establishment in full against any claim, by whatever name, which the Guest and/or any third party may lodge against the Catering Establishment, if and insofar as this claim has any connection in the broadest sense with any (Catering) Service to be provided or which has been provided by the Catering Establishment under the terms of any agreement with the Customer or has any connection with the accommodation where such a (Catering) Service was provided or was to be provided.

12.10 The liability to indemnify referred to in Clause 12.9 also applies if the Catering Agreement with the Customer and/or the Guest is cancelled in full or in part for any reason.

## LIABILITY OF THE GUEST AND/OR CUSTOMER

13.1 The Customer and the Guest and anyone accompanying them are severally liable for all damage which has occurred and/or may occur to the Catering Establishment and/or to any third party as a direct or indirect result of any non-fulfilment of obligations (culpable deficiency) and/or wrongful action, including breaking the house rules, committed by the Customer and/or the Guest and/or anyone accompanying them, as well as for all damage caused by any animal and/or any substance and/or any article which is in their possession or which is under their supervision.

## SETTLEMENT OF ACCOUNTS AND PAYMENT

14.1 The Customer has to pay the price fixed in the Catering Agreement or, insofar as the Catering Agreement was signed more than three months before the time when the Catering Services arising out of that Agreement have to be provided, the prices which apply at the time that the Catering Service(s) has/ have to be provided, which are understood to be the prices stated on the lists displayed by the Catering Establishment in a place visible to the Guest or which are included in a list which is handed to the Customer/Guest, if necessary at the request of said Customer/Guest.

14.2 A list is considered to be displayed in a place visible to the Guest if the list is visible in rooms which are normally accessible in the Catering Establishment.

14.3 An extra charge can be made by the Catering Establishment for special services, such as the use of a cloakroom, garage, safe, laundry, telephone, telex, TV rental, etc.

14.4 All accounts, including accounts relating to Cancellation or No-show, are due for payment by the Customer and/or Guest at the time they are presented to him. The Customer is responsible for paying in cash unless otherwise agreed in writing or unless agreed otherwise.

14.5 If an invoice is sent out for an account which is below e 150,-according to the conditions in the fourth subclause, then the Catering Establishment may add e 15,-for administration costs to the account. The stipulations in this clause correspondingly apply to that amount.

14.6 The Guest and the Customer are severally liable for all amounts which one or both of them may owe the Catering Establishment on any account. Neither of them may appeal to benefit of excussion. Except where stipulated otherwise, Catering Agreements are considered to be concluded jointly on behalf of every Guest. By turning up the Guest acknowledges that the Customer was competent to represent him in concluding the relevant Catering Agreement.

14.7 As long as the Guest and/or Customer has not entirely fulfilled all his obligations to the Catering Establishment, the Catering Establishment is entitled to take over and keep all Goods which the Guest and/or Customer has brought with him to the Catering Establishment, until the Guest and/or Customer has fulfilled all his obligations to the Catering Establishment to the satisfaction of the Catering Establishment. Should this situation arise, the Catering Establishment has a right of lien as well as a right of retention on the Goods in question.

14.8 If payment otherwise than in cash is agreed, all invoices for any amount must be paid by the Customer to the Catering Establishment within fourteen days of the invoice date. If an invoice is sent out, the Catering Establishment is at all times entitled to add an extra 2% to the invoice to cover the restriction of its credit, which is removed if the Customer pays the invoice within fourteen days.

14.9 If and insofar as payment is not made in good time, the Customer is in default without any notice of default being necessary.

14.10 If the Customer is in default he must reimburse the Catering Establishment for all costs, both judicial and extrajudicial, arising from collection. The set level of extrajudicial collection costs is at least 15% of the principal amount owed, with a minimum of e 100.-all to be increased by the VAT due on that amount.

14.11 Over and above this, if the Customer is in default he will be charged interest at 2% above the legal interest rate. When the amount of interest due is calculated, part of a month is counted as a full month.

14.12 If the Catering Establishment has in its keeping Goods as referred to in Clause 14.7 and if the Customer from whom the Catering Establishment has received the Goods into keeping is in default for three months, the Catering Establishment is entitled to sell these Goods publicly or privately and to recover the amount owed from the proceeds. The costs associated with the sale are also the responsibility of the Customer, and the Catering Establishment can also recover these costs from the proceeds of the sale. After the Catering Establishment has recovered everything it is owed, any remaining money shall be paid to the Customer.

14.13 Every payment shall, regardless of any endorsements or observations made by the Customer at the time of payment, be considered as serving to reduce the debt of the Customer to the Catering Establishment in the following order:

1. the costs of execution
2. the judicial and extrajudicial collection costs
3. the interest
4. the damage
5. the principal amount.

14.14 Payment shall take place in Dutch currency. If the Catering Establishment accepts foreign instruments of payment then the market exchange rate in force at the time of payment shall apply. The Catering Establishment may charge administration costs amounting to a maximum of 10% of the amount offered in foreign currency. The Catering Establishment can effectuate this by adjusting the market exchange rate then in force by a maximum of 10%.

14.15 The Catering Establishment is never obliged to accept cheques, giro payment cards and other such instruments of payment and may attach conditions to the acceptance of such instruments of payment. The same applies to other instruments of payment not referred to here.

**FORCE MAJEURE**

15.1 Force majeure for the Catering Establishment, which means that any deficiency caused by this cannot be attributed to the Catering Establishment, shall be defined as every foreseen or unforeseen, foreseeable or unforeseeable circumstance which interferes with the fulfilment of the Catering Agreement by the Catering Establishment to such an extent that the fulfilment of the Catering Agreement becomes impossible or difficult.

15.2 Such circumstances are also understood to include such circumstances involving persons and/or services and/or institutions which the Catering Establishment is planning to use in fulfilling the Catering Agreement, as well as everything that applies to the aforementioned in terms of force majeure or reasons for postponement or cancellation, as well as non-fulfilment by the aforementioned.

15.3 If one of the parties to a Catering Agreement is not in a position to fulfil any obligation in that Catering Agreement, he is obliged to inform the other party of this as soon as possible.

**LOST AND FOUND**

16.1 Any objects which are lost or left behind in the building and appurtenances of the Catering Establishment and which are found by the Guest, must be handed in to the Catering Establishment by the Guest with all convenient speed.

16.2 Any objects which the rightful owner has not claimed from the Catering Establishment within a year of their being handed in become the property of the Catering Establishment.

16.3 If the Catering Establishment sends the Guest any objects that have been left behind, this shall take place entirely for account and risk of the Guest. The Catering Establishment is never obliged to send on such objects.

**CORKAGE**

17.1 If the Guest and/or Customer consumes drink that has not been provided by a Catering Establishment on the premises of that Catering Establishment, the Customer has to pay Corkage for each bottle consumed.

17.2 If the Guest and/or Customer consumes food that has not been provided by a Catering Establishment on the premises of that Catering Establishment, the Customer has to pay a Food Charge.

17.3 The amounts referred to in Clauses 17.1 and 17.2 shall be agreed in advance or, in the absence of prior agreement, shall be fixed at a reasonable level by the Catering Establishment.

## APPLICABLE LAW AND DISPUTES

18.1 Catering Agreements shall be governed exclusively by the laws of the Netherlands.

18.2 Any dispute between the Catering Establishment and the Customer (not being a natural person who is not acting in the exercise of a profession or business) shall be exclusively subject to the jurisdiction of the court in the domicile of the Catering Establishment, unless another court is competent under the strictly binding provisions of the law and without prejudice to the authority of the Catering Establishment to settle the dispute through the court which would have jurisdiction in the absence of this condition.

18.3 If and as soon as an arbitration committee is established under the auspices of Koninklijk Horeca Nederland and any other organisations which may be involved, the disputes which the arbitration committee is set up to mediate shall be settled in accordance with the regulations drawn up for this purpose.

18.4 All claims from the Customer become barred after one year has elapsed from the time of their origination.

18.5 The nullity of one or more clauses in these general terms and conditions does not affect the validity of all the other clauses. If a clause in these general terms and conditions turns out to be invalid for any reason, then the parties are assumed to have agreed a valid replacement clause which comes as close as possible to the meaning and scope of the invalid clause.

# 11

# Safety Rules

## INTRODUCTION

The hotel and catering industry is both large and diverse in character. It employs over two million full and part-time workers and embraces a wide range and scale of catering activities; from large scale food processing to individual cook to order catering. Accident rates in the catering industry have shown a rising trend since the Reporting of Injuries Diseases and Dangerous Occurrences Regulations (RIDDOR) first came into force in 1986/87. Statistics show that the rate is high when compared with other parts of the services sector. Accidents give rise to unnecessary pain and suffering. They also place an enormous financial burden on the catering industry.

In addition to the worrying news about accident trends, the industry also needs to be aware of a range of health and safety legislation which came into force on 1 January 1993. Health and safety is an issue which the catering industry cannot afford to ignore.

## THE COSTS OF ACCIDENTS

Every working day in Great Britain two people are killed and over 6000 are injured at work. Every year three-quarters of a million people take time off work because of what they regard as work-related illness. Around 31 million work days are lost as a result; more than 30 times that lost through strikes. The catering industry is a significant contributor to these statistics.

Workplace accidents and ill health cause unnecessary misery to the individuals concerned and to their families. They can also cripple companies because, in addition to the direct costs of personal injuries, they may also incur other far greater costs such as damage to property or equipment and lost production. Only a small proportion of these are recoverable from insurance.

A recent HSE study costed 6000 accidents from a range of companies. All were considered to be preventable by improved management control. The costs were alarming:

— accidents cost one organisation 8.5% of turnover;

— in another, costs represented 37% of profits;

— in a third, costs were 5% of operating costs.

In all cases the losses were between eight and 36 times greater than the insured costs.

A key outcome of the study was the recognition that the investment needed to increase market share and generate extra profits to cover accidental losses could be much greater than the investment needed to reduce the losses.

## THE COMMITTEE

The Health and Safety Executive (HSE) and the catering industry have established the Health and Safety in Catering Industry Liaison Committee as a direct response to these issues. The Committee comprises representatives of HSE and local authorities (LAs), together with employers, employees and trade associations from the catering industry. The committee will act as a network to develop and communicate information and guidance through the industry and will provide a forum where issues can be identified and resolved.

## NEW REGULATIONS

Six sets of Health and Safety at Work Regulations came into force on 1 January 1993 in order to implement six European Community directives. The Regulations are written in such a way as to encourage proper health and safety management. They also require risk assessments to be carried out. It is good practice to ensure that money spent on health and safety matters is directed at the hazards presenting the greatest risk. The assessment requirements in the new Regulations seek to ensure that you identify such risks before moving down the path of providing adequate control. The key will be to make systems efficient and effective: mountains of paper will not impress inspectors, but assessment of risk conducted at a level appropriate to the nature of the business and its work activities, leading to effective risk control, should find favour.

The Regulations cover health and safety management, manual handling, safety in the workplace and with work equipment, personal protective equipment, and display screen equipment (VDUs). The existing Health and Safety at Work etc Act 1974 will remain almost totally unchanged. Most of the duties in the six sets of Regulations are not new: they clarify and make more explicit duties which were already legal requirements. Exceptions to this are new requirements concerning health and safety management, manual handling and the use of display screens. Each of the sets of Regulations are backed up by either an Approved Code of Practice or guidance, giving comprehensive advice on compliance.

The catering industry should be in a particularly strong position to respond to the new Regulations because businesses will be able to draw on experience gained from operating within the requirements of the Food Safety Act. The systems needed to meet customers' quality assurance standards should also tie in well with the systems approach to health and safety management.

Initial action should be concentrated on the areas which experience has shown present the highest levels of risk. In the catering industry these are SLIPS, TRIPS AND FALLS; LIFTING AND MANUAL HANDLING; CONTACT WITH HOT SURFACES, HARMFUL SUBSTANCES ETC; BEING STRUCK BY AN OBJECT; DERMATITIS; AND WORK-RELATED UPPER LIMB DISORDERS.

The following paragraphs give further information on the new Regulations, how they are likely to be enforced and the priorities for the catering industry.

## Priorities

The new Regulations introduce a number of requirements which deal specifically with the hazards responsible for most of the deaths, injuries and ill health in the catering industry. Employers will therefore need to concentrate on these high priority areas.

The key requirement to which all businesses will need to give priority is the management of health and safety. The Management of Health and Safety at Work Regulations 1992 ('The Management Regulations') require every employer and self-employed person to make a risk assessment. They also cover the need for health surveillance (which you should already be looking at under The Control of Substances Hazardous to Health Regulations 1994, better known as COSHH) and training. When looking at training needs, new recruits, part-timers and temporary staff will have to be considered. Additional information on managing health and safety and on risk assessment is given later.

The Management Regulations contain two other important items. Firstly, they require employers to appoint competent people to help the company to comply with the legislation. The Approved Code makes it clear that in most cases this can be done using existing staff, provided they are given the facilities to acquaint themselves with best practice etc. Secondly, the more detailed requirements for making arrangements for health and safety may mean it is necessary to revise any existing safety policy to expand on how it is proposed to plan, organise, control, monitor and review the arrangements.

Between them, slips, trips and falls and being struck by an object, account for over half of all reported injuries in the catering sector. The Workplace (Health, Safety and Welfare) Regulations 1992 ('the Workplace Regulations') address these problems. They require floors to be of suitable construction, non-slip where appropriate, and to be kept free from any article or substance which might cause a person to slip.

The Workplace Regulations also require effective measures to be taken to prevent people falling any distance likely to cause injury (unlike the previous legislation, which was concerned with falls of 6 feet or more). Precautions have to be taken to prevent falling objects causing injury, including simple things like pots and pans falling from high shelves. A further specific duty aimed at preventing falls involves the design of windows, which must take account of those who use them normally and those who are required to clean them

Handling, lifting and carrying accidents account for 14% of all accidents in catering. The Manual Handling Operations Regulations 1992 ('the Manual Handling Regulations') require employers to avoid the need for hazardous manual handling operations, so far as is reasonably practicable. Those hazardous operations which can't be avoided have to be assessed and the risk of injury reduced. It should be remembered that manual handling does not just mean lifting: pushing, pulling etc also need to be taken into account. Training in proper lifting techniques is important, but is not an alternative to reducing the risk in the first place.

The catering industry is unique in having a high level of accidents involving contact with hot surfaces and harmful substances. The Workplace Regulations contain a requirement for appropriate protection to be provided wherever there is a risk of contact with equipment or substances that are at high or low temperature. The health problems prevalent in the catering industry are dermatitis and work-related upper limb disorders. Those caused by contact with harmful substances are covered by COSHH so little change may be required to comply with the new Regulations.

Think positively about this new legislation. Look at the work you do and try to foresee the major problem areas, then implement changes to reduce the risks. This approach will help you to meet your legal requirements and may prevent the tragedy of an accident or case of ill health at work.

## ENFORCING THE REGULATIONS

Responsibility for the enforcement of health and safety legislation in the industry is divided between HSE and local authorities, (usually through their Environmental Health

Department). HSE is the enforcing authority for institutional catering, for example in prisons, hospitals and schools. Local authority enforcement officers have responsibility for retail catering establishments such as pubs, restaurants, hotels, fast food establishments and small catering firms.

HSE inspectors' approach to employers in the period immediately after the coming into force of the new Regulations will be to promote awareness of the Regulations and the duties they place on employers. They will point employers in the direction of sources of advice and guidance as necessary.

Consideration of formal enforcement is not likely unless:

— the risks to health and safety are evident and immediate; or .

— what needs to be done is not new (ie existing duties transposed into new legislation); or

— employers appear deliberately obdurate and unwilling to recognise their responsibilities to ensure the long-term health, safety and welfare of employees and others affected by their activities.

Local authorities have yet to develop their own uniform enforcement policy. The joint Chairman and Local Authority Leader of the HSE/Local Authority Enforcement Liaison Committee (HELA) has, however, written to LAs saying that HELA recommendations on enforcement would be unlikely to differ significantly from the HSE approach.

## Managing Health and Safety

The most effective way of preventing accidents and ill health at work is to manage the business in such a way as to encourage all staff to develop a positive culture towards health and safety. The aim should be to control all accidental loss, because the mistakes that can cause injuries and illness can also lead to property damage and interrupt production.

Any company health and safety policy should be based on commitment at the very top. Where possible, it should be developed in consultation with staff, to give them a feeling of ownership. The policy should aim to ensure that commitment and accountability are shared by all staff, including supervisors and managers, and that they are aware of their health and safety responsibilities and have the competence and training necessary to carry them out.

Planning is the key to ensuring that your health and safety efforts really work. This means setting objectives; identifying hazards; assessing risks; implementing standards of performance for the protection of people, and safeguards for plant and production; and developing a positive culture. These are all management concepts which the catering industry has used to implement its general move towards improved standards of food safety and quality assurance.

In the catering industry there is a wealth of information on hazard identification and assessment of risk.

Once appropriate measures have been taken to try and reduce risks, you need to consider how to measure performance, just as you would for finance, production or sales. This should involve two types of monitoring. Firstly, regular inspections, which take place before things go wrong and show whether the standards you have set are being met. Secondly, reactive monitoring, after things go wrong. This includes investigating accidents, property damage and near misses.

The monitoring described above provides information to enable you to review your activities and improve performance. However, it is also recommended that health and safety is occasionally subjected to a more comprehensive review (audit), either by your own staff or outsiders. The audit should complement monitoring activities by looking to see if your policy, organisation and systems are achieving the right results. It should tell you about the reliability and effectiveness of your systems and enable you to learn from your experiences. Although not a legal requirement, audits are worthwhile, particularly in larger organisations, to ensure that money spent on health and safety is not being wasted.

## Risk Assessment

Risk assessment is a concept which is common to all of the new sets of Regulations. Confusion can arise because the term sounds more complicated than the process it describes. The underlying concept is, in fact, very simple. We all carry out risk assessments every day. When crossing the road the HAZARD of being knocked down by a car is always there. For this reason you assess the RISK of being run over before deciding to cross. If you think the risk is too great because the traffic is particularly heavy, then you may decide to eliminate it by not crossing, or to reduce it to an acceptable level by waiting until there is a gap, or walking to a pedestrian crossing. The new health and safety laws work in a similar way. They require an employer to identify all the hazards in the premises eg mincers, slicers, slippery floors etc. Any associated risks must then be assessed, ie are the hazards likely to cause harm to the employees? If the answer for any hazard is yes, then the employer needs to think of ways of eliminating it or reducing the risk to an acceptable level. Failure to do this can have the most tragic consequences.

The main requirement to carry out a risk assessment is contained in the Management Regulations. The Approved Code of Practice, which gives advice on how to comply with the Regulations, clearly states that for small undertakings presenting few or simple hazards, a suitable and sufficient risk assessment can be a very straightforward process based on judgement and requiring no specialist skills or complicated techniques. In addition to looking at the risks and the people affected by them, it should consider existing precautions and how these can be improved.

In practice it may be easier to look at risk assessment as a two stage process, the first stage being an initial judgement which screens out those activities where a risk assessment is not needed. Employers with five or more employees need to record the SIGNIFICANT findings of the risk assessment. For the catering industry this will most probably include those associated with slips, trips and falls, manual handling, contact with hot surfaces or harmful substances, dermatitis, and upper limb disorders.

Where risk assessments have already been done to meet the requirements of Regulations covering specific aspects of work, for example the Manual Handling Regulations, there is no need to duplicate the work when conducting the overall assessment required by the Management Regulations, but care should be taken to ensure that all significant risks are covered.

The requirement for a risk assessment should be regarded as a means of identifying the likely safety and health problems in a premise, and of putting them in some order of priority, so that the activities presenting the greatest risk can be dealt with first. THIS HELPS TO ENSURE THAT YOU GET MAXIMUM BENEFIT FROM ANY MONEY SPENT. The process is not meant to be complicated, and in the main it relies far more on common sense and good judgement than any complicated paper analysis.

12

# Career in Catering Industry

There are many different occupations available within the catering industry:

## KITCHEN ATTENDANT

Kitchen hands assist cooks and chefs in preparing and storing food, washing dishes and utensils, and cleaning work areas. Kitchen hands work in hotels, motels, restaurants, cafes, hospitals, takeaway food bars, boarding schools, and factory or office canteens.

### Work

Kitchen hands may perform the following tasks:

- wash and clean utensils and dishes that are returned to the kitchen and make sure they are stored appropriately
- handle, sort, store and distribute food items
- wash, peel, chop, cut and cook foodstuffs and help to prepare salads and desserts
- dispose of rubbish
- organise laundering of linen
- wash dishes
- clean food preparation equipment, floors and other kitchen tools or areas.

The particular duties of a kitchen hand may vary depending upon the type of workplace and their level of experience. Inexperienced kitchen hands or those in larger restaurants or hotels may focus on cleaning and housekeeping tasks such as scrubbing pots, sweeping floors and putting utensils and crockery away. Other kitchen hands may be involved in preparing ingredients: cleaning, chopping, slicing, grating, peeling and trimming. Kitchen hands usually aren't involved in cooking the food, though in smaller establishments there may be opportunities to be more involved in the cooking side of things.

**Work Conditions**

The role of the kitchen hand tends to involve repetitive work. Commercial kitchens can be very hot and noisy, and working conditions may be uncomfortable. However, the work is varied and working as part of a team in a busy kitchen can be fun.

Kitchen hands are often employed on a part-time, casual or seasonal basis and usually work in shifts. They must be prepared to work irregular hours and to stand for long periods.

Protective clothing such as overalls or gloves may be provided. Kitchen hands must be able to use knives and other cooking equipment efficiently and safely.

**Personal Requirements**

- interested in practical work
- good hand-eye coordination
- able to work quickly and safely
- good personal hygiene
- free from skin allergies to foods and detergents
- good communication skills
- able to work as part of a team

**Education/Training**

You can work as a kitchen hand without formal qualifications. However, there are formal qualifications available, and these may assist you in gaining employment and advancing within the industry.

Certificate I in Hospitality (Kitchen Operations) This certificate will provide you with the basic skills to work as a kitchen hand. Other qualifications are available to help kitchen hands move forward into other cookery positions.

These qualifications can be completed in a number of ways. For more information on the main options, see the following pages:

- New Apprenticeships
- Find training

## Employment and career opportunities

Most kitchen hands work on a part-time or casual basis.

It is a very large occupation with high staff turnover and there is usually a steady demand for experienced kitchen hands.

The job provides the opportunity to learn about other kitchen work and can serve as a good introduction to the catering and hospitality industries. Many people in the industry suggest that people interested in a career in hospitality, especially those intending to be a chef, should get some experience as a kitchen hand. It's a great way to help decide whether you want to become a chef before committing to an apprenticeship. Many chefs have worked their way through the ranks starting out as the kitchen hand.

## COOK

If you like cooking, want to work in an energetic and dynamic environment, are creative, like doing things with your hands and don't mind working hard, you could become a cook.

Cooks prepare and cook food in a commercial setting. Cooks may work in restaurants, cafes, hotels, motels, clubs, cafes, hospitals, take-away outlets, function centres, catering firms, flight catering centres and ships.

The range of duties carried out by cooks will vary depending on where they work. In hotels, clubs, restaurants and take-away food outlets, cooks often specialise in preparing and cooking a particular type of food (e.g. fried chicken, pizza or barbecued meat). They may also specialise in national cuisine (e.g. Thai, Vietnamese, French, or Italian). Other specialisations include entrees, desserts,international and pastry cooking.

**Duties and Tasks**

A cook may perform the following tasks:

- check food to make sure of its quality
- regulate temperatures of ovens, grills and other cooking equipment
- prepare food for cooking
- cook food by a range of methods (i.e. baking, braising, frying, roasting or steaming)
- divide food into portions and make sure that the food is well-presented
- clean food preparation areas and equipment
- store food in temperature-controlled facilities
- receive and store supplies
- make sure kitchen is hygienic and functional
- plan menus and estimate food requirements
- prepare food to meet special dietary requirements
- train and supervise other staff.

**Work Conditions**

Commercial kitchens can be very hot and noisy, and working conditions may be uncomfortable.

Cooks are required to do shift work, including weekends and public holidays. The work can be tiring, and involve long hours, and it may be stressful, particularly at peak hours of the day. Cooks spend a lot of time on their feet. On the other hand, it's a very sociable occupation where you work in a team environment.

Cooks work with sharp knives and around hot appliances. Cuts and burns are the most common occupational dangers. High standards of personal hygiene are a must, as a lack of attention to health and hygiene can spread disease and put clients at risk.

It is challenging work as you have to work long hours and nights and weekends, however it is extremely rewarding and offers great career options and job satisfaction.

## Personal Requirements

- a high level of personal cleanliness
- able to plan your time and work under pressure
- good communication skills
- punctuality
- flexibility to perform shift work (sometimes on a 24-hour rotating roster)
- able to stay calm in difficult situations
- able to work well in a team

## Education and Training

Cooks generally require formal qualifications. There are a number of nationally-recognised qualifications available, depending upon the type of cookery you choose to specialise in.

**Certificate II:** Kitchen Operations-This certificate will enable you to be a short order cook, a breakfast cook or a cook in a café or bistro. It is also the pathway to Certificates III in Asian Cookery, Patisserie or Catering

**Certificate III:** Commercial Cookery-is the standard 'trade' qualification required to become a qualified cook

**Certificate III:** Asian Cookery-is the trade qualification for those specialising in Asian cookery

**Certificate III:** Commercial Catering-will enable you to work as a caterer in a catering firm

**Certificate III:** Patisserie-will enable you to work as a patissier, specialising in fine pastries, cakes and desserts

These qualifications can be completed in a number of ways. For more information on the main options, see the following pages:

- New Apprenticeships
- Find training

Other qualifications are available to help cooks move forward into chef and management roles.

### Career and Employment Opportunities

There are excellent job opportunities for cooks, and good cooks are always in demand. Continued growth in the tourist industry has generated a strong demand for cooks, and there is currently a shortage of cooks in all States and Territories.

Cooks can work in a variety of locations and can become a chef or catering manager, or can own their own restaurant or catering company. They can also be specialists in areas such as ethnic cooking, Asian cookery, baking and patisserie or dietary catering. They can even be TV chefs! There is lots of variety and good travel opportunities. Many young cooks get experience overseas before progressing in their chosen career area.

With experience and further training, qualified cooks may be promoted to supervisory positions. Movement between employers within the industry may be required in order to gain experience and promotion.

## CHEF

Chefs may work in restaurants, cafes, hotels, motels, clubs, cafes, function centres, catering firms, flight catering centres and ships. Chefs (Heads of kitchens) are in charge of the kitchen and the staff working there as well as responsible for designing the menu and selecting and ordering the food. They are often responsible for planning and organising of the food for a special event such as a wedding, dinner or conference.

Chefs and cooks, particularly those working in larger establishments, often specialise in a particular cuisine or the preparation of a particular food. These range from Asian to African cuisines, to sauces (chef saucier) and to salads. And with confidence, creativity and experience, the possibilities are endless for creating new styles of cooking or combining different ingredients.

### Duties and Tasks

Chefs can take on any of a wide range of tasks or specialities depending upon their skills and where they work. They are responsible for managing kitchens, purchasing foodstuffs, preparing and cooking food and presenting it. They are also responsible for keeping kitchens clean and hygienic. They are supported by people working as kitchen hands and fast food cooks.

Chefs perform the following tasks:

- Plan menus and estimate food requirements
- Prepare and cook different kinds of foods
- Portion, present and serve food
- Monitor food quality at all stages
- Store food safely and hygienically
- Prepare food to meet different requirements such as dietary or cultural needs
- Discuss food preparation issues with managers, dieticians and other staff
- Demonstrate techniques and advise on cooking procedures
- Plan staff rosters and supervise the activities of cooks and assistants
- Work out food and labour costs together with the head chef
- Discuss food preparation issues with managers, dieticians and other staff members
- Order food, kitchen supplies and equipment
- Explain and enforce hygiene regulations
- Select and train staff
- Freeze and preserve foods.

The particular duties will depend upon the specific role and the type of kitchen. There are four main 'levels' of chef:

*A commis chef: a commis chef is a qualified cook, who works under the direct supervision of other chefs in the kitchen. Commis chefs have often just completed their qualification. Commis chefs are generally the least experienced chefs in the kitchen.*

A chef de partie controls a particular section of the kitchen. Chefs de partie can include chefs specialising as larder cooks, butchers, pastry cooks, sauce cooks, roast cooks, relief cooks, side-dish cooks, breakfast cooks, canteen cooks or fish cooks.

A sous chef (also known as second chef) is the second-in-charge in the kitchen.

A chef de cuisine (also known as head chef or executive chef) is in charge of the kitchen. They plan menus, oversee all staff, and supervise the overall operation of the kitchen. In larger establishments, the chef de cuisine or head chef generally does more supervision than cooking. Senior chefs have to attend staff meetings, where they discuss problems related to their areas and receive or issue instructions to other managerial staff. In small restaurants, the head chef may prepare food, assisted by other cooks or apprentices. As well as expert cooking knowledge, chefs involved in supervision need a general knowledge of the skills and activities of all their workers.

## Work Conditions

Commercial kitchens can be very hot and noisy, and working conditions may be uncomfortable. Chefs are required to do shift work, including weekends and public holidays. The work can be tiring, and involve long hours, and it may be stressful, particularly at peak hours of the day. Chefs work with sharp knives and around hot appliances. Cuts and burns are the most common occupational dangers. High standards of personal hygiene are a must, as a lack of attention to health and hygiene can spread disease and put clients at risk.

It is challenging work as you have to work long hours and nights and weekends, however it is extremely rewarding and offers great career options and job satisfaction.

## Personal Requirements

- a high level of personal cleanliness
- enjoy cooking
- able to organise efficient work schedules
- good communication skills

- punctuality
- flexibility to perform shift work on a 24-hour rotating roster as required
- able to work under pressure and stay calm in difficult situations

## What Training do you Need?

A commis chef:

**Certificate III:** Commercial Cookery-is the standard 'trade' qualification required to become a qualified cook

**Certificate III:** Asian Cookery-is the trade qualification for those specialising in Asian cookery

**Certificate III:** Commercial Catering-will enable you to work as a caterer in a catering firm

A chef de partie or sous chef:

**Certificate IV:** Commercial Cookery-is designed for qualified cooks who want to develop their skills in kitchen supervision

**Certificate IV:** Asian Cookery-is designed for qualified cooks who want to develop their skills in kitchen supervision in an Asian kitchen

**Certificate IV:** Patisserie-is designed to give you high level patisserie skills as well as supervisory skills required for running a café or cake shop

**Certificate IV:** Catering Operations-will enable you to develop more catering skills such as managing functions or catering for hospitals, as well as supervisory skills

## A CHEF DE CUISINE (HEAD CHEF OR EXECUTIVE CHEF)

The Diploma of Hospitality Management or Advanced Diploma of Hospitality Management are the qualifications for chefs who wish to acquire skills in management to manage a kitchen or their own restaurant.

These qualifications can be completed in a number of ways. For more information on the main options, see the following pages:

- New Apprenticeships
- Find training

### Career and Employment Opportunities

There are excellent job opportunities for chefs. It is a large occupation and employment prospects are good, with relatively strong job growth predicted nationally. Expanded tourism has increased demand for highly skilled chefs, particularly in establishments of international standard. The majority of chefs work in capital cities and in large country centres, particularly in areas where there are tourist resorts.

In large kitchens the progression is usually from commis chef, to chef de partie, to sous chef, to head chef, to executive chef or food manager. Movement between employers within the industry may be required in order to gain experience and promotion.

Chefs with sufficient capital may become the owners of restaurants.

## FOOD SERVICE MANAGER

Food service managers plan, organise and control the operation of establishments where food and beverages are served, such as restaurants, cafes, cafeterias and canteens.

### Duties and Tasks

A food service manager may perform the following tasks:

- talk with the chef to plan the menu
- supervise the purchase and storage of food
- supervise provision of all crockery, cutlery, detergents and kitchenware
- make sure there is adequate security for food and equipment
- keep records of payments and expenses
- plan, coordinate and supervise the activities of workers in dining rooms, kitchens, bars and other areas
- manage staff hiring and rostering

- provide some staff training
- discuss catering arrangements with clients
- make sure that the dining rooms, kitchen, storage facilities and other work areas are kept clean and conform to the sanitary regulations
- attend to complaints concerning food and service.

**Work Conditions**

Food service managers spend most of their time in the dining area and in the kitchen. Most of the time is spent on their feet. They often work in the evenings and on weekends and on public holidays.

The work can be tiring, and involve long hours, and it may be stressful, particularly at peak hours of the day.

There is a high level of customer contact involved, and the job may involve dealing with difficult customers and complaints.

**Personal Requirements**

- willing and able to work for long hours, on shifts, and on public holidays and weekends
- good communication and organisation skills
- able to remain calm and in control in difficult situations
- able to work as part of a team

**Education/Training**

There is no specific requirement to have formal qualifications to work as a food service manager. However, there are formal qualifications available, and these may assist you in gaining employment and advancing within the industry.

Diploma of Hospitality Management provides the skills required to work as a manager in the hospitality industry. Advanced Diploma of Hospitality Management provides the skills required to work as a senior manager in the hospitality industry. Most restaurant/catering managers are also expected to have a significant level of experience in the hospitality industry, and many people work their way up through the industry. These qualifications can be completed in a number of ways. For more information on the main options, see the following pages:

- New Apprenticeships
- Find training

### Employment Opportunities

It is a large occupation with good job prospects. Growth in the tourism and hospitality industries indicate that there will probably be increased demand for good staff. Positions tend to be filled by promoting an experienced person from within the organisation.

Self-employment is possible. People who intend to run their own business are advised to gain several years of experience, both on the job and by completing an appropriate qualification. The costs to purchase or establish your own business are high, so you will need a significant amount of capital.

## WAITER (FOOD AND BEVERAGE SERVICE)

Waiters serve food and drinks to guests in hotels, restaurants, clubs and similar establishments. Waiters greet patrons, present them with menus, make recommendations on available food and beverage choices and answer any questions they might have.

### Duties and Tasks

A waiter may perform the following tasks:

- set tables with clean linen or place mats, cutlery, crockery and glasses
- welcome and seat customers and hand menus to them
- tell guests about the menu and drinks and appropriate combinations of food and drinks
- in some cases promote local produce and attractions to visitors from interstate and overseas
- take customers' orders and pass them to kitchen staff or bar attendants

- serve food and drinks
- carve meat
- make up bills and present them to customers
- handle money or credit cards
- take restaurant reservations
- clear tables and return dishes and cutlery to kitchens.

## Work Conditions

It is busy, exciting work and requires someone with lots of energy and good communication and customer service skills. You will have to work nights and weekends, however, it gives you lots of opportunities to meet people and even to travel. Imagine the fun of working on a cruise ship or in a ski resort!

Waiters often work split shifts and in the evenings, weekends and public holidays. Uniforms may be supplied by employers. Waiters must be a minimum age of 18 years to serve alcohol.

Waiters spend long periods on their feet, and may have to deal with difficult or dissatisfied customers.

## Personal Requirements

- well presented
- good communication skills
- good memory
- polite and patient
- friendly, efficient and speedy
- enjoy working with people
- able to work as part of a team
- prepared to work weekends and evenings
- able to handle money
- stamina

## Education/Training

You can work as a waiter without formal qualifications. You will probably get some informal training on the job.

However, there are formal qualifications available, and these may assist you in gaining employment and advancing within the industry.

To be a qualified food and beverage attendant, you should have a Certificate II in Hospitality (Operations) as a minimum, although some places will let you start with no training as they offer training on the job. A Certificate III in Hospitality (Operations) is the qualification for a waiter or bar attendant. You can specialise through electives in whatever best meets your job needs.

**The Certificate II:** Operations-is the entry-level qualification which provides the basic skills to work as a food and beverage attendant

**The Certificate III:** Operations-is the certificate for a qualified waiter, in both food and beverage

Other qualifications are available to help waiters to move into supervisory or more specialised roles:

**The Certificate IV:** Supervision-is designed to provide the supervisory skills to be a head waiter, sommelier or supervisor

The Diploma of Hospitality Management is designed to provide the management skills as well as the operational skills and knowledge needed to be a food and beverage manager

The Advanced Diploma of Hospitality Management provides the advanced management skills for those who are interested in managing a restaurant, heading up a large department or owning their own business.

These qualifications can be completed in a number of ways. For more information on the main options, see the following pages:

- New Apprenticeships
- Find training.

## Employment and Career Opportunities

There are many opportunities in a huge variety of places including hotels, motels, cafes, restaurants, clubs, recreation and convention centres and other entertainment venues. Most waiters are employed in cities, although many work in larger country centres, particularly those which are tourist resorts.

There are good job prospects. As turnover is high in this occupation there is usually a steady demand for replacement staff. As the tourism and hospitality industry continues to grow, with a growing number of hotels, cafes and restaurants, there are likely to be increased employment opportunities for skilled waiters.

Waiters who have undertaken appropriate training or who have suitable experience are highly regarded by employers. You can start as a waiter or bar attendant, and with experience and further training, progress to head waiter (maitre d'), supervisor or Food and Beverage Manager. If you are interested in wine, you can become a sommelier. Some waiters also specialise in silver service (serving food, using a fork and spoon, directly from platters on a the guest's plate at the table).

Career paths are flexible and there are many associated jobs in areas such as training, marketing and events management.

## BAR ATTENDANT

Bar attendants prepare, mix and serve drinks to customers in hotels, bars, cafes, restaurants and clubs.

### Duties and Tasks

A bar attendant may perform the following tasks:

- serve alcoholic and non-alcoholic drinks
- draw beer from the tap or pour from bottles
- mix ingredients to make cocktails and slice fruit to garnish drinks
- prepare and serve a variety of coffees
- refill drink and cigarette dispensers
- collect glasses from tables and place them in glasswashing machines
- wipe down tables and empty ashtrays

- collect payment, operate cash registers and give change
- arrange bottles and glasses on shelves
- clean bar service area and polish glasses
- operate TAB and Keno or gaming machine terminals
- assist in the cellar
- assist in stock control
- make coffee using an espresso coffee machine or filter system
- observe workplace hygiene, occupational health and safety, and security procedures.

Bar attendants may also provide drinks to waiters or serve them to tables, depending on the type of business.

**Work Conditions**

Bar attendants generally do shift work, often in the evenings, weekends and public holidays. Many bar attendants are employed on a part-time or casual basis. Uniforms may be supplied by employers.

The work environment can be busy and noisy, and may be hot and stuffy, especially during peak periods. While legislation can vary between states, many licensed premises permit smoking, so it can also be smoky.

Bar attendants must be at least 18 years of age, and are required to comply with legislation on the responsible service of alcohol. Bar attendants spend long periods on their feet, and may have to deal with difficult or intoxicated customers.

**Personal Requirements**

- good interpersonal skills
- good memory
- efficient and speedy
- enjoy working with people
- prepared to work weekends and evenings
- good cash-handling skills
- able to stand for long periods

**Education/Training**

You can work as a bar attendant without formal qualifications. You will probably get some informal training on the job. However, there are formal qualifications available, and these may assist you in gaining employment and advancing within the industry.

To be a qualified bar attendant, you should have a Certificate II in Hospitality (Operations) as a minimum, although some places will let you start with no training as they offer training on the job. A Certificate III in Hospitality (Operations) is the qualification for a waiter or bar attendant. You can specialise through electives in whatever best meets your job needs.

The Certificate II in Hospitality (Operations) is the entry-level qualification which provides the basic skills to work as a bar attendant

The Certificate III in Hospitality (Operations) is the certificate for a qualified waiter, in both food and beverage

Other qualifications are available to help bar attendants to move into supervisory or more specialised roles:

The Certificate IV in Hospitality (Supervision) is designed to provide the supervisory skills to be a head waiter, sommelier or supervisor

The Diploma of Hospitality Management is designed to provide the management skills as well as the operational skills and knowledge needed to be a food and beverage manager

The Advanced Diploma of Hospitality Management provides the advanced management skills for those who are interested in managing a restaurant, heading up a large department or owning their own business.

These qualifications can be completed in a number of ways. For more information on the main options, see the following pages:

- New Apprenticeships
- Find training

## Career and Employment Opportunities

Bar attendants can work in hotels, bars, restaurants, cafes, clubs, recreation and convention centres, and other licensed entertainment venues. There are good job prospects. Most bar attendants are employed on a part-time or casual basis. As turnover is relatively high, there is generally a constant demand to replace those leaving the job. As the tourism and hospitality industry continues to grow, with a growing number of hotels, cafes and restaurants, there are likely to be increased employment opportunities for skilled bar staff. Bar attendants who have undertaken training or are experienced are highly regarded and sought by employers. Bar attendants with experience and additional training may progress to supervisory or management positions. Career paths are flexible and there are many associated jobs in other areas of the hospitality industry, as well as related areas such as training, marketing and events management.

## CONCIERGE/PORTER

Luggage porters carry luggage for guests in hotels and passengers in transport terminals, show them to their rooms, berths or cabins, and provide other guest services.

Concierges provide additional services to guests, such as organising and booking tickets for tours and entertainment for guests, and advising them on the services and attractions available in the local area.

## Duties and Tasks

A luggage porter may perform the following tasks:

- take baggage, tag it and give identification slips to guests or passengers
- load or unload luggage and take it to the receiving area
- carry luggage and show incoming guests to rooms
- explain details of hotel room services and facilities to guests as they arrive
- carry the luggage of departing guests to cars, buses or taxis

- talk with transport carriers to make travel arrangements and retrieve lost luggage
- page guests and run errands
- park guests' vehicles.

A concierge may perform the following additional tasks:

- provide guests with information on the local area, attractions and events
- organise and book tours, transport and entertainment for guests
- assist guests and staff with safety and emergency procedures

## Personal Requirements

- interested in working with people
- well-presented, alert and perceptive
- interpersonal skills
- physically fit
- good communication skills
- good knowledge of the local area

## Work Conditions

Porters and concierges are required to do shift work, including nights, weekends and public holidays. These jobs have a high level of contact with the public. Uniforms are generally provided by the employer.

They need to be physically fit to handle luggage, and may be required to stand for long periods of time.

## Education/Training

You can work as a porter or concierge without formal qualifications. You will probably get some informal training on the job. However, there are formal qualifications available, and these may assist you in gaining employment and advancing within the industry. Luggage porters should have a good command of the English language, and the ability to speak a second language may be an advantage. A current driver's licence is often required. To be a qualified porter, you should have a Certificate II in Hospitality (Operations) as a minimum, although some places will let you start with no training. A Certificate III in Hospitality (Operations) is the qualification for a concierge. You can specialise through electives in whatever best meets your job needs. The Certificate II in Hospitality (Operations) is the entry-level qualification which provides the basic skills to work as a porter.

### Concierge

These qualifications can be completed in a number of ways. For more information on the main options, see the following pages:

### Career and Employment Opportunities

Porters and concierges are mainly employed in the larger international standard hotels, so available jobs tend to be in capital cities and regional centres that cater to large numbers of tourists. There are only a limited number of job openings in this occupation, although once you gain a position there are good career opportunities in the tourism and hospitality industries. Experienced porters and concierges may eventually be promoted to duty managers or front office managers.

## HOUSEKEEPING ATTENDANT

Housekeeping attendants (room attendants) clean and maintain rooms in hotels, motels and other lodging places.

### Duties and Tasks

A housekeeping attendant may perform the following tasks:

- check that rooms have been vacated before cleaning
- make beds daily and change bed linen
- vacuum carpets, floors and upholstery
- clean bathrooms and supply with fresh towels and toiletries
- check and re-stock tea, coffee, sugar, milk and mini bar supplies

- make sure that televisions, radios, lights and air-conditioning equipment are working
- report to a supervisor articles left behind by guests, damage to rooms and any items which appear to have been stolen
- take laundry and dry cleaning orders from guests.

## Work Conditions

Working conditions and hours vary greatly, depending on where room attendants work. The work is not usually heavy, but lifting, carrying and bending are involved.

## Personal Requirements

- interested in practical work
- neat personal appearance
- good personal hygiene
- honest and reliable
- physically fit
- able to stay calm in difficult situations

## Education/Training

You can work as a housekeeping attendant without formal qualifications. You will probably get some informal training on the job. However, there are formal qualifications available, and these may assist you in gaining employment and advancing within the industry.

To be a qualified housekeeping attendant, you should have a Certificate II in Hospitality (Operations) as a minimum, although some places will let you start with no training. You can specialise through electives in whatever best meets your job needs.

The Certificate I in Hospitality (Operations) is the entry-level qualification which provides the basic skills to work as a housekeeping assistant

The Certificate II in Hospitality (Operations) is the certificate for a qualified housekeeping attendant

Other qualifications are available to help housekeeping attendants move forward into supervisory positions.

These qualifications can be completed in a number of ways. For more information on the main options, see the following pages:

**Employment and Career Opportunities**

Housekeeping attendants are employed by individual hotels, motels or guest houses, or by companies that operate a chain of establishments. Most housekeeping attendants work in capital cities and surrounding suburbs and in those country centres where there are tourist resorts.

Demand for housekeeping attendants depends on growth in the tourism and travel industries and on the general level of economic activity. As turnover is relatively high, there is generally a constant demand to replace those leaving the job. With experience and training, housekeeping attendants may be promoted to supervisory levels and to the position of executive housekeeper.

## HOTEL/MOTEL FRONT OFFICE CLERK

Hotel and motel front office clerks look after the needs of guests on arrival and during their stay in the hotel or motel.

**Duties and Tasks**

A front office clerk may perform the following tasks:

- receive reservations for accommodation from clients either in person or by telephone, fax or email
- take guests' details as they arrive and allocate them a room
- talk to transport carriers (e.g. airlines, bus companies, rental car agencies) to make travel arrangements for guests and to find lost luggage
- inform guests about the hotel/motel's facilities, policies and procedures
- provide tourist information to guests

- make reservations for sight-seeing tours, restaurants, the cinema and live entertainment
- deal with enquiries and requests from guests
- take messages for guests
- calculate guests' bills and issue receipts upon payment
- arrange accommodation for guests travelling to other destinations
- perform cashier duties, cash travellers' cheques and exchange foreign currency
- place guests' possessions in a safe if requested
- coordinate the cleaning of guests' personal laundry, shoe shining and room service deliveries
- follow in-house procedures to help make sure of the security of guests and employees
- perform general secretarial duties such as preparing correspondence and attending to a switchboard.

In a small or medium-sized hotel all of the above duties may be carried out by one person. However, in an international standard hotel several clerks may be employed. Each clerk is allocated a set of specific duties to perform (e.g. one may attend to guest reception, another may be responsible for the switchboard, while another works as an information officer).

## Work Conditions

Hotel and motel front office clerks usually work shifts including evenings, weekends and public holidays.

The role involves a high level of public contact, and may involve dealing with difficult customers and solving problems.

## Personal Requirements

- enjoy working with people
- friendly, helpful and patient
- able to assist guests with a limited understanding of English

- good communication skills
- able to record information accurately
- able to work as part of a team
- able to project a professional manner at all times
- good interpersonal skills
- flexible
- able to stay calm in difficult situations

**Education and Training**

You can work as a front office clerk without formal qualifications. You will probably get some informal training on the job. Experience in word processing and operating office machinery such as switchboards is desirable. The ability to speak a second language is an advantage if working in an international hotel. However, there are formal qualifications available, and these may assist you in gaining employment and advancing within the industry.

To be a qualified front office clerk, you should have a Certificate II or Certificate III in Hospitality (Operations) as a minimum, although some places will let you start with no training. You can specialise through electives in whatever best meets your job needs.

The Certificate II in Hospitality (Operations) is the entry-level qualification which provides the basic skills to work as a front office clerk

The Certificate III in Hospitality (Operations) provides additional training to develop a broader range of skills

Other qualifications are also available to help front office clerks move forward into supervisory positions.

These qualifications can be completed in a number of ways. For more information on the main options, see the following pages:

**Employment and Career Opportunities**

Hotel and motel front office clerks are employed by hotels, motels, guesthouses and hostels throughout the country. They may work in privately-owned hotels or motels, or in companies that operate a chain of establishments. It is a large occupation and employment prospects are good. With experience and training, front office clerks may be promoted to supervisory or managerial levels.

## HOTEL SERVICE SUPERVISOR

Hotel service supervisors coordinate and supervise the activities of hotel service workers including domestic staff, luggage porters and doorpersons.

### Duties and Tasks

Hotel service supervisors may perform the following tasks:

- determine work requirements and allocate duties to domestic housekeepers, luggage porters and doorpersons
- talk to managers to coordinate activities with other organisational units
- maintain attendance records and rosters
- explain and enforce safety regulations
- oversee the work of the unit and suggest improvements and changes
- talk to workers to resolve problems
- perform front office and reception duties
- perform the tasks of a domestic housekeeper, luggage porter or doorperson.

### Work Conditions

Hotel service supervisors often work evenings, weekends and public holidays. In some hotels and motels, the hotel service supervisor may work mostly behind the scenes. In an international standard hotel, however, they are likely to have a high level of contact with the public and may have to deal with difficult guests and be on call if major problems arise.

### Personal Requirements

- interested in working with people

- friendly, helpful and patient
- able to assist guests with a limited understanding of English
- good communication skills
- good interpersonal skills
- good organisational skills
- able to record information accurately
- able to work as part of a team
- able to project a professional manner at all times
- able to stay calm in difficult situations.

**Education and Training**

Hotel service supervisors would generally be expected to be experienced employees with a strong background in front office operations. There is no specific requirement to have formal qualifications to work as a service supervisor, but there are formal qualifications available, and these may assist you in gaining employment and advancing within the industry.

To be a qualified service supervisor, you should have a minimum of a Certificate IV in Hospitality (Supervision). You can specialise through electives in whatever best meets your job needs. The Certificate IV in Hospitality (Supervision) provides the skills required to work as a service supervisor.

The Diploma of Hospitality Management provides the advanced skills required to supervise a large department or the services of a small hotel, motel or restaurant. Other qualifications are available to help service supervisors move forward into further management positions:

*The Advanced Diploma of Hospitality Management provides the advanced management skills for those who are interested in managing a hotel, heading up a large department or owning their own business.*

These qualifications can be completed through a training program plus some on-the-job experience, or through a New Apprenticeship.

## Career and Employment Opportunities

Hotel service supervisors are employed by hotels and motels throughout the country. They may work in privately-owned hotels or motels, or in companies that operate a chain of establishments.

Job prospects depend on the level of tourism and economic activity. It is a small occupation, but high turnover may provide additional job openings.

However, there is very strong competition for available jobs.

## HOTEL/MOTEL MANAGER

Hotel and motel managers plan, supervise and control the operations of a hotel or motel, including food and beverage, front office, housekeeping, budgeting, marketing/advertising and recruiting and managing staff.

Hotel and motel managers may work in privately-owned hotels, motels or resorts, or they may be employed by companies that operate a chain of businesses.

## Duties and Tasks

Hotel and motel managers may perform the following tasks:

- plan, direct and coordinate the services of accounting, food and beverages, guest services, maintenance, staff development, and sales and marketing
- allocate tasks and priorities, coordinate resources, develop business plans and marketing strategies
- undertake management tasks such as looking after building costs, rents, maintenance, lighting, power, heating, air conditioning, floorings and furniture
- control capital and operational expenditure
- make sure government health, occupational safety and licensing regulations are followed
- carry out marketing and sales activities for rooms, conventions, banquets and conferences

- supervise arrangement and re-arrangement of furnishings
- prepare reports
- manage the security of the hotel and its staff
- publicise the hotel/motel through public relations activities in the local business community.

The specific duties of the manager will vary with the size and nature of the workplace. In larger hotels/motels, the manager's role is often more administrative, with many of their responsibilities being delegated to others, such as food and beverage managers and function coordinators. In hotel or motel chains, the purchasing and advertising functions are usually centralised.

## Work Conditions

Hotel and motel managers often work evenings, weekends and public holidays. Whether in a small or medium-sized hotel or motel or an international standard hotel, most hotel and motel managers are very 'hands-on'.

They have a high level of contact with the public and may have to deal with difficult guests and be on call if major problems arise.

## Personal Requirements

- interested in working with people
- friendly, helpful and patient
- able to assist guests with a limited understanding of English
- good communication and organisational skills
- able to record information accurately
- able to work as part of a team
- able to project a professional manner at all times
- good interpersonal skills
- able to maintain control and composure in difficult situations

**Education/Training**

There is no specific requirement to have formal qualifications to work as a hotel or motel manager. However, there are formal qualifications available, and these may assist you in gaining employment and advancing within the industry.

The Diploma of Hospitality Management provides the skills required to work as a manager in the hospitality industry

The Advanced Diploma of Hospitality Management provides the skills required to work as a senior manager in the hospitality industry

These qualifications are generally completed through a full-time or part-time training course. Most hotel/motel managers are also expected to have a significant amount of experience in the hospitality industry, and many people work their way up through the industry.

University degrees in related areas, such as business or marketing, may also be an advantage.

The ability to speak a second language is an advantage if working in an international hotel.

# Bibliography


Angel, Bradley: *Toxic Threat to Indian Lands: A Greenpeace Report*, San Francisco, Greenpeace, 1991.

Auguste, E.: *Escoffier Cook Book: A Guide to the Fine Art Cookery*, New York, Crown, 1969.

Baum, T.: *Managing the Development and Implementation of National Human Resource Policies for Tourism*, England, Wiley, 1994.

Berry, A., Jarvis, R.: *Business Accounting for Hospitality and Tourism*, London, Chapman and Hall, 1995.

Black, Wendy: *Elegant Hotels of Europe*, Glen Cove, PBC International, 1994.

Boissevain, J.: *Coping withTourists*, Oxford, Berghahn Books, 1996.

Bryson, McDowell: *Concierge: Key to Hospitality: A Training Manual*, New York, Wiley, 1992.

Clark, Mona: *Interpersonal Skills for Hospitality Managers*, London, Chapman Hill, 1995.

Cracknell, H. L.: *Escoffier: The Complete Guide to the Art of Modern Cookery*, New York, John Wiley, 1979.

Donald E. : *Public Personnel Management: Contexts and Strategies, Upper Saddle River*, NJ: Prentice Hall, 1998.

Eberts, Marjorie: *Careers in Travel, Tourism, and Hospitality*, Lincolnwood, VGM Career Horizons, 1997.

Gilligan, C. : *Strategic Marketing Management*, Oxford, Butterworth-Heinemann Ltd., 1992.

Gisslen, Wayne: *Professional Cooking*, New York, Wiley, 1999.

James, M. : *The Meeting Planner's Legal Handbook*, Washington, D.C.: Goldberg & Associates, 1996.

Johnson, Hazel: *Financial Institutions and Markets: A Global Perspective*, NY, McGraw Hill, 1993.

Koontz, H.: *Management: A Global Perspective*, New York, McGraw Hill, 1993.

Lawrence, J.: *Principles of Managerial Finance*, MA: Addison Wesley Longman, 2000.

Medlik, S.: *Managing Tourism*, Oxford, Butterworth-Heinemann Ltd., 1991.

Michael, John: *Principles of Hospitality Law*, London, Cassell, 1999.

Nancy, N.: *Choosing a Career in Hotels, Motels, and Resorts*, New York, Rosen Pub. Group, 1997.

Pearson, D. J.: *Strategic Marketing Management*, Oxford, Butterworth-Heinemann Ltd., 1992.

Peter, J.: *College & University Foodservice Management Standards*, Westport, AVI Pub. Company, 1985.

Robert, W.: *Site Selection: New Advancements in Methods and Technology*, New York, Lebhar-Friedman Books, 1998.

Rosemary, E.: *Managing Employee Relations in the Hotel and Catering Industry*, London, Cassell, 1995.

Sherman, Barry: *Telecommunications Management*, New York, McGraw Hill, 1995.

Thomas, F. : *Introduction to the Hospitality Industry*, New York, Wiley, 1995.

Timothy, R.: *Cases in Hospitality Management: A Critical Incident Approach*, New York, Wiley, 1995.

Walden, Richard: *Genetic Transformation in Plants*, England, Open University Press, 1988.

Ware, Richard: *How to Open Your Own Restaurant: A Guide for Entrepreneurs*, New York, Penguin Books, 1991.

William, H.: *The Chef's Guide to Practical Restaurant Cookery*, New York, Van Nostrand Reinhold, 1988.

Zaccarelli, Herman E. : *Food Service Management by Checklist: A Handbook of Control Techniques*, New York, Wiley, 1991.

# Index

## N



## O



## P



## R



## S



## T



## U



## W



□□□